0171419

£16.99

QLR HH
(Ain)

YOUNG PEOPLE LEAVING HOME

CARLISLE

030 432 4469

Available in the Cassell Education series:

P. Ainley: *Young People Leaving Home*

P. Ainley and M. Corney: *Training for the Future: The Rise and Fall of the Manpower Services Commission*

G. Antonouris and J. Wilson: *Equal Opportunities in Schools*

N. Bennett and A. Cass: *From Special to Ordinary Schools*

D. E. Bland: *Managing Higher Education*

M. Booth, J. Furlong and M. Wilkin: *Partnership in Initial Teacher Training*

M. Bottery: *The Morality of the School*

L. Burton (ed.): *Gender and Mathematics*

C. Christofi: *Assessment and Profiling in Science*

G. Claxton: *Being a Teacher: A Positive Approach to Change and Stress*

G. Claxton: *Teaching to Learn: A Direction for Education*

D. Coulby and S. Ward: *The Primary Core National Curriculum*

C. Cullingford (ed.): *The Primary Teacher*

L. B. Curzon: *Teaching in Further Education* (4th edition)

B. Goacher *et al.*: *Policy and Provision for Special Educational Needs*

H. Gray (ed.): *Management Consultancy in Schools*

L. Hall: *Poetry for Life*

J. Nias, G. Southworth and R. Yeomans: *Staff Relationships in the Primary School*

A. Pollard: *The Social World of the Primary School*

J. Sayer and V. Williams (eds): *Schools and External Relations*

B. Spiecker and R. Straughan: *Freedom and Indoctrination in Education: International Perspectives*

R. Straughan: *Beliefs, Behaviour and Education*

H. Thomas: *Education Costs and Performances*

H. Thomas, G. Kirkpatrick and E. Nicholson: *Financial Delegation and the Local Management of Schools*

D. Thyer and J. Maggs: *Teaching Mathematics to Young Children* (3rd edition)

M. Watts: *The Science of Problem-Solving*

J. Wilson: *A New Introduction to Moral Education*

S. Wolfendale (ed.): *Parental Involvement*

Young People Leaving Home

Pat Ainley

with 86 young people in Kirkcaldy, Liverpool, Sheffield and Swindon
and an afterword by Sheena Ashford

CASSELL

Cassell Educational Limited
Villiers House
41/47 Strand
London WC2N 5JE, England

387 Park Avenue South
New York, NY 10016-8810, USA

First published 1991

British Library Cataloguing in Publication Data
Ainley, Pat
    Young people leaving home. – (Cassell Education).
    1. Great Britain. Labour market. Participation of
adolescents.
    I. Title
    331.340941

ISBN 0-304-32443-4
ISBN 0-304-32446-9 pbk

Printed and bound by Dotesios Ltd,
Trowbridge, Wiltshire

Contents

Acknowledgements

Acknowledgements are due to the following for their assistance: to the staff of the Social Statistics Research Unit, City University, especially its Director, Professor John Bynner, Deputy Director, Dr Angela Dale, and Art and Design Director, Kevin Dodwell, and particularly to Bob Edwards for his help with the spreadsheet and graphs; to all those involved in the ESRC's 16–19 Initiative at the Universities of Dundee, Edinburgh, Liverpool, Sheffield and Surrey, and to the councillors and council officers in Fife Regional Council, Kirkcaldy District Council, Liverpool, Sheffield and Thamesdown Councils who provided so much background information; to Sharon Clarke, Brian Dudgeon, Gill Jones, Beverly Katai and Fiona Tasker for reading through the draft, and to the person from Kirkcaldy, who helped in the transcription of those interviews but wishes to remain anonymous; to Tom Spears, Joan Hare, John Lockwood and Molly for their hospitality; to Beulah and Adam for their more than usual forbearance, also to my publisher, Naomi Roth, for her usual help and encouragement. Finally, I would like to thank the young people and their parents for their help and patience in providing the information, without which nothing could have been written. Their names are pseudonymous but I hope their experiences have been faithfully represented.

Readers' attention is also drawn to *Leaving Home, a Training Course and Resources Guide*, full of invaluable help and ideas, from the Youth Work Press (1991).

The work described in this book was funded by ESRC award number XC05250021 with additional support from City University.

Outline

Social science research is usually undertaken at the more or less direct behest of policy-makers and written for the benefit of other social scientists. This inevitably colours its entire conception, execution and presentation. This study was part of a larger piece of unusually 'pure' research into the lives of young people in the late 1980s and early 1990s. While it deals with important policy issues, the futility is recognized of trying to influence by reasoned argument and logical demonstration alone those in power to act on behalf of anyone else. Rather the study merely aims to describe what is going on within certain limited social parameters and relate this to larger economic and historical developments. It is not presented primarily for the so-called 'community' of researchers. Instead, I hope that young people themselves, perhaps not so different from those described, might be interested in the accounts of others in the similar situation of starting out in life. While it may therefore find readers in sixth forms, at FE colleges and in the first years of undergraduate courses, the book is still bound by some of the conventions of academic research. So it begins with a review of the literature – a necessary ritual to establish the author's familiarity with the field and containing the usual fulsome references to all his previous publications. This introduction also raises some of the questions the research initially hoped to answer. From there on it tries to give a sense of the process of collecting the interview cases. This may be familiar to fellow researchers and may or may not encourage others in similar undertakings. Such an account also gives the reader an opportunity to judge the validity of the findings. The four succeeding chapters introduce each labour market area of the study in turn and the first section in each sets the scene for the interviews that follow by briefly describing the locality. To an extent, interviewees are allowed to tell their own stories and analysis is left largely to the reader at this stage. Finally, the last chapter sums up the results of the study and divides the interviewees, so far presented individually, into representative types. The conclusion then anticipates future matters of interest and concern, pointing, as is habitual, towards new areas for further research. Lastly, an Afterword by Sheena Ashford compares the advantages and disadvantages of qualitative and quantitative methods of social study with reference to this less than perfect attempt to combine them.

'Home is the place where, when you have to go there,
They have to let you in.'

Robert Frost, 'The Death of the Hired Man' in *Selected Poems*,
Penguin, 1955.

Chapter 1

A Necessary Introduction

THE 'PROBLEM' WITH YOUTH

'Youth' was not an area for specific study until psychologist Stanley Hall identified it as 'adolescence' in his 1904 book of that title. As a social construction rather than a psychological stage of development youth was not recognized until the study of age-graded societies by anthropologists (e.g. Mead, 1935). In tribal societies ruled by elders, age along with gender were the principles of social organization with clear demarcations and highly structured rites of passage for individuals passing through the recurrent traditional cycle from one age status to another. By contrast, in dynamic industrial societies, where the principle of social order follows lines of class, constant change and ambiguity attach to stages of life that once seemed clearly defined.

During the period of relative affluence for these industrially developed societies after the Second World War, extended education systems separated learning and labour for still longer. Young people acquired their own economic identity for the first time with the creation of a youth market for products particularly aimed at their increased spending power. Without the responsibilities of their elders but with money to spend, this group came to be regarded as a special social problem and proliferating studies blossomed into a sociology of youth. It may seem strange that to a society for which eternal youth was the ideal sold by advertising to millions, young people themselves appeared as a growing problem. Yet, 'Increasingly', as Gill Jones wrote, 'the emphasis was on generational conflict: far from representing the nation's hopes for the future, the young were coming to be seen as a threat to the established order' (1988).

Not all young people were a threat of course; it was predominantly working-class youngsters who were the focus of attention as they created the increasingly bizarre and exotic series of youth cultures that were incorporated into popular culture from the 1950s Teddy Boys on through the Mods and Rockers to Punk. It has even been suggested (by Cohen, 1986) that the interest in youth of ageing sociologists nostalgic for lost working-class roots was sustained by the same desire to stay forever young that seemed to grip the rest of society. More fundamentally, of course, research followed political priorities as succeeding 'moral panics' constructed delinquents through to football hooligans as threats to the established order. For the first time, Bernard Davies argued *(Threatening Youth*, 1986), a coherent national youth policy was in the making in the UK, designed to contain as well as 'threaten' young men. At the same time the series of ethnographic studies of various more or less threatening youth groups was integrated into sociology's concern with structure through a focus upon social reproduction, for example in Paul Willis's romanticized portrait of working-class 'lads', *Learning to Labour* (1977).

Research interest shifted when youth subcultures could no longer be so easily sustained by a buoyant youth labour market. In the late 1970s it was the transition from school to work that came to be seen as critical, as schools were blamed for creating the latest youth problem (or problem for youth) of mass unemployment (see Ainley, 1988). Workless youth, and the succession of 'training' schemes that were devised to occupy them, then became the focus of study. As these involved up to a third of working-class school leavers and indirectly affected many others, there was an emphasis upon studying '"ordinary" or "non-problem" young people', as Hutson and Jenkins put it (1989, p. 5). 'Ordinary Kids', as Brown – also in Swansea – called them (1987), were now the problem, pushed, as Coffield and his colleagues in the North-East wrote, into *Growing Up at the Margins* (1986). So much so that for Mac an Ghaill, 'The concept of "youth" now appears as a metaphor for limited and limiting opportunities' (1990, p. 121).

When the economy revived somewhat after 1986, demographic factors also contributed to making youth itself less of a problem and more of a marketable commodity (at least in some parts of the country). Now the problems for youth were associated ones like housing. Cusack and Roll (1985) asserted that unemployment and simultaneous loss of young people's welfare rights were exacerbating a growing problem of teenage homelessness. Also there was continued study of 'disadvantaged' (i.e. discriminated against) groups such as black youth. Changes in the labour market also contributed to recognition of young women's importance and youth studies became less male-centred.

Now new technology, by blurring the distinction between manual and mental labour and with rapid technical change requiring lifelong instead of once-and-for-all school/college learning, is extending youth beyond its old association with teenage years upwards. Later marriage with fewer children, both due largely to wider contraceptive use, is reinforcing this trend, leading to a new 'post-adolescent youth' when adult rights exist without adult responsibilities. Twenty-five is the new age of majority according to Britain's 1988 social security legislation. This pays a lower rate of Income Support and Housing Benefit to those under 25 on the grounds that most are not householders and that they should not be encouraged to leave their parents' home. This seems a purely arbitrary division, although the latest directions at the time of writing from the government for its ever-changing programme of Youth Training envisage the training of skilled workers continuing to 'generally by the time of a young person's 23rd birthday'.

There is also some popular resonance for a divide at 25; for example, Mansfield and Collard wrote that for most of their sample of newly-weds:

> twenty-five years was the watershed . . . by this time (the 'end of youth' according to one young man) the free-living period should be abandoned in order to settle down into marriage. Public recognition of 16–25 as the 'travelling years' is perhaps neatly symbolised by concessionary fares to the under-25s. (1988, p. 57)

Indeed, the distinguished Romanian sociologist Fred Mahler suggested that prolonged education and vocational preparation have pushed young people beyond 30
into a new limbo of 'post-adolescence' requiring a new science of 'juventology' to
describe their situation adequately (in Adamski and Grootings, 1989).

At the same time as protracted education and training is raising the threshold of
adulthood, there is a simultaneous lowering of the formal adult threshold. For
example, the voting age has been lowered, along with the age for marriage without
parental consent, for undertaking hire-purchase agreements, etc. These simultaneous
and contradictory developments are the source of much confusion, not least for
young people themselves.

LEAVING HOME IN THE '16–19 INITIATIVE'

The Economic and Social Science Research Council's 16–19 Initiative, of which this
study was a part, was launched in 1986 when concern about youth was at a new high,
especially after the 1981–5 riots or uprisings in the inner cities. The year 1985, as
Kiernan pointed out, was the peak year for the cohort born in the early 1960s so that
'there were more young people aged 16–24 years than at any time for half a century'
(1986, p. 2). In addition, it was no longer clear what was happening to young people
after they left school, compared to twenty years previously when 'school leavers were
sorted by the schools in the proportions 20:40:40, corresponding to the traditional
hierarchy in manufacturing industry between non-manual, skilled manual and
unskilled manual labour' (Ainley, 1989, p. 11). At the same time the claims for
success that were being made for the government's Youth Training Scheme were
growing more strident (see Ainley and Corney, 1990).

Unlike the Manpower Services Commission's monitoring of its own programmes
of Youth Training, independent academic study did not attempt a large national
follow-up. Instead, it followed the ESRC's previous Young People in Society
programme to embrace a number of independent studies of adolescent development
in areas such as occupational and political socialization, drinking and smoking,
friendship and delinquency (see Bynner, 1987). It similarly used questionnaire surveys
linked to interviews and ethnographies in area studies. This followed the example of
Ashton and Maguire, whose study *Young Adults in the Labour Market* (1986) had
concluded that local labour market factors outweighed virtually all other influences
upon young people's employment careers. Four areas were selected, two of them
(Swindon and Kirkcaldy) because they had already been extensively studied by a
previous ESRC Economic Life Initiative. Two others (Liverpool and Sheffield) were
chosen because they reflected the academic interests in sociology and psychology that
the Initiative aimed to combine to describe and explain the contemporary economic
and political socialization of young people.

In each area 800 young people in their fifth year in state secondary (but not special)
schools were randomly selected along with another 800 two years older. These two
groups were followed up from 1987 to 1989. The core study of the Initiative aimed to
chart the economic and political socialization of these school-leavers in their contrasted local labour markets. Associated studies concentrated upon particular groups
of ethnic minority youth, stepchildren, rural youth, etc. (See Banks *et al.*, 1991 and
Bates *et al.*, 1991, forthcoming, for the overall findings.) Among these special groups
were those who left home during the survey at an atypically early age. While this was

unusual, it was not necessarily a problem, and the study that is reported here differs from many of the youth studies very briefly outlined above in that the young people who were studied did not present a particular problem. For example, they were not (by definition) among the 50 000 young people estimated to become homeless each year (SHAC, 1990). They were unusual only in having moved from their original home at an earlier age than average.

'The main period of leaving home activity amongst women spans ages 19 to 23 and amongst men ages 20 to 25' (Kiernan, 1986, p. 6). This activity, as Kiernan went on to say, is still associated with 'leaving home and marriage being coincident or people marrying fairly quickly after leaving home' (ibid., p. 7). Since age of marriage has been rising since its low point of 22.4 (average both sexes combined) in 1970, it could be expected that age of home-leaving would rise along with it. However, it was suggested by Young (1987) that in the context of Australia and by Harris (1983, p. 221) that in the context of modern industrial society as a whole there is emerging 'a period early in adult life when the individual defines him/herself independently of their familial status'. Certainly, as Kiernan wrote elsewhere (1987), 'there has been a dramatic reversal in marriage behaviour; young people are marrying less and marrying at later ages'. This seems to contradict the greater popularity of marriage as an institution, which several commentators have pointed to and which is clearly evidenced in representative surveys such as *Social Trends*. Nevertheless cohabitation as a preliminary or 'trial' stage of marriage, if not (yet?) as a substitute for it, is increasingly common. Some of these new trends should be visible in a sample of young people who had left home before the age of 20.

How home-leaving was affected by the local economy for young people entering the labour market should also be apparent in the four different labour market areas; also the effects of very different local housing situations – in other words, the interrelation of the employment and housing markets in the four areas. Differences would be particularly marked in the two poles of Liverpool and Swindon. On the Isle of Sheppey, Wallace (1987) had shown that young unemployed people were twice as likely to be still living in their parents' home as those young people who were regularly employed. In larger and more representative labour markets, initial analysis of the '16–19' data showed that many of the unemployed youth in the depressed areas in the North had moved to work, although it later appeared that many of them had subsequently moved back again. Indeed the 1984 and 1987 national Labour Force Surveys showed quite clearly not only that young people with fewer ties were, unsurprisingly, more likely to move to find work than people older than 24 but that the unemployed, older and younger, were also more likely to move in search of jobs (Wells, 1989). Sullivan and Falkingham also confirmed that

> Young hardcore unemployed people tend to be more mobile than average: 40% of them had lived in four or more places since age 16, compared with 28% of the permanently employed group (although the unemployed group were more likely to be living at home than the others). (reported in Murphy, 1990)

Eversley speculated, 'It is possible that the propensity of young people to leave home and to set up their own households has been slowed down by the recession', adding '"Love on the Dole" is possible, but unemployment still acts as a deterrent' (1983, pp. 82, 92). Subsequent social security changes have made it still more difficult.

If moving in search of work applied especially to young men, it had also been proposed by Griffin (1985), among others, that young women's response to unemployment was to get married and have children earlier than usual and as an alternative to paid labour. Or, as Margaret Thatcher put it, 'These young single girls deliberately become pregnant in order to jump a housing queue and get welfare payments' (*The Times* 10.11.88). This 'immorality' was the female equivalent to the 'threat' of male violence. Mrs Thatcher's comment did not appear to be borne out by national figures which showed that as a percentage of all live births to unmarried women, births to women under twenty have been decreasing since 1976 while unemployment was rising (*Population Trends*, Vol. 56). However, Penhale's 1989 analysis of the 1981 Census showed 'that the effect of unemployment is to advance the timing of motherhood among women from all social backgrounds' (p. 29), even though he cautioned that while 'some young women may indeed have children in response to unemployment, most do not' (p. 27). Whether this was the case in the high-unemployment areas in the North as compared with Swindon in the then more prosperous South should also be clear from the '16–19' sample.

These then were some of the questions initially posed for this research into the young people in the '16–19' sample who had left home during the period of study.

TRAJECTORIES AND TRANSITIONS

Career trajectory was a central organizing concept of the ESRC's 16–19 Initiative from its inception. As summarized by Roberts and Parsell,

> Trajectory implies linear and predictable progression . . . that the sequences of positions in education, training schemes and jobs through which most 16–18 year olds progress are determined independently of their own inclinations. (1988a, pp. 3–4)

Their notion derived from Erik Olin Wright's 'A general framework for the analysis of class structure' and his idea of 'contradictory locations within class relations' (1984). This applied not only to the managers and professional experts he was especially concerned with but also to young people, who, Wright said, are in 'pre-class positions, linked with greater or less certainty to specific class destinations' (1978, p. 94). This might seem to constitute youth as a class in themselves – as Musgrove had once proposed, 'relatively independent of the stratification system of adults' (1969, p. 50). While that is going too far, the notion of trajectory allowed for changes from class of origin to class of destination and for the perpetual change of occupations and statuses within and between classes that distinguishes a class from a caste system.

How individuals experience their personal trajectories was to be illuminated by the psychological perspective that also informed the '16–19' study, 'focusing upon the social psychological processes of identity formation, social representation and attribution, and agency and self-efficacy' (Breakwell, 1987). This might go some way towards answering what Phil Cohen in *Rethinking the Youth Question* (1986), called 'the 64 000 dollar question. . . . How has the decline in the political cultures of the manual working class, and the rise of structural youth unemployment affected the formation and outlook of non-student youth?' (p. 62). The '16–19' could not attempt to answer this question save in terms of a series of transitions and the stages between them.

British society as a whole lacks shared communal rituals to confirm adult status, like the religious rites of First Communion or Bar-Mitzvah, or the secular ceremonies of the US school-leaving 'prom'. For young people in the UK therefore, as Bazalgette wrote, 'The key transition is the act of leaving school, which becomes in the young person's mind, the ritual changeover point from being a child to becoming an adult' (1978, p. 47). This continues to be the case even when there is no work available to transit to and is one reason why, as Bynner (1989) pointed out, 'Of all the industrial countries Britain retains among a substantial section of its population a profound aversion to education.' The crucial importance of the transition from school to work as marking the difference between dependent child and independent adult had been emphasized by Kitchen to describe what he saw as the 'culture shock' involved in the passage 'from learning to earning' (1944). Although in the full employment conditions of the long boom after the Second World War, as Roberts wrote towards the end of the period in 1971, 'Repeated empirical studies [showed] . . . that most young people make the transition into employment without experiencing any major difficulty' (pp. 133–4).

'Transition' has a comforting ring because it is by definition only temporary.

> The concept of a 'transition phase' in adolescence is often employed as a palliative for society's functional problems of recruiting and integrating youth into adult worlds. If it is merely 'a stage they are going through', then adults frankly need not confront the problems their behaviour raises, because, after all, 'they'll grow out of it'. (Berger, 1963)

As well as the transition from school and childhood, there is also 'the transition from the youth to adult labour markets' (Ashton, Maguire and Spilsbury, 1990, p. 168). As well as the complication that transitions vary as between boys and girls and for the different segments of the labour market that they enter, 'transitions, far from representing a simple progression, vary in their timing and ordering (or whether they are ordered at all) according to class' (Jones, 1986, p. 1). As Cohen wrote, 'each class culture throws its own grid of representation over the life cycle, and what is a mark of maturity in one may be a sign of backwardness in another'. These different transitions at separate levels are not experienced discretely by those involved in them but are part of what Riseborough (1988, p. 28) called 'the osmotic totality' of their biographies. Moreover, new markers of maturity are continually being improvised, although what Kernan designated 'perhaps the definitive step to adulthood' remains 'the transition to parenthood' (1986, p. 11). This confirms the final socially approved step from family of origin to family of destination.

Wage, dole or training allowance gives at least some independent control to the young person for the first time, although a succession of social security changes has increased the enforced dependence of young people upon their parents and pushed back the age of adult independence for the young unemployed. Even if this only substitutes dependence upon the state for dependence upon parents or guardians, there is a change in responsibility. Instead of someone else having total responsibility for you, you have at least some responsibility for yourself. With the creation of your own family as the last step to adulthood, you have responsibility for others. As a first step on this royal road the social significance of physically moving from the childhood home to 'your own home' is second only in symbolic and actual significance to the transition from school to the labour market if not to work. This

> transition from dependent adult-in-waiting to autonomous adult involves a process of dislocation and relocation, both physical and psychological. This is why 'a place of one's own' is of such significance, both as a means and as an expression of the transition which is being made. (Mansfield and Collard, 1988, p. 55)

'Natural' though it may seem, this emphasis upon autonomy and independence is historically and culturally specific. For example:

In normal family life in Japan there is an emphasis on interdependence and reliance upon others, while in America the emphasis is on independence and self-assertion. In Japan the infant is seen more as a separate biological organism who from the beginning, in order to develop, needs to be drawn into increasingly interdependent relations with others. In America, the infant is seen more as a dependent biological organism who, in order to develop, needs to be made increasingly independent of others. (Caudill and Weinstein, 1972)

In the 1981 UK Census only 10 per cent of 17-year-olds had left home but by age 25 only 10 per cent of daughters and 25 per cent of sons remained in their parents' home (Wall and Penhale, 1989). The few studies of this process agree that it is not necessarily a simple once and for all step but rather likely to be prolonged. As Young stated of Australia,

The evidence suggests that the major part of the movement from home and back again is completed by age 25 years. Only beyond that age has the adult child finally established independent and permanent living arrangements away from the parents' household. (1987, p. 19)

So that 'What seems to be happening is that a preliminary stage of leaving home now exists, occurring at a younger age and involving a high incidence of returning home' (p. 35). There is thus 'a duration of the leaving home process of almost five years' (p. 41).

Some of the consequences of this period were indicated by Goldscheider and Waite (1987), who claimed on demographic evidence from large-scale US surveys that

Whatever the type of living arrangement, the experience of a role hiatus that removes young women physically from one family context seems to result in a delay in their entering a new one. Among men, the effects are inconsistent, or even opposing. It is possible therefore that women gain more from independence than men.

As Waite had speculated previously,

Young women appear to be building a set of new expectations that increasingly reduce their orientation to traditional family roles and to the likelihood of marriage. These include increased education and work experience, as well as non-family living. Even the increases in parental divorce experienced by young people seem to have a greater impact on marriage for women than for men. (with Kobrin, 1984).

They concluded:

Pressure to find alternatives to traditional marriage can be expected to increase as a result of these combined experiences. For some, this may mean non-marriage, at least for a while. However, some of the pressure is likely to be felt on the institution of marriage itself, further reducing its dependence on the traditional division of labour and placing more emphasis on companionship and equality.

The fluidity of the situation is shown by demographic research published in Canada, where, similarly to other industrially developed countries, 'While more elderly Canadians have been living alone, the young have been leaving the parental home at earlier ages than in the past'. But Boyd and Pryor (1989) found 'empirical evidence for the impressionistic reports of increased tendencies among never-married young

Canadian adults to live with parents', returning home to form a 'cluttered nest'. Van Vliet (1988) related these changes to economic conditions, pointing out that the percentage of young Americans living with their parents reached a peak during the 1930s depression, fell after 1945 and has risen again during the 1970s. Schnaiberg and Goldenberg (1989) also point to what they called 'the returning young adult syndrome' in the USA, where they saw it as 'the major symptom of certain recent changes in the American middle-class family system' and 'a significant traumatic event for many of the families experiencing it'. They see it as reinforced by the rising age of marriage but caused by 'constricted opportunity structures for many young adults' leaving college and unable to find jobs, or at least jobs that enable them to live independently. In Britain also, with student loans and other changes associated with 'enterprise' in higher education, students are an increasingly problematic group of young people.

In a rapidly changing social situation transitions between stages in the individual life course can thus extend into stages in their own right with effects upon preceding and successive stages and upon other dimensions of the transition process. Could any of this be observed in this '16–19' sample of young people who had moved, albeit at an earlier than average age, from their parental or original home? The questionnaires which the young people filled in covered a three-year period from, in the case of the younger cohort, 15–16 to 18–19, or, in that of the older, from 17–18 to 20–21. Although an interview towards the end of that period would retrospectively cover the events prior to it, only a section of the individual's life history would be recorded. This could be but a part of their life course, as of their career trajectory, or their family's life cycle.

In any case, 'The central problem in using the concept of the family life cycle is that it refers only to the nuclear family' (Hohn and Mackensen, 1989, p. 4). 'Life cycle' has often been associated with the related idea of a cycle of poverty which the then Sir Keith Joseph reimported from the USA. Cycles of poverty were supposed to trap families within a new 'underclass' and there was much talk about breaking the cycle. The notion of a new 'underclass' was given sociological substance by Pahl's influential 1984 study, again in the peculiar and isolated conditions of Sheppey. However, if any such 'underclass' existed elsewhere, with its own distinct pattern of life totally removed from any involvement in orthodox paid labour, it would surely be apparent in the continuously depressed economy of Merseyside. However, even here, Roberts (1990) concluded that there was no evidence for the emergence of such an underclass that would remain unemployed if by some miracle full employment returned.

Dissatisfaction with the functionalist model of the life cycle had led family historians and sociologists to use the alternative of life-course analysis. As described by Elder, 'A life-course framework . . . facilitates study of divergent or non-conventional family patterns, as well as the conventional, by working with the life histories of individuals' (1978, p. 26). Whereas the life-cycle approach records stages of parenthood, the life-course perspective examines the processes of transition between these stages. Moreover, it sees them in the context of the individuals' autobiographic sense of the timing of their own life, together with what Haraven (1982) called 'family time and industrial time'. In interviews with young people at a particular stage in their lives it would be a privilege to share with them their sense of how what they were doing related to the rest of their lives past and future, as well as to those of their relatives in the older generation and their contemporaries in the same generation.

Interviews would also record how this connected with the wider economic life of the locality in which the young people had grown up – with revival in Swindon, partial recovery in Sheffield, more mixed fortunes in Kirkcaldy District and unabated decline in Liverpool; overall, the North as against the South. Beyond that again they would perhaps comprehend a still larger historical conjuncture of which interviewees would be more or less conscious.

HISTORICAL AND CLASS PERSPECTIVES

'To leave home is the most straightforward of all migratory moves. It is something that nearly all of us do at some stage in our lives, yet paradoxically, very little is known about it' (Wall, 1978). The picture of how it was, and perhaps how many people think it still should be, is presented in Diana Leonard's classic study, published only in 1980, of growing up in working-class Swansea during the 1960s. Then 'it was almost unheard of for young people to leave home prior to marriage' (p. 61). The transition from parental to own home happened at the same time as marriage and both were enfolded with becoming adult. They involved a long period of preparation and saving for young men who had graduated from apprenticed boys 'mated' to an older man into proper (trades-)men, while women filled their bottom drawers on the proceeds of lower-paid and less skilled work. The event was surrounded by all the rituals of romance, courtship and engagement. As summarized by Hutson and Jenkins,

> Sexuality was only acceptably expressed within marriage; considerable stigma attached to unmarried pregnancy, which almost inevitably led quickly to the Register Office. There was a clear preference for 'white' weddings in church, one of the central components of an elaborate ritual cycle of prestation and counter-prestation between the two kin groups involved. (p. 65)

Although this is the popular stereotype that used to be followed by all the respectable classes and which is still modelled upon the ideal sustained by the faery world of wedding cards and Royal ritual, it was not always so.

In an historical study of four areas (including Swindon coincidentally) Wall showed that 'the age at leaving home' (1978) has varied considerably over time. Marriage in late-medieval England was characteristically later, so that households consisted of parents and their unmarried children up to their late twenties. Children often remained at home to work, acquiring hereditary skills from the older generation, e.g. lace-making. Thirteen per cent of the population were servants, generally young, unmarried and often related to the head of the household whom they served. Apprenticed boys lived in the workshops of their masters, when not wandering around Europe acquiring a varied practical experience in their craft. Boys left home before girls, even though women, as now, married younger than men. Indeed, Wall quotes an Italian visitor to England in the seventeenth century (cited in MacFarlane, 1970) who was appalled at the cruelty of the English when he witnessed children away from their parents in service at age 8.

During the two to three hundred-year-long pre-industrial phase, homeworking, even though it kept families together, as they had been on the farm, undermined the traditional structures of inheritance of land and property in the countryside. This process reduced parental control over children and loosened the bonds between the generations. Early marriage became more frequent, often to a partner of choice rather than one arranged by fathers. Within artisan families the sexual divisions of labour also became blurred and more flexible than within traditional peasant families (see Mendick, 1976, p. 296).

It is a commonplace to note that industrialization, among its many other effects, separated production from reproduction; most people no longer worked at home but went out to work in factories instead of nearby fields. This new division of public and private life, so important for the later construction of the notion of the Englishman's home as his castle, and the Victorian ideals of masculinity and femininity, was first experienced as dislocation. As Levine wrote, 'The ethic of equality and mutuality . . . disappeared from the marriage itself, replaced by a highly segmented form of nuptuality in which the worlds of husbands and wives barely overlapped' (1985, p. 178). As for children, 'Under the factory system, children and parents were working in different places. . . . The result was a frequent desertion of the home by the children and a considerable juvenile vagrancy problem' (Sanderson, 1972, p. 79). For Engels, this heralded the 'utter' and 'necessary' 'dissolution of the family', for

> The children who grow up under such conditions are utterly ruined for later family life, can never feel at home in the family which they themselves found, because they have always been accustomed to isolation, and they contribute therefore to the already general undermining of the family of the working class. (1969, 172–3)

By the mid-nineteenth century, related Wall, 'The conditions of life in large towns gave rise to situations in which children would remain longer in the parental household than they had either in pre-industrial England or in rural areas'. Without effective contraception but with the new need to limit family size, marriage was often delayed. Still, around ten per cent of children of all ages lived separately from their parents, mostly with relatives but others orphaned, left behind by migrating parents, avoiding overcrowding by sharing with others, in lodgings, apprenticed or in domestic service. 'From age ten onwards,' according to Anderson,

> the proportion who had 'left home' rose rapidly. By age 25 over three quarters of boys were no longer at home but under half were household heads. Indeed 30 per cent or more of boys and 46 per cent of girls were neither 'children' nor heads of households. At the peak age of 20 some 49 per cent of boys and 46 per cent of girls were in this 'intermediate' residential status. (1983, p. 10)

In sum, there were not the clear distinctions that later emerged, with no 'sudden rush' or 'set age', so that, as Wall wrote, 'The exodus from the parental household was a very much more gradual process than today'. By comparison, to quote Anderson again,

> an important characteristic of family life – indeed of all life – in the years after the Second World War was its greater age-gradedness and predictability. A young person aged, say, 14, looking forward in the 1960s could, with a reasonable probability of being right, have predicted within a very few years the timing of his or her future life course – leaving school, entering employment, leaving home, marrying and setting up home, early patterns of child-bearing and rearing. None of this would have been possible in the nineteenth century; much would still have been difficult before 1945. (ibid, p. 13)

Neither was it so important who young children resided with; as still in many Third World countries today, even quite young children might be brought up by neighbours or relatives if their parents were unable to look after them for any reason – often because of migration. Smaller families, as compared with these larger extended ones, mean that child-rearing in the metropolitan countries is now compressed into the early years of marriage. The phenomenon of 'an empty nest' once children have left is also a new one, giving parents the potential for a new start in life, so long as they do not then have to take on the care of their own aged parents.

Wall noted that children of the gentry also left home early but states that there was a subsequent divergence, so that 'in contemporary Western society the higher the status of the family, the longer the child will remain at home'. Prolonged childhood, as opposed to early child labour, became the ideal which the ruling class set their inferiors. This was, as has often been pointed out, a childhood in which parents played small part, despatching their offspring to the care of nurses, nannies, schools and colleges from an early age. Less education and early marriage and childbirth is still widely regarded as characteristically lower class. While it is rising, the average age at marriage of women of social class five is 22 compared with 26 for social class one women (the average age at birth of first child for class one and two is 27.9 compared with 23.7 for classes four and five). There is also a social class gradient in divorce, which is four times as likely in social class five as in classes one and two (Haskey, 1983). This phenomenon is compounded by the increasing likelihood of divorce the younger are the partners, so that teenage marriages are least likely of any to survive.

Jones (1986) proposed a 'typology of youth class' in which 'it is the middle class who are likely to leave the parental home earliest' (p. 11). However, drawing upon Leonard's popularly understood distinction between 'leaving home' and just 'living away', she qualified this as referring to students who '"live away" at a younger age' while 'the working class "leave home", later but more permanently' (p. 13). She also associated the emerging 'intermediate household status of "living with others"' with what she called 'the stable middle class' (ibid.) – whereas 'When the stable working class leave home for reasons other than marriage, they follow a pattern which is similar to that of the stable middle class, but are more likely to live with kin'. This is not 'a move towards independent living . . . since the resident is still likely to be in a dependent relationship with the relative who is the head of the household' (p. 15). The other two groups of her typology – upwardly mobile working class and downwardly mobile middle class – showed 'patterns which are between those of the two "extreme" groups' (p. 12).

Payne and Payne (1977) suggested that social division was shaped by housing opportunities, so that the direction of housing careers was determined at an early stage since young couples faced the choice between on the one hand delaying conception while saving for home-ownership and on the other early childbirth to gain eligibility to council housing. Reworking their findings, Murphy and Sullivan (1983) associated home ownership with low fertility and council housing with high fertility. Later (1986) they noted 'the effect of childbearing filtering couples into different tenures' but added, 'Unemployment is strongly reinforcing the stratification of British housing both within and between tenures'. This underlies what Hutson and Jenkins, following Pahl, suspected is 'increasingly a defining feature of British society . . . the polarisation between "no wage" and "two wage" households' (1989, p. 15).

Ineichen (1981), tracing the 'housing careers' of a sample of newly married couples in Bristol, showed that 'despite some overlap of age, income and occupational status, owner-occupiers and council tenants develop as groups with contrasting social characteristics, partly as a response to structural factors within the housing market'.

Again, he indicated associated differences in life patterns: 'probable eventual owner-occupiers' knew each other longer before marriage and had fewer children later, compared with council tenants 'typified by extreme youth, low occupational class, low earnings and rapid fertility'. 'Within eighteen months of marriage, therefore, two distinct housing groups had appeared, with marked differences of age, class and income'. Ineichen used the 'career' approach to 'illustrate the ways motivation is restricted and shaped by the housing choices available; in other words, one of the processes by which structure is formed'.

The notion of a housing career might be valuable to trace the initial transitions of young people setting out to independent living in very different areas of the country with different housing choices available to them. These choices had been constrained during the 1980s by the rise in mortgage rates and, in most places if not continuously, the rise of house prices and rents, public and private. Choices were also narrowed by the lack of new public housing starts, the deterioration of much existing housing and the loss of local authority stock through council right to buy schemes. In this situation the importance of 'having a home of one's own' has changed, as Crow and Allen noted (p. 19).

All these accounts suggested distinct types of parental home leaving, with separate starting points leading to still further segregation, if not polarization. However, Anderson speculated, 'Possibly we are returning to a situation of much greater diversity of experience . . . in the harsher, more uncertain and more diversified economy in the 1980s.' He warned: 'the resultant changes would by no means necessarily be for the better' (1983, p. 14). Instead of clear stratification, this suggests a broadening spectrum of positions and their associated behaviour patterns while the distance grows between the two extreme poles.

Kiernan in the same volume attributed the fact of 'conjugal links being more varied and vulnerable than in the recent past' (p. 17) to 'a shift in the timing of marriage' (p. 22). Elsewhere (*New Society* 16.2.90) she claimed, 'It is now virtually a majority practice to cohabit before marrying' and saw in this 'nubile cohabitation' of young people living together a prelude, or alternative, to marriage, the reason for more than 25 per cent of children now being born outside wedlock. 'Is Britain likely to follow Sweden?' she asked, where marriage and cohabitation are largely indistinguishable.

The future behaviour of today's adolescents, 'the largest potential category of additional family founders (and household formers)', is, Eversley admitted, 'anybody's guess'.

> They may stay with their parents; they may form single sex groups, or cohabiting heterosexual partnerships; they may marry, live in communes, or even become vagrants. . . . If there is, therefore one over-riding policy question which needs to be faced in the field of the family and the housing system, it is the future of those youngsters who would, in former times, now be forming their own households. What they will do, where they will live, whether they will form partnerships, and when and where they will be able to accomplish this, that is the main area of uncertainty. (1983, pp. 93, 94)

The study of young people leaving home in the ESRC's 16–19 Initiative should at least go some way towards answering some of these questions.

A FIRST LOOK AT THE DATA

A first look at the data from the questionnaires returned by the 6400 16–19 year olds sent them showed 1073 (= 16.77 per cent) had recorded that they had lived with people other than their parents or 'in their own home', as the 1988 questionnaire phrased it. Of these 329 were in the first year of the survey (=10.28 per cent of that total) and 744 (= 23.25 per cent) when the sample was one year older in 1988. Even though it was evident that some of those early movers had gone back to their parental home (c. 17.8 per cent of them) this total seemed unexpectedly high. Knocking on a number of doors in Swindon to be told by indignant parents that 'She's never left home; she's always lived with us!', or by puzzled children that 'There must be some mistake', soon made it clear that this initial figure was an overestimate of the number of movers by about 20 per cent. It was necessary to double-check who respondents, recorded as living 'in their own home', were living with and to drop those who listed parents. In addition, not all of the 329 who recorded an address different from that of their parents or step-parents in 1987 would have moved from their parental home recently, though the increase in numbers at an address different from their parental home by the next year indicated that many of them might have done so. They could have been living with people other than their parents/step-parents – 'other relatives', 'friends or relations', 'other people' or just 'other', as the questionnaire defined them – for some time. However, all of them, even in the extreme hypothetical case of adopted children, would have moved from their mothers at some time. So in this sense all of the 1073 less 20 per cent (= 858) were movers and not just 'living at an address other than their parental home'.

Overall, more young women than young men had left home (in a ratio of 3:2). This corresponded with the well known finding that, as summarized by Kiernan, 'Women leave home at younger ages and at a faster pace than men, one half having left for the first time before their twentieth birthday' (1986, p. 10). Since women on average also marry younger than men, there is clearly still an association between home-leaving and marriage, although, as Jones noted, 'There is likely to be less association now than before between the age at marriage and that of leaving home' (1986, p. 6–7).

Among the 744 movers by 1988, 115 were students, 290 in the home of a relative or friend, 218 said they were in their own house or flat, 77 in lodgings or digs, plus 44 'others'. Compared with the 329 movers one year earlier, 11 were then students, 204 in the home of a relative or friend, 83 'in their own house or flat', 26 in lodgings, plus 29 'others'.

Of the 290 in the home of a relative or friend by April 1988, 160 were female and 130 male. Only 2 of these men and 2 of the women said they had their own children, one of the mothers reporting that she was married, though 6 women (one with a child) and 5 men recorded that they were cohabiting, and 13 women (one with a child and one expecting) said they were engaged, as did 4 of the men. Moving to marry, cohabit or start a family did not seem therefore to be a reason for these young people to have moved into the homes of friends or relatives. By area, 67 were in Kirkcaldy (36F:31M), the same number in Liverpool (34F:33M) with 77 in Swindon (44F:33M) and 79 in Sheffield (45F:34M). Nearly half those living with friends or relatives in Swindon were working, which might have stimulated them to move from their (in most cases) parents' home. However, the virtually equal numbers of those living with friends or relatives in Sheffield, where only 20 per cent of them were employed and

18 per cent unemployed, showed that other influences than purely economic were at work. In Kirkcaldy a similar percentage were employed, though many more were unemployed in Liverpool.

Of the 218 who recorded that they were living in their own house or flat, 148 were female and only 70 male. However, this was misleading because many had misunderstood the question to mean living with their parents 'in their own (family) home' and not, as intended, to mean living on their own or with friends in their own accommodation. Of these young women 28 had their own child (= 19 per cent of them compared with 2 per cent teenage mothers in the sample altogether). Nineteen were married, 21 cohabiting and 20 engaged (cf: 4, 4 and 10 of the men). Numbers married, engaged or cohabiting were highest in Sheffield and lowest in Liverpool. Numbers were too low to show significant differences between the areas, for example in local council housing policies for young people. A number of those in their own house or flat had moved, as would be expected, to form their own domestic unit with or without a child, and many of them were otherwise unemployed. The same proportion of these movers as those with relatives or friends were unemployed and this was again the largest group amongst these young people. However, the fact that a larger proportion of this group, especially males, were also working (more than the average for the whole cohort) perhaps showed the necessity for a wage to maintain their independent living.

Sheffield was again the area in which the young people sampled were likeliest to move, perhaps reflecting something of housing conditions locally, though it was now equalled by Kirkcaldy (14 out of 30 being married, engaged or cohabiting, six with children). Swindon had 14 out of 25 of these movers married, engaged or cohabiting, nine with children. Those least likely to move to set up their own domestic unit appeared to be in Liverpool, with 5 out of 22 married, engaged or cohabiting, only one with a child. Compared with the sample overall, in the first year of data collection the number of respondents with children was 1 per cent and Swindon was the area where there were most young mothers (20), contrary to the prediction that this would be a reaction to unemployment. By the second sweep however, 3.9 per cent of females reported that they either had or were expecting a child, with most of them (39) now being in the high unemployment area of Liverpool. The fact that not as many of these young mothers had reported moving as reported having a child or being pregnant showed that there were already a number of 'hidden homeless' – people who presumably needed their own accommodation but had not yet got it. This was another group (along with the homeless) who would not be covered by interviewing only those who had changed their address. (Some cases of homeless youngsters and 'hidden homeless' families were, however, discovered among the interviewees who were eventually interviewed.)

Among the 77 (32F:45M) recorded as living in lodgings or digs, 14 said they were married, cohabiting or engaged of whom only two had children. Moving into private, rented accommodation, even though it might include temporary hotel accommodation prior to rehousing, did not seem therefore to be much of an option for those moving to form their own family. Nor did it account for many of the students in the sample; only 7 of those living in lodgings or digs could be identified as students. It might be natural to think that Kirkcaldy's large share of these movers (43 of the total) might reflect the higher numbers of students from that area over any other, or indicate that lodgings/digs were more easily available there and/or the lack of other accommodation. But later investigation showed Kirkcaldy District had in many ways the best housing situation for young people of the areas studied. The anomaly can therefore be attributed to the larger number of students from the district, most of whom had to move out of the area at least for higher education. Also, many respondents had moved out of the area to find work – nearly as many as for Liverpool and more than for Sheffield.

Looking briefly at the returns for the first questionnaire in 1987, 253 of the 15–18-year-olds then recorded that they were living with relations other than their parents or step-parents. The fact that 140 were in the younger 15–16 age group, and fewer (113) were in the group that was a year older, perhaps showed that they were already living with, and had possibly been brought up by, other relatives and were not, as might have been supposed from the 1988 questionnaire returns, using their other relatives as a staging post or half-way house to independent living. On the other hand, in the 1988 questionnaire 'friends or relatives' were included together, whereas in the first questionnaire these were listed separately, with 76 recording that they lived with 'other people'. For this younger sample, unlike the other one year later, Liverpool was the most, instead of the least, likely area for young people to be living with relatives other than parents or step-parents (78), followed by Kirkcaldy and Swindon (60 cases each) and Sheffield now last with 55 cases.

The picture was clearly complicated! Instead of sitting in front of a screen struggling to make sense both of the figures which it threw up and of the SPSS-X program which produced them, it was necessary to go out into the areas and have a look. This reality came a step nearer as for the first time case numbers were converted into names and addresses and individual lives began to emerge from behind the mass of figures.

Chapter 2

Swindon

ONE OF THE FASTEST GROWING AND MOST RESEARCHED TOWNS IN EUROPE

Swindon is no longer the 'plain country town' William Cobbett passed by nearly two centuries ago at the dawn of an industrial transformation he apprehended but could not understand. 'As a market town on the fringe of the Wiltshire dairying area', where 'textiles and clothing followed leather in importance', in the nineteenth century the town 'enjoyed a larger role than its size alone would have warranted' (Wall, 1978); until, that is, it became 'the workshop of an empire that stretched from Paddington to Penzance', as Howard Newby, the Director of the Economic and Social Science Research Council, put it in his radio programme 'Changing Tracks' (BBC4 22.12.89). The decline of the Great Western Railway works (employing over 14 000 at its 1925 peak) mirrored that of British industry as a whole, although it was offset by Austin-Rover's car plant, employing 4000 by 1959, Peugeot-Citroën (3000) and, more lately, Honda, employing 2000 in the most advanced automated engine plant in Europe. Still, only the superior engineering of Brunel's Great Western Railway allowed high-speed trains to pioneer the M4 artery which fed Swindon's renaissance as a new centre of office services and high-technology manufacturing – 'the pulsing heart of Britain's industrial resurgence', to quote Professor Newby again. It enabled the relocation first of people, as a London overspill town, and later of offices from the capital, including those of the ESRC itself, and it carries the growing numbers who sleep locally but commute daily to Cobbett's 'Great Wen'. Now that there is a general apprehension that humanity stands again at the threshold of changes as awesome in their unforeseeable consequences as those unleashed by the first industrial revolution, Swindon, as Professor Newby said, 'gives us a glimpse of what towns up and down the country might become in the 1990s'.

Swindon's projected 1990 population (147 566; surrounding Thamesdown area, 171 613) makes it one of the fastest growing and also one of the most researched towns in Europe. Yet not only is the role of the railway in sustaining its modern as well as its past development often ignored but so too is that of the military. Indeed Swindon's revival can be dated from the relocation of Plessey and Vickers to the town during the Second World War. As the Greater London Council's 'Industrial

Strategy' stated, 'The South East as a whole is something of a defence-orientated economy.' So Morgan and Sayer note, 'The prominence of the arms industry in Britain's sunbelt is particularly clear in the M4 corridor' (1988, p. 204). They trace the emigration of defence-related precision electronics industries out from central London during the Second World War and link their spread in a 'Golden Crescent', stretching around the capital from Cambridge to Southampton and reaching out towards Bristol, to nearby defence and nuclear establishments at Porton Down, Aldermaston, Harwell, Slough and West Drayton, related in turn to adjacent university research departments. This undermines the view of the area as a showcase for the free play of market forces when 'the corridor's success owes much to state-provided infrastructure and military expenditure, while the most advanced parts of its industry are foreign owned' (ibid., p. 219).

Increasingly though image creates 'success' and even Hall *et al.* (1987), who show 'how accidental the whole process of high technology growth has been' (p. 8) and are not certain that 'phenomena like the M4 corridor are much more than convenient vehicles for features in the business pages or for estate agency promotions' (p. 3), note 'the image or cachet high technology companies give to an area' (p. 58). Yet high-technology industry by the broadest definition accounted for only 6 per cent of employment in Swindon by 1986 (although 20 per cent of manufacturing). The work involved is not necessarily complex; as one of the Swindon interviewees said of her work in an electronics factory, 'It's just fitting little things that go in the back of cars and tellies.' No qualifications were required for this £120 a week shift-work, nor had she been given any training for it.

New offices, however, dominate the townscape, while Morgan and Sayer recall Orwell's description of Kent in their account of the surrounding ' "fat-cat" country of shallow valleys, rolling downlands, patchwork quilts of fields, punctuated by public schools, market towns and twee villages with stone-walled and thatched-roofed cottages . . .' (p. 149). These amenities compensate for the lack of executive housing and other facilities in Swindon, so that the managers and higher professionals live outside the town. Swindon, 'soulless' and 'centreless', compared with nearby Marl-borough, Cirencester or Bath, thus remains a working-class town, even if now largely white collar instead of blue collar. People have come to work there not only from London but from Ireland and the North, for as 'a major beneficiary of overheating further East' Swindon 'owes much to its ability, as an "expanded" town, to grow at a time when development in most of the other South East towns was restricted' (p. 216). Its ethnic minority population is, however, relatively small – Poles who have been there since the war made up around 2 per cent in the 1971 census and in 1981 2.7 per cent were listed as born in the Republic of Ireland, 3.0 from the new Commonwealth and 3.8 from 'the rest of the world'.

Following the 1952 New Town Development Act, and as an 'overspill' town for London, the workforce doubled in size between 1951 and 1981. Spacious estates were laid out with integrated public and private housing that tended to polarize throughout the 1980s. This left not only a small inner urban core but also large public-sector estates with a concentration of social problems. The local authority lost a quarter of its 15 000 housing stock through its tenants' taking advantage of the government's right to buy scheme and was unable to build any more even though the housing waiting list rose towards 5000. However, owner occupation has always been high – even by 1900 60 per cent of households were owner occupiers, 'possibly the highest in the UK' (ESRC, no date), and 70 per cent by 1938. As a result of the Planned

Expansion Scheme initiated in 1954, by 1981 the percentage of private owners had dropped to 63 per cent but was still above the 56 per cent national average. (The private rented sector is small – 7 per cent compared with 13 per cent nationally.) The council itself initiated a build-for-sale programme in the 1960s. Possibly because of this long tradition of owner occupation, the identification of home owners with Conservatism did not occur in Swindon, which is one factor that allowed it to retain a Labour council while sending Tory MPs to Parliament.

As a result of so much in-migration, Swindon's population is generally younger than the national average, particularly in some parts of the town. Many people who came to live in Swindon were employed in offices relocated from high costs in the capital but communicating through the latest technology; so much so that Swindon for a time almost became again a company town, this time serving Allied Dunbar (1800 employees) instead of the railway works, which closed in 1986. However, there was also much foreign penetration following the general trend.

> In particular, multinationals from advanced, high-wage economies establish operations in Britain to obtain the advantage of cheap (and well-qualified) labour and to establish a European market and servicing base. They tend to establish such a base in an existing area of industrial concentration, with particular reference to international communications, implying a location in the M4 Corridor close to Heathrow. Since they are large, they may well decentralise routine assembly operations to lower-wage peripheral regions. (Hall *et al.*, p. 89) [For example to Scotland (see p. 75).]

This results in 'spatial divisions of labour' (Massey, 1984) 'from Palo Alto, California, to the Masan Free Production Zone, Korea' (p. 137). Swindon lies along this line. Amidst all the talk of de- and post-industrialization, of service industries serving other services, these real connections should not be lost. So, as Sivanandan records,

> the arduous, toxic work of bonding tiny, hair-thin wires to circuit boards in wafers of silicon is done by the unskilled, female labour of South East Asia, while the cleaner, safer, more straight-forward task of operating the machinery is done by the deskilled workers of the centre. (1989)

The social and political response to this overdevelopment, as Sivanandan calls it, presents what a previous ESRC study, 'Changing Urban Regional Systems', described as 'a double paradox'. First, in the days of the railway town, 'a solidaristic, working class community largely failed to generate radical politics'. The failure is partly explained by the deliberate policy of the Great Western Railway Company of locating its works in rural areas with little experience of industrial organization. But secondly, and more recently,

> the eclipse of the 'traditional' working class, heavy in-migration, the disruption of ties between work, community and household, and the rise of the 'new service economy' – all the ingredients of 'class dealignment' – coincided with the consolidation of Labour control.

In this respect Swindon afforded a contrast with the other areas of this study, particularly Liverpool, as representing 'the acceptable face of Labour local government'. With unemployment rising above the national average for 1975–78 (it peaked at 11.4 per cent in 1985, 2.3 per cent below the national average), Swindon went through a crisis similar to the one that later hit Sheffield, and the one by which Liverpool remained blighted. Although Swindon was rate-capped in 1984/5 and

1985/6, this was a consequence of its previous commitment of resources to infrastructural support rather than out of any ideological conviction, as in Liverpool.

Instead, the Labour Thamesdown borough council (a 1974 amalgamation with outlying Highworth Rural District Council) actively promoted a public-sector-led effort to attract new investment. This was in contrast to Conservative and squirarchical Wiltshire County Council which for a long time blocked growth. With its success, the private sector took the lead, and the Council's own 1987 'Economic Development Strategy' estimates the aggregated total of jobs created in the area since 1978 as a result of companies relocating to be 30 000. However, it is often overlooked that three of the largest four employers in Thamesdown are the council (1800), county council (7000) and the local health authority (4000). The council continues to provide such amenities as exist and is consequently one of the highest spenders nationally on leisure and recreation. The Community Development Department makes great efforts to welcome new arrivals to the identical and box-like houses on the private estates that now ring the town. Two Arrivals Officers work in the north and west of Swindon visiting newcomers to provide information about local facilities. Yet here the image of Dallas Avenue, as one of the new streets is named, is belied by the so-called 'Swindon syndrome'. This affects what the local branch of the marriage guidance service Relate called 'bed and breakfast couples', who both work shifts to pay their mortgage, and has led to allegedly the highest divorce rate in Europe. Rapid growth has also produced physical and infrastructural problems, such as a water supply that is running dry, especially in west Swindon, where, as everyone says, a new town the size of Salisbury was for a long time served by only four pubs.

However, while many people in Swindon regret the loss of so much countryside around them (see, for example, pp. 106–7), until recently, young people found themselves in a seller's labour market. Even so, as late as October 1986, 3254 16–24-year-olds were registered unemployed in the Swindon travel-to-work area and 749 of them had been without work for over a year. Two years earlier the Council had undertaken its own extensive research as part of its contribution to International Youth Year, giving questionnaires to 1500 14–25-year-olds, 5 per cent of the age range. The conclusion then was that 'Without question the over-riding issue for young people is unemployment' (Curphey and Grant, p. 41). Unemployed young people were more likely to face difficulties at home and to be evicted by their parents, so that in its response to the report the council noted, 'It is clear that the problems of bringing up a family are not just restricted to parents with babies and young children.' It concluded, 'young people (as a whole) seem to be one of the most disadvantaged groups in the community. They seem to be the least competitive (along with older workers) in the employment market, and their access to decent housing is very limited' (Community Planning Committee 1984, pp. 18 and 29).

How much youth homelessness persisted and how much it was aggravated by newcomers to the area was a matter of dispute between Thamesdown Social Services and Wiltshire Education Committee, which ran the youth service. The *Swindon Advertiser* reported, 'Free breakfasts are being served to the homeless as booming Swindon turns the clock back more than 100 years' (9.3.89) and again: 'Homeless are turning to vice' (29.3.89) and 'Shocking Problem on Our Streets' (30.3.89). At the same time a local campaign was fighting to save a hostel threatened with closure by changes in the board and lodging regulations for young people, and eighteen squatters were evicted from a house in the centre of town (required by the probation service for new offices!). A Thamesdown councillor meanwhile had visited a hostel in

Sheffield and concluded that a similar project was needed for single young people in Swindon (Minutes Community Planning Committee 2.2.87). In the last complete year for which figures were available 42 per cent of the 949 people applying to Thamesdown's Homeless Families Unit were under 21, 'the majority of them not getting on with their parents but they've outstayed their welcome with friends,' as a worker at the unit reported, adding, 'If youngsters could pay their way at home we'd halve our problem.' She thought that when the poll tax was introduced it would make matters much worse.

At least the youth labour market had picked up by the time of this study to the extent that 'competition in Swindon . . . is likely to be competition between employers for youth labour rather than the converse' (Bynner, 1990). Employers actively recruited in local schools, offering incentive schemes to those they signed on. As in other parts of then sunny Loseland (London and the South-East) this led to early collapse of the Youth Training Scheme, almost before it was launched in 1983 (q.v. Marsden *et al.*, 1990). Where Youth Training, as it has since been renamed, survives it does so only by offering employed status or as a modified apprenticeship; although as far as most young interviewees were concerned it remained a last resort. Yet the unemployment rate in Swindon still stood at 4 per cent in January 1990, compared with the 'official' national rate then of 5.9, and 8 per cent of the total 3035 unemployed were under 20 with 20 per cent aged between 20 and 24.

Careers Office lists record the initial destinations of the c. 3000 leavers each year from Swindon's nine large secondary schools and showed that, in line with national levels, about half of all young people left full-time education at the minimum age of 16. Most of them entered employment directly. Of female school leavers, 43 per cent started clerical jobs. Sixty per cent of males went into engineering, construction and manufacturing. From preliminary examination of the careers trajectories of the Swindon '16–19' cohorts, it appeared both that more young people were leaving school for work at the earliest opportunity and that more were also staying on for vocational courses in the tertiary/further education system (introduced as the top tier of the local comprehensive system in 1977) that led to improved job prospects. Traditional vocational 'day release' courses also continued at the FHE college. Employers also sought youngsters who had completed sixth form to A-level; most of those seeking further study have to move out of the area. Swindon's lack of a polytechnic may be hindering its economic development (Ball, 1990, p. 11).

For women, who traditionally depended upon the male bread-winner in the railway workforce, there were a range of opportunities, not only in the new offices. These increased female participation in paid labour locally, particularly part-time working. A number of employers in competition for female labour had introduced shift systems and hours of work to attract women workers and were talking about collaborating to introduce a shared crèche, though this proposal did not meet with approval from some interviewees with young children since it would be too expensive to be worthwhile. However, in Thamesdown, as in the rest of the UK, women are underrepresented at the higher professional and managerial level, and make up the bulk of clerical intermediate posts, being concentrated in the worst-paid and lower grades. In the 1981 Census 41 per cent of women in Thamesdown worked part-time compared with 1.5 per cent of men. While this built upon traditions of temporary seasonal work linked to agriculture, to an extent new working practices have affected the whole workforce. They have moved towards casualization and deskilling, equalizing and 'feminizing' men's work and wages, with a minimal role for trade unions and including part-time and shift working, job-splitting, home-working, contract labour, flexibility and personnel management modelled on the USA or Japan. One consequence was that interviewing was not restricted to particular hours of the day or night. Young people who were working were as likely (and as unlikely) to be at home in the morning as in the evening.

'WOO'D, AND MARRIED, AND A' '

Another consequence of all the research done in Swindon was that it was not possible even to attempt to interview all of the 141 16–19-year-olds initially indicated by the information from the first two questionnaires to be living at different addresses from their parents. Some were part of the random core sample being undertaken in all the areas of the '16–19 Initiative'. Others were stepchildren who were part of a special study, while another investigation removed still more for in-depth videotaping on the subject of their sex-lives. Another group were paired with comparable young people in Padderborn, the West German equivalent of Swindon. This left only 71, who were each sent an introductory letter (Appendix 1). However, 16 of these turned out to be still with their parents (see p. 13), only 1 of whom had ever possibly moved but whose parents it seemed were reluctant to disclose the fact. Ten had moved but left no forwarding address at their last known abode. It was not possible to trace them back to their original address because the agency administering the questionnaires no longer had it. Seven more had moved out of the area (to Birmingham, Bristol, Cardiff, Newcastle upon Tyne, and Madrid – with her mother after the latter remarried a US serviceman), including two students (one in Aberystwyth and one in Brighton). Five no longer wished to take part. Three others were never at home despite repeated calls. Three more did not reply to a message asking them to phone to arrange an interview. Three boys were in the army and one in the air force. Two girls were in hospital, one having a baby. One boy was in prison and one could not be found in any of the many 'New Roads' in Swindon and its environing travel-to-work area.

In an effort to find a selection of cases to interview, rather than attempt to phone and arrange interviews with the remaining 20 (not all of whom were on the phone in any case), it seemed best to follow traditional salesman's lore and doorstep them. It is harder to refuse a caller at the door than to put down the phone. However, this also has disadvantages, particularly for a male interviewer asking to see a female who may be alone in the house. A briefcase can provide a presentable image, though in Swindon it is likely to lead to confusion with the many door-to-door salespeople and an answer of 'Not today, thank you.' Most interviews were conducted in the interviewee's home, though since the letter had offered to meet them anywhere that was convenient for them, some also took place at their work and in pubs and cafés. Interviews were usually in private, though where other members of their family or friends were present it is mentioned. Interviews followed a structured schedule that became increasingly open-ended (see Appendix 2). They were transcribed in short-hand with a tape-recorder as back-up. With some interviewees this faithful transcription provided an opportunity to dictate a detailed autobiography or even confession. One exclaimed, 'I've found someone to listen to me at last!'

Eight of the 20 cases interviewed in the Swindon travel-to-work area had bought their own house, six young women and two young men, though two of the girls had subsequently lost their property, being unable to keep up their mortgage payments and repay other debts they had incurred. All of these young people who had bought their new homes, excepting one boy who had bought on his own, had done so in partnership. However, none of them was actually married to their partner when they moved, except one girl whose marriage had been arranged for her in Pakistan.

Beverley came closest to the stereotypically female pattern of moving to marry and have children, stopping work to do so. Indeed she followed a family tradition of marrying young:

> 'All the girls in our family got married young and had children pretty well straight away. That's why we've got so many generations in our family – my daughter's great-great-grandfather, for instance. That's why it's quite a big family as well.'

She had left school after taking five CSEs and got work 'five days after – flower arranging in a florist's for £35 a week.' After the summer she went to work in a factory as a sewing machinist for £72 a week. 'I left for more money. I got fed up after a while.' After another factory job 'inspecting microchips', 'the factories got to me so I worked as a cashier at a garage. The money was the same (£87 a week) but it was meeting people, seeing different faces – a lot better.' She left to have a baby, having met her husband 'just after I left school' through playing in a darts team at the local pub. They become engaged on her seventeenth birthday and married two-and-a-half years later, ten months after they had moved into their own house and eight months before their daughter was born.

Their one-bedroom house with lounge–diner and adjoining kitchenette downstairs was typical of the small, identical private houses compacted tightly together around winding closes in Swindon's Western Extension. There was a general westward movement into these new estates among those who had bought. In Beverley's case she had moved only half a mile from her parents, who had previously bought a three-bedroom house nearby. Only Beverley's younger brother remained there with them now. Like her mother who was also a housewife, Beverley looked after her child full-time. 'I don't plan to go back to work if I can help it,' she said. 'Keep the house tidy, that's my job. Unless we get into real money difficulties, I would go back full-time then. I'll settle for one more child but I would like another two more.' Her 23-year-old husband, like her father who drove a lorry, was self-employed – a carpenter earning around £400 a week. Her older sister had also worked as a self-employed hairdresser before she too had left home to marry. With a mortgage of £450 a month, Beverley found it 'a lot cheaper' at her parents', where she had paid only £10 a week. Nevertheless she and her husband were saving and planned to sell their house. 'We did have another place but we lost it, so we're waiting now and when somebody buys this we'll look again. We want a two-bedroom, older house with a garden, in an older part of town.' Beverley didn't really like the new estate, even though 'It's nice and quiet. But I've only got one friend down the street and I see her nearly every day. We take it in turns, I go to her house and then she comes to mine for about four hours every day.'

Since hers was a Catholic household (Beverley was an irregular church-goer), 'My mother didn't like it when we moved. She thought I ought to get married first. She thought it wasn't right not to be married before you moved. Father didn't say a lot; he keeps his mouth shut.' Nevertheless, 'I see my mum every day to visit and I stay there when my husband goes away for a week. Plus they come here sometimes and I phone as well as visit.' Apart from these past differences with her parents, there had been no other difficulties in carrying out the resolve she had shared with her husband to move. 'There was quite a lot of houses about at the time.' The estate agent had helped them and they had physically moved their own possessions themselves. Beverley compared herself with other people her age:

> 'A lot of people I was at school with are still living at home so I suppose I went ahead a bit early when I was young. I liked it like that. A lot of people say they want to go out and enjoy themselves but I'd rather be sat at home. Going out and that doesn't appeal to me really.'

Her peers were catching up with her in any case because 'I've been to a lot of parties recently as there've been a lot of weddings recently.' Not interested in politics – 'I don't take much notice, I just get on with my life' – Beverley had voted once for the SDP and 'probably will' again. She considered herself 'working class, I suppose'.

Three other young women, all in the older (20–21) cohort interviewed in Swindon, also owned their own homes. One had sold her first one-bedroom maisonette for a two-bedroom one and was saving for a third. One was married and one engaged but neither of them yet had any plans for children. Both were working at jobs they were dissatisfied with, in an electronics factory and as a telephonist, but rather than retire to housewifery like Beverley, they aspired to something 'better' and 'more interesting'. However, with mortgages of £365 and £350 a month on weekly wages combined with their partners of £285 and £377, they could not afford to take a drop in income. Like Beverley, they had met their older partners (25 and 24, a computer operator and a foundry serviceman) after school, 'courting'/'going steady' for about two-and-a-half years before getting married or engaged. The one who had married became engaged nineteen months earlier when she moved into her first new home; the other became engaged on her nineteenth birthday and moved one month later. Their parents also owned their own homes and had supported their daughters' moves, being in regular contact with them. One was within a few roads on the same private new-built estate, the other, like Beverley, felt 'a bit in the sticks' out on the Western Extension. They did not think they were unusual; many of their friends were living with boyfriends and had bought or were saving to buy their own homes. However, one of these interviewees said she would have preferred to have stayed longer at home and felt her mother had pushed her out. It had been her fiancé's idea to move – 'I would quite happily have plodded on otherwise.'

This last case illustrates the difficulties of the case study method being pursued and the dangers of taking individual cases as overly representative. While the situation of this interviewee was typical of those who had left home earlier than is usual, to buy their own home, her reasons for doing so were individual ones. Unlike others (e.g. p. 26 and p. 28), she did not feel under any pressure to buy as soon as possible to get a foot on the housing ladder. Indeed, she did not really want to leave at all but her reasons for doing so and her mother's pressure upon her were obviously deeply affected by a family tragedy. The death of her elder and only sister one year previously after a long illness had, as she said, 'changed my life a lot'. It perhaps explained why, although she had good school qualifications, she did not go on as her sister had done to higher education, even though her teachers encouraged her to. Perhaps it also contributed to her description of herself as 'very negative'. She had no plans to have children or to marry. Indeed, she did not know whether she would still be with her partner in five or ten years' time. Nor was her home important to her – 'I'm not materialistic and I don't plan for the next thing like that.' Nor her job – 'I haven't got any aims and ambitions any more.' How these expressions related to her experience would take individual psychology rather than sociological inquiry, which can only point towards the individual motives that result in what – to be significant – must be typical patterns of social behaviour.

The fourth girl who had bought her own house conformed to a pattern typical of a different culture. Nazreen (20), who had lived in Swindon since she was two, left school before the Christmas of her last compulsory year to return to Pakistan where she was born and where her father arranged her marriage. For the first seven months she stayed with relatives and then after the ceremony moved to her husband's family before returning with him to Swindon a year and a half later. Here they stayed rent-free with her parents in their own house in the area of town most resembling an inner city. (It is also supposedly the 'red light' district and the location of many of the bed-and-breakfast hotels used by the council for homeless families.) With grandmother, four younger sisters and a younger brother,

> 'We needed our own place. It was overcrowded, although the council said we weren't. We were looking for ages, going down to the council, looking in the papers, going to estate agents that we'd heard about from friends. We were on the council waiting list but they couldn't help. [Swindon's] Homeless Families [agency] offered hostel accommodation but we didn't want to share. My parents said we should stay with them and save money up to buy our own place. I wouldn't have minded staying here and saving up to buy but my husband and my father didn't get on too well. My father treated him like a little kid, always sending him on errands, like "go and get some cigarettes, fetch this, do that".'

Consequently it was her husband's idea to move, and when after two-and-a-half years with Nazreen's parents they found a two-bedroom house a mile and a half away that they sublet from another Pakistani family for £50 a week, 'We were glad to have made it to get our independence. We were lucky; some people pay so much more rent.' They didn't need any help to move: 'We didn't have no stuff to get help with.' Their second child was born there.

Now, after a year and a half renting,

> 'We're in the middle of moving again. At the moment the mortgage is going through. We'd been looking for ages. We'll be half a mile away from here, which is nearer town and a lot better, nearer all the facilities.'

Their new two-bedroom house with garden required a £484 a month mortgage, Nazreen's husband's wage as a machine operator being £220 a week. 'We'll be able to do it if I start work. It'll be really difficult if not.' Before her first child was born Nazreen had been working part-time catering for £47 for a 20-hour week – 'Rubbish wages!' Then she worked full-time as a clerical assistant for £140 a week, having taken evening classes to get GCSE English, Maths and Business Studies. 'As soon as this little one gets old enough I'll go to evening class again.' She would soon be returning to work, leaving her children in her mother's care. Meanwhile, 'I come round here every weekday during the day', so 'I still say this is my own home for the moment 'cos I come round here when my husband's at work.' Later, 'if my husband's wages go up and we can afford the mortgage, he said I can go training for what I want'. Nazreen did not see herself as a housewife or mother – 'Office worker, 'cos I'm going back to work hopefully' – even though, 'I want another two kids, but not for a long time yet. Not for ages 'cos we'll have to get a bigger house first. We're also planning to go away on holiday if dad gives me money for it – a month or two in Pakistan.' 'Class? What are we? We're working class aren't we? We're working people.'

MORE HOUSE-BUYERS AND SOME LOSERS

John (20) was one of two young men interviewed in Swindon who had bought their own home. It was a small one-bedroom house in a new development of twenty others squeezed like a concertina into a fork of the road from town to the Western Extension. Like one of the young women discussed above, he and his fiancée moved in at the time of their engagement with no immediate plans to marry but would perhaps do so when they had children. His fiancée was the same age as himself, and they had been 'regularly dating . . . since we left school'. Like the other young women so far described, she had moved straight from her parents' home, but John had lived independently for a time, first in a lodging house belonging to a friend: 'Well, I didn't pay as much as everybody else. They offered to take me.' Then, after fifteen months, 'I had to leave because they sold the house.' An uncle and aunt took him in for six months at the same rate (£25 for board) while he and his girlfriend saved to buy.

> 'This was the first place we looked at but it was hard finding a place for the money we had. I'd have liked to have got my own place a bit earlier but we couldn't afford it. It was very important – I just wanted something to call my own.'

He could not call his parents' three-bedroom privately owned home his own 'because of my stepfather – say no more!' and had left under 'a sort of joint agreement: my mum said, "Get out!" and I said, "I'm going anyhow!" We were on each other's backs all the time and it was like a bad atmosphere.' They had not helped him since he left:

> 'When I moved out of mum's the boss of the small shop where I'd been working since I left school helped me move. I moved on my own to the second place with the car and the third time hired a van and got help from my uncle and cousins.'

Now, however, 'We visit them [my parents and my younger sister] about once a week. They think it's a good idea to buy but they don't seem to worry about me, except how we'll manage moneywise.'

John's parents had reason to worry. His wages as a produce foreman at a large supermarket were £130 a week, while his fiancée brought home £92 a week from her office job. At the time of interview their mortgage was £500 and must have increased since. Since John estimated he spent £20 a week running his car, this left them only £38.50 a week each to live on. Nevertheless, said John, 'I think things in general are getting better for us because we're on our way up in our lives.' Training in-store to become a produce manager, John was confident he could move to a bigger house and start a family in four years. In fact, 'Some people would call us yuppies' – 'Because we've got our own car and our own place and our own lives,' his fiancée explained. 'Old people would call us that and blame us for putting the prices up.' But they themselves did not feel they were different from other people and considered their move quite usual for people their age.

Mike (20) was also struggling to meet the mortgage he had taken on his own for a one-bedroom house. This was on a newly built estate at the edge of town a quarter of a mile from where his parents also owned their three-bedroomed home. In fact Mike was rescheduling the mortgage on the evening of interview. This extended it from £4680 p.a., more than half his wages of £170 a week with bonus and overtime as a glass-cutter in a double-glazing factory, to £3456 (42 per cent of his salary). He had felt that he had to move because

> 'It was a situation where the house prices were going up so fast in Swindon that I said to myself it's going to be now or never. It's a good stepping-stone for my future 'cos it's got my foot on the step. It'll help in the future when I get married, instead of like a lot of people get married and then worry about the house. Someone of my age buying their own house on their own at 19 is unusual but normally people that age are not earning the money for it, they are still getting a trade or at university, still in the learning process, but I felt I was ready for it and could afford it and didn't want to wait until I was married 'cos it might be too late then.'

His parents had supported him: 'They backed me fully and they helped with the painting and decorating.' They also advised him, 'and I could go to my two brothers for advice 'cos they own their own houses'. However, 'It was quite easy, although the first house I went for fell through due to the mortgage not coming through quickly enough.' 'In fact, I see my parents more now than I did then 'cos ever since I was 14 my dad's called me a lodger 'cos they only used to see me for meals. I'd be out and about 'cos I was into the Scouts then and liked to keep active with quite a busy social life.' Now 'I see them four or five times a week. I normally pop in on my way home from work and I see them at weekends, on Sundays – the gathering time.' He took three meals a week there and brought his washing round – 'Well, I only take towels and sheets 'cos I haven't got a washing line and they take so long to dry'. 'Plus I've stayed there a week once when they were away to look after the house and feed the dog. They don't come here 'cos they work nights. I see my brothers and sisters at mum's and sometimes they come here or I go there and I've got an aunt who comes to see me quite a bit.' So, 'It's pretty well the same [as being at home] 'cos everybody in the family is so close' – geographically and socially.

While he considered himself 'settled' in his new home, Mike was not sure that he would stay there. 'With the house I've got two options: the one I would prefer is to rent it out but the more likely one is to sell it.' This was not (only) because of the expense but because

> 'at the back of my mind I've got the idea of going round the world on a working holiday in about two years time, like a friend who's gone over to America with a summer camp, so I might do that and travel on from there. So ideally I'd rent it 'cos at least I'll have something to come back to. Eventually I'll sell this house and get a bigger one with three bedrooms in my next stage.'

Before this, though, 'I want to get a trade under my belt so I plan to go to evening classes, hopefully this September join a welding course.' For Mike, like the two young women mentioned in the last section (pp. 23–4), was discontented with his present occupation which he had taken after a couple of short shop assistant jobs and a year's catering YTS that he did not complete.

> 'They call me a "glass operative", but if you narrow it down the factory name is a snipper because I run a machine that snips off the bits we don't want for double glazing. It's not a skilled job really – the cutters are the only skilled people in the factory.'

While holding to the traditional, but in Swindon increasingly obsolete, working-class ideal of becoming a skilled tradesman, Mike sought other certainties in his life. He had recently begun to attend an ecumenical church, the only member of his family to do so. 'It was a sort of social thing to start with but then I started going to the church and meeting all the people but I don't know which way to turn at the moment.' Still in a stage of exploration, Mike, while he saw his life organized in a series of stages, did not see these as necessarily age-related. Marriage for instance: 'I don't think there's any particular age to get married. No particular age is right. It's just when you meet the right person.' He considered, however, that his acquisition of a property could possibly make him an attractive target for a relationship that might tie him down prematurely: 'Then it would be difficult finding the motivation to get up and go. That could change my life and shatter my dreams.'

For two young women interviewed in Swindon their dreams of owning their own homes had already been shattered. Debi (20) was renting a bedsit for £105 a month in a house near the centre of town.

'You have to share the bath and toilet but I go to my mum's for a bath twice a week. I used to take my washing home but now we have to go to a laundrette since mum said she's not going to do it, or my brother's, any more. My brother is living in a room upstairs, and I'm waiting for the flat upstairs, but my brother has stirred it up between me and my sister, who's on and off with her husband, and if she decides to leave him she'll nag me to get in here and take the flat upstairs. So I'm not settled here. If I'm here for another five years it might change but we're planning to move again so I don't put too much effort into it, decorating and making the place seem like our own home. I've given up waiting for the council. I'm hoping to move into the flat upstairs; then I'll start to settle.'

The reason why all three children had left their parents' council home seemed to have to do with their mother.

'My mother and father wanted some peace, that's what they kept saying: "We've had you lot for so many years. It's time you went off on your own." I wanted to move anyway because we were getting on each other's nerves a bit – the way she keeps everything so tidy. It's the way my mother has been brought up. She wasn't wanted either so she doesn't want us. I wish she wasn't like that but she is. I've never met her parents. She never talks about it but I think there must've been something really horrible that my mum's dad did to her when she was young. [Now] I see them twice a week, usually every Sunday, but not for dinner – just go down there. Mum never offers dinner. She's visited twice.'

Debi left home first when she was seventeen to share with the sister of her employer at the butcher's shop she was then working in. 'I left because I was only young then and I didn't realize I wasn't supposed to tell the DSS I was living there.' This also led to her leaving her job and she was unemployed for three months before working first in a greengrocer's and then in a sports shop earning £87 a week. After fourteen months back with her parents, to whom she paid digs money of £10.15, she left again to share a bedsit with her boyfriend for £30 a week.

'He's two years older than me. I met him at school and I've been going out with him ever since. I think one of the reasons we left that place was he was paying the rent while I was buying the food and the landlady started asking for more.'

He earned £120 as a forklift-truck driver. Debi returned home again, for eight months before leaving again, this time to buy.

'The boyfriend's sister and her husband helped us find a place and helped us out a bit. Plus the family gives you bits and pieces of furniture. It's not hard to buy. There are thousands around but I didn't like going around looking at people's houses who you don't know so I preferred to do it through people we knew. The problem is in Swindon it's so hard and expensive. We found a one-bedroom house about five miles out of town but I quite liked it there, although the neighbours were snobby and it was half an hour on the bus but it was just too expensive with a £400 mortgage, bills, rates and everything else so we rented it out, advertising in the paper. We were going to go through an agency but they weren't charging as much as we needed [£260 a month]. We were just stuck. The only people we could talk to were the building society. They were awful as well as the solicitors. They wouldn't help you in the least. They offered to put it down £50 a month for the months around Christmas but then asked for it all back in the next payment. They just said if you can't afford it then sell it and we couldn't transfer the mortgage because we were in arrears. We're going to sell it, which is terrible really as the prices have gone down now.'

They moved back to his parents' privately owned four-bedroom house.

'We used to give them £20 a week but I couldn't get on with them so I moved here. His mother drove me up the wall. [Now] I'm just doing temporary work – warehousing for £3 an hour but it depends on where the agency sends you. I'm fed up with shop work. I thought I'd look for something else. I'm waiting to hear about two jobs: the Post Office and buying in a menswear shop. I'm looking around and going to the job centre. If I get stuck my boyfriend will always help me out. He plans to buy a house with his sister and rent it out to commuters from London or people moving in and then sell it and get the money to put down on our own house. It'll be a few years though. If he buys a house I'll probably stay as I am but I don't like to plan too far ahead. We might not be talking to each other by then. We stretched ourselves to the limit buying that house and then the mortgage rate went up again. . . . We wouldn't do that so much next time and not for at least four years. Anyway, I don't want to get tied down to marriage. I want to have a career first. What I really want to do is to run my own shop. Like now, I'm going down to the Job Centre looking for assistant manager jobs. What I'd really like to do is run a sports shop. There is a real need for a proper specialist one in Swindon 'cos there's nothing at the moment really and there are a lot of new people coming in who would go there. Twenty-eight's a good age for a family. It wouldn't bother me if we did get married to live upstairs for a while.'

Nor did Debi seem to mind living on her own:

'They always used to be shocked at work when I said I was on my own so I suppose it is unusual but I quite like it. They're most surprised if you're a girl on your own; they always think you're with your boyfriend. I couldn't live at home now because I want to do what I want my own way. I like my independence.'

The other young woman (also 20) who had bought a house but been unable to keep up the payments and lost it was living rent free in a friend's house at the time of interview but this was a temporary arrangement that would end when her friend's parents sold the house. Like John (p. 25), she had moved from her parents before buying because she did not get on with her stepfather. She had gone to her grandparents whilst in her last year at school. She was then already regularly dating her boyfriend and after three years at her grandparents' they moved into their own one-bedroomed flat six miles away, getting engaged as they did so.

After a year they could no longer pay £470 a month for this out of his wages of £120 a week as a warehouseman and hers of £160 as a key-to-disc operator shiftworking with a computer company. They also owed debts from credit cards, loans and hire purchase but were able to pay these off with the profits from the sale of the flat. They split up when they left and he returned to his parents while she went to her friend but they reunited after a month. They now planned to rent and were saving to buy again in three or four years. This set back their plans for two or three years' marriage before having children, ideally at 25. In retrospect:

> 'We would've done things a lot different because a lot of my friends did it the right way. They saved up for a deposit but me and my boyfriend rushed into it, we even took out a loan for solicitor's fees. We rushed into it without saving first. It certainly taught me a lesson. We'll save up before we move next time and no credit cards ever again!'

Her grandparents' reservations had been proven correct. Her parents, whom she saw less, had been indifferent.

RENTING, PRIVATE AND PUBLIC

If two out of twenty young movers had lost the homes they had bought in Swindon this was likely to be a common and recurrent problem, and other young people were well aware of it and had learnt from the bad experiences of acquaintances or friends. Lindsay (20) and her fiancé (21) were saving to buy a house but, partly because of the example of people their age whom they knew, they had decided not to buy straight away. 'We looked into it but it was too much.' However, her fiancé had a pressing reason to move: 'His parents had their house up for sale and they were looking for a two-bedroom bungalow so there wouldn't be room for him as well.' They had been going out together for four years, becoming engaged after three. 'We were on the council waiting list for two years but the only way to get a house with them is to have a baby.' The council's Housing Department had advised them to apply to a housing association, which they did, moving into a one-bedroom flat, for £25 a week, one year after they had become engaged and a year before they planned to get married. Now they were saving out of his wages of £130 a week as a fork-lift truck driver and hers of £121 as a packer in a store, a job she had moved into via a year's probation on YTS straight from school. 'We'll stay in the flat and if the mortgages come down we might go into it or we might transfer from the housing association to the council, then we might do that up and buy it.' Their stay in the flat had something of the nature of a trial marriage before the full commitments of the church ceremony they planned and the joint mortgage they would be taking on.

> 'We've started a shared account now to learn how to do it for when we get married so that arguments won't start. I've never lived with him before and even when you've been going out with someone for four years it's different when you live with them.'

There was in any case plenty of time – 'About 25, that's a good age to start a family.'

Even if she had not moved the five miles from her original home into the flat Lindsay would have appeared on the list of movers because she had been brought up since infancy by her grandparents and therefore was listed as not living with her parents. Calling at her grandparents' three-bedroomed, privately owned house on the outskirts of town, Lindsay happened to have returned for one of her regular visits. 'I visit them a couple of nights a week' and 'I stay with them occasionally. I also phone about thee times a week. I don't know why I was brought up by my grandparents. I don't really ask about it but I regard my gran as my family more than anyone.' She was until recently in touch with her mother, who had another family now: 'I'd see her about once a week if I hadn't fallen out with her.' Her grandparents, both retired – her grandfather from the old railway works – were 'pleased' that Lindsay moved but 'Nan was a bit iffy 'cos she's old-fashioned and she still regards me as her daughter, her little girl.' Like the interviewee who had gone to stay with her grandparents while at school but had not returned to them after losing her home (p. 28), Lindsay felt she was imposing upon her grandparents by staying with them longer, although, unlike some of the parents of these young movers, it did not seem her grandparents wanted her to go.

Two other young women, aged 19 and 20, were also renting privately. They were both married, one with two children. This latter interviewee had married one month after her first baby was born and described her occupation as 'housewife and mother', saying 'I don't have to work any more' after listing a succession of YTS, shop, factory and packing jobs she had done since leaving school. She had walked out of her parents' privately owned ex-council house to rent a bed-sit because she, like others, did not get on with her stepfather. She got on better with her family after she moved, which was also not unusual. She had moved to rent with her husband twice since. They had their names down with the council, although they planned to buy a house 'in the end' but were not saving for it and did not give much thought to this, or to the eventuality and inevitability of going back to work (any work) at least part-time when her children went to school. 'We just carry on bimbling along from day to day.'

In contrast with this attitude and the traditional feminine pattern of moving to marry, stop work and raise children, the other of these two interviewees considered herself a career woman. She had stayed on at school to take additional O-levels, trained in silver-service catering but then left for office work. Here she was training with computers on the job and even though she earned only £90 a week considered she had good prospects of becoming a manageress. She wanted to establish herself in this position before having a family and was prepared to move to another part of the country if necessary to further her career. Her husband would move with her since 'he can work anywhere'. He had had a series of jobs since leaving the army, his present one for a cleaning contractor paying £450 a week. They had married a year previously, meeting nine months before that, when she was 17 and he 23 and still in the army. For the first four months of their marriage they lived rent-free with her parents in her father's curator's cottage but then moved to rent a bed-sit flat for £50 a week where they were saving to buy a house in two to five years.

Two young men in the sample held council tenancies. Both were 20 and married with two children. One had obtained his council house via a four-month stay in a homeless families' hostel which he described as 'a glamorized Colditz'. He and his wife had been school sweethearts and married a year after they both left at 16, having a baby six months after that and another two-and-a-half years later. She stayed at home looking after these infants while he had held the same job in a builder's merchants since leaving school, starting as a 'dogsbody' on £30 and now earning £140 with overtime. They did not plan a larger family but were saving to buy their three-bedroom council house, having built a patio and an extension on to it.

The other young father had met his wife in London where he went to work roofing. They could not get housed there even though she was pregnant and he had returned to stay with his parents in Swindon for four months before they found a flat to rent.

After a year they were rehoused into a three-bedroomed council house for which he paid £33 a week rent. Labouring on building sites for £140 a week, he hoped to buy a house within five years. If he bought his own council house he would hope to sell it and move to a better area. He also hoped to have two more children 'but not twins again!'. As with Beverley (p. 22), family tradition played a part in influencing the course of his life. Comparing himself to his peers, he conceded that leaving home and marrying with a family at 19 was unusual but by comparison with his older brother and sister it was not. Like Beverley, it meant that his was a large family with several generations still alive.

OTHERS

Three other young movers interviewed in Swindon were also living in council accommodation; however, their lives did not conform to the varieties of moving to cohabit and/or to buy that have been outlined but followed other patterns of transition and return. In one case this was closely connected to work: a lad of 18 had moved 200 yards down the road from his parents' council house into his 17-year-old girlfriend/fiancée's council house. From here her father operated the subcontracting asphalt business that employed the interviewee along with his fiancée's brothers. He regarded this as a convenient arrangement which saved him getting up so early in the morning and left more room in his parents' house, where they had taken in a lodger. Since he still had a bed at his parents', he was only 'sort of living away' and found it hard to say where his home was. He was saving money but for a car not a house, though his girlfriend had other plans and hoped they would marry and move when she was 21.

Another male interviewee (20) had returned to his father's privately owned house but, like the case referred to on p. 23, in unusual and individual circumstances. His mother had committed suicide when he was 17, although he had moved out before this after a row with his religiously fundamental father. Since then he had been 'in and out of this house ten times in the last two years'. During that time he had slept on friends' floors and occasionally slept rough. He had also sublet rooms in households and rented bed-sits. He had become involved with the police after 'getting mixed up with the wrong crowd . . . people who take drugs and sniff glue'. He left his office job because 'people wouldn't let me forget . . . they kept trying to help me'. Only a girlfriend he had been going steady with for the last year had helped him to 'quieten down a lot', to get a new job as a trainee manager and to stop fighting with his younger brothers, though relations with his father were still tense. He explained, 'You need a family round you but when the family explodes all you can do is walk out.'

Two other interviewees had returned home. One was a young man who had never really left but gone to live with grandparents so as to remain at the same school when his parents bought a house in a village on the edge of Thamesdown. He had also stayed with a sister and her boyfriend near this new house when his great-grandmother moved into it. When his parents completed an extension for her he moved back again. He did not regard any of these moves within the family as living away, partly because he saw his parents every day throughout. The other interviewee had returned to her parents after only one month away in a one-bedroom flat 'just down the road' she had rented privately with a boyfriend. She had been going out with him since her last school year and they were engaged four months after she left school. They were going to wait for a council flat but moved when 'it fell into our laps' three months after they got engaged. Her parents were 'not too chuffed but they said if that's what I wanted . . .'. She returned to their four-bedroomed council house one month later but now had a year-old child to look after. She no longer saw her boyfriend and he made no contribution for his child. She typed part-time for £40 a week and planned to stay where she was, eventually taking over the tenancy from her parents.

The other single mother in the Swindon interview sample had not yet got her own council tenancy. Diane (18) was waiting for it in a run-down bed and breakfast hotel in the same street as the one where Nazreen's mother lived (p. 24). This was the first stability she had had since leaving home fourteen months before: 'I've just been bouncing around like a pea in a pod.' But, 'I have settled down here. When I get a council place I'll be properly settled. That's what we're all waiting here for.' She would move first into the hostel accommodation used by the other interviewee rehoused through Swindon's Homeless Families Unit (p. 30) and be rehoused from there, a process Diane optimistically hoped would be completed by Christmas in five months' time. 'If I can get it all sorted out before the baby's born I'll be happy 'cos I wouldn't like it to come into the world homeless.'

Diane had first left home when

> 'I ran away a couple of times. The first time I was about 11. I slept on the streets. I was only away for a couple of days then my dad came looking for me. I never got on with my mum. We were always rowing as I used to get all the attention off my dad and my mum didn't like it.'

At 14, 'When my dad died I tried to commit suicide four times. Also when I split up with my boyfriend. But I wouldn't do it again because I've got the baby to think about now.' After her father's death,

> 'I was fed up with my mum's boyfriend beating me up. My mum was going mad but her boyfriend told her to keep out of it and that I had to stand on my own two feet. If I'd stayed living with my mum I would've done something to her boyfriend that I would've regretted as I've got a temper like a bull.'

She went first to friends in a nearby council house on the same estate but that only lasted for two months. 'They were all boys, all on the dole and they were doing my head in so I went to the homeless and they sent me to the hostel.' A local councillor on the estate 'told me the only way he could get me a place would be if I got myself pregnant'. However, Diane stressed that when she did get pregnant, 'It wasn't planned. We weren't intending to have kids until I was at least twenty-two or -three.' The councillor on Swindon's 'homeless families' had put her in touch with social services but the hostel was expensive (£40 out of the £80–£90 she got from irregular jobs packing first computer discs and then vegetables). 'I got kicked out 'cos you can only stay there a short time' (three months). She then moved in with her boyfriend's family, paying them £20 a week for board. He was 22 and 'he had all sorts of jobs. Then he was with a car-hire company. I don't know how much he earned; he kept that to himself.' After another three months she split up with him and rented a room in a privately owned ex-council house with two other couples for £35 a week. This did not last long either because after two months 'I went back to him 'cos he came creeping to me to do it. We were going to get married in June but I told him I was pregnant and he told me to fuck off.' She had never found it hard to find places that were all within two miles of each other, once through an advert in the local paper but usually through friends. Friends had also helped her to move her belongings. 'If ever I got stuck I went to the Homeless and they found me a place and this time as soon as I said I was pregnant they found me a place straight away.'

Diane now shared bed and breakfast accommodation with six other people, 'all housewives/mothers', aged from 18 to 23, and one of their partners (22) who worked as a plasterer, plus five infants – 'we're like a big family'. Their rent of £40 a week each was paid by the council:

'We've worked out the landlady gets £1040 a week with the hotel and the other houses she's got. We're supposed to get breakfast but we don't. The Health Inspector's been in after we found a slug in the bathroom plus the wiring's all loose and fibreglass is coming through the wall . . . I suppose the council's so desperate for places they've got no choice but to use her and we don't like to make a fuss 'cos we've got nowhere else to go.

'I would have preferred to have done things differently. I didn't want to make the mistakes my mum made but I seem to have done them. Moving about has caused it. If I'd stayed with my mum I wouldn't be in the position I'm in now 'cos there's a lot of people my age still living with their parents. So it's her boyfriend's fault. I wouldn't be able to visit her if her boyfriend had his way [so] I meet mum off the bus after she finishes work at the factory and she comes round every night to see how I am and I see her in the pub on Saturdays. So it's only Sunday I don't see her.

'The doctor says I'm not allowed to work at the moment but I might get a part-time job when the baby's a year old and get a full-time one when it starts school. Any job – one that pays the best money I suppose. Jobs are OK if you go through agencies and with the council it's OK once there's a place in the hostel. They've got their own list of houses and you move out after six months and then they give you a grant to get you all fixed up. I might buy the council house they move us into – I'll see what it's like. So hopefully I'll be a married old woman [in five or ten years' time], a housewife with another two children.'

TWO STUDENTS

It was not part of the original intention of this research to interview students and they were eliminated from the questionnaire data on those in the whole sample who had moved. With few exceptions, student youth have not been a subject of concern to sociology because their situation has been taken for granted by both their lecturers and students themselves. Ever since the 1963 Robbins Report *Higher Education* it has been recognized that, as the report stated in an appendix,

Children with fathers in professional and managerial occupations are twenty times more likely to enter full-time higher education than are those with fathers in semi- and un-skilled jobs. The differences are again much greater for girls than for boys. (HMSO, 1963b: 38)

This division was only reinforced by the expansion of higher education in the 1960s, which catered mainly for middle-class youth, offering them a route to preferred non-manual employment in the growing service and state sectors. In addition,

The trend in recent years has been for more occupations that aspire to professional status to become closed to applicants without degrees. So completing higher education has likewise tended to become confirmation of professional/managerial, or, even more loosely, 'middle-class', status. (Ainley, 1990b, p. 97)

In a complex dynamic, professional and other 'non-manual' occupations are, at the same time as they attempt to professionalize themselves, being proletarianized by the way new technology is being introduced. For the higher education which prepares students for professional occupations this means an opening out with new types of courses to new types of student, making the situation of HE students increasingly problematic. Indeed, it already is so with students who have been taught following the new methods of the Technical and Vocational Education Initiative and GCSEs in schools now entering higher education. At the same time it is predictable that the introduction of student loans for the payment of the full fees which colleges are already charging will restrict the access of wider numbers of people to higher education. 'Nevertheless the writing is clearly on the wall for the traditional three-year finishing course as the accepted transition from school to work for middle-class youth' (ibid., p. 100).

Housing for students is also a growing problem. The collapse of the private rented sector has resulted in a shortage of cheap accommodation for students. Reductions in student eligibility to Housing Benefit have further weakened students' market position. Deregulation of the private rented sector will result in rising rent levels and reduced security of tenure, as it did in Scotland following the 1988 Housing (Scotland) Act. Robbins had recommended 'a great expansion of university residence' but by the end of the 1970s university funds for residential accommodation were terminated. Now the beginning of every academic year sees students sleeping in the corridors and classrooms of colleges up and down the country. In Edinburgh a University survey found that

> The high cost of living in the city has generated a new breed of 'student landlord' which has eluded previous studies of student private rented accommodation. For those students (or parents) who possess the financial means to enter owner occupation, and consequently let to fellow students, the purchase of flats in popular student areas represents a sound investment. (Nicholson and Wasoff, p. 98)

The report concludes,

> Given the current trend towards student owner occupation this could well mean that in the area of student housing there will increasingly develop a social division of students. On the one hand there will be those students (or their parents) who possess the financial capacity to enter owner occupation for the duration of their degree course, while on the other, those who through necessity seek accommodation in the private rented sector. The outcome of this scenario will be that 'student owner occupiers' leave university with a substantial capital asset and a significant advantage in their future housing prospects, while 'student tenants' leave university to begin their professional and housing careers with a substantial debt to repay. (ibid., pp. 99–100)

Further, one predictable effect of student loans will be towards a North American pattern of students living at home and working their way through college while studying locally. For students from parts of the country without higher education institutions, like Swindon, this will be a further disincentive from pursuing their studies to a higher level (see p. 20).

The two students among the 20 movers in Swindon who remained after all the others in the sample had been accounted for happened to have just arrived home for their summer vacation at the time interviews were being undertaken. They typify both the housing problems increasingly facing students and the growing divisions between them. At the same time they also throw into relief some of the characteristics of a student status which is becoming more problematic. As far as housing is concerned this status implies that young people who leave home to study are only 'living away' and have not yet 'left home'. However, in the majority of cases, studentship is an institutionalized transition from living dependently upon parents/ guardians to independent living, just as it is an accepted and prolonged transition from school to work.

George (19) had just completed his first year as a drama student at a college in London. His father was a site supervisor for a cable TV company and his mother a part-time clerk. Their only child, he had been brought up in their privately owned three-bedroomed bungalow in a village on the outskirts of Swindon. He had two A-levels from two years at tertiary college during which time he worked two nights a week for £25 in the McDonald's in town. He also worked for two months during the summer vacation for between £150 and £200 labouring on local building sites. Despite saving out of this he found that he ran up an overdraft at the end of every term. Since going to London in October 1988 he had moved house six different times, more than anyone else in the Swindon sample except Diane.

> 'It was very difficult – a nightmare – initially and subsequently. I think I've been more unsettled than most partly because I came from outside London. Also other students at polytechnics and colleges get help and are more organized generally. I would have preferred more organized accommodation and halls of residence, especially the first year. You can go to the college accommodation office but they just give you what you can get anyway. It's all just left up to you basically. I joined agencies but the deposit etcetera is just crippling. Like one place it was nearly £500 for the first week.'

Rents at the houses and flats he had shared with other students within the same area of east London varied between £20 and £50 a week per person. He had managed to gain a rent rebate of £15 on the flat charging him £50 a week. Tenancies were generally short, however, and, although George had succeeded in finding somewhere he could return to in the autumn, this meant some of the other tenants had had to stay there working through the vacation in the capital. His parents had helped him to transport his belongings by car but could offer little further assistance. George returned home every holiday and phoned 'a few times' during term.

> 'But things will change because I'm going to have to make my base up there because of the career I want to go into and the opportunities I want to pursue, there is more chance of finding things up in London. My ambition lies with my job rather than settling down with a family, etcetera. Because of the insecurity of it, I can't think of saving up for my own home, for instance, as an immediate prospect but I would like eventually to own my own home and to have a family, but definitely not before 26. It'll become harder if I can't find more than part-time work. It could wear on your tolerance living like that in and out of digs. You have to be determined to keep going. So it's very difficult to say how I see myself in the future in the career I'm going into. I couldn't even tell you what I'll be doing when I've finished my course. It'll always be striving to reach a certain standard, struggling is probably a good word.'

Daksha (20) was a student at the private University of Buckingham where she was approaching the end of her two-year law degree course. Her family, which had arrived in Swindon in 1976, had just moved from an ordinary three-bedroomed house to a four-bedroomed house on one of the better private housing estates. Her father and mother owned their own business. Like her two younger brothers, Daksha had taken A-levels at tertiary college, working the while at a £20 Saturday shop job. At university she had for her first year been in halls of residence and then moved into a house which she had found through an estate agent and which she shared with other female students for £35 a week each. It was difficult to find places because 'Buckingham is very small'. Although her parents were 'not that keen' on her going to college, her father helped her to move in the family car and gave her the money to study in the form of a 'loan'. Even so, she found 'You run out of money a lot'. She returned to visit her parents for a weekend once a month and every vacation; she phoned them once a week. Daksha regarded 'both places equally as home. Even though it's only a temporary home, your friends are there and they become like a family to you.' Talking of her friends from school, she said:

> 'Most of them didn't go to university. They've stayed in Swindon doing the same things so I can't communicate with them 'cos we don't have anything to talk about so I've only got one friend here now and she's at Bristol University.'

Daksha's plans were

> 'to become a very successful City solicitor. I would like to buy my own house sometime in the future. I would like to buy that for myself first [before marriage]. I think of myself as a career person but all I can think about now are my exams.'

However, Daksha here gave two interviews, one when her father was in the room and one when he was out. When he was out she revealed that she had already applied without his knowledge for a place at law school.

> 'My father wouldn't like it at all though. He would like me to finish my degree and get married 'cos with the arranged marriage system you're sort of worth more if you've got a degree. That was probably one of the reasons I wanted to be away in the first place or I might have been stuck in all that.'

Daksha's dilemma illustrates very clearly the crunch point for students when it comes to leaving their parents' home finally and no longer just 'living away'.

Chapter 3

Sheffield

CRYSTAL PEAKS AND THE REST OF ENGLAND'S FOURTH CITY

On the outskirts of Sheffield there is a little Swindon, or rather a smaller version of the Western Extension, called Crystal Peaks. The name of this private housing development alludes presumably to nearby Derbyshire and explains the peculiar pinnacles of its glass and plastic shopping centre-cum-cinema and entertainment complex. This is surrounded by tiny, identical houses with sloping red rooves, each with its own fenced garden patch. In the absence of public open space the flat fields around them are being criss-crossed by roads and roundabouts and dotted with warehouses selling home care and garden ware. As a shopping centre, however, Crystal Peaks has recently been dwarfed by nearby Meadowhall, the largest covered shopping area in Europe.

With the restrictions upon new public house building (97 completions in 1988–9), the 900 houses built for sale each year in Sheffield, many of them on Crystal Peaks, provided virtually the only chance of new housing in the city (cf. 100 completions annually by housing associations). Thirty-nine per cent of house-buyers in the city during 1988–9 were first-time buyers, 24 per cent of all buyers being under 25. The rise in rate rebates to owner occupiers, the majority of claims in some areas, shows the financial liabilities many buyers have incurred. Average house prices in Sheffield that year ranged from £66 500 for a detached house with garden through £40 000 for a semi to £28 000 for a flat or maisonnette, £27 000 for a terrace house. Amounts loaned increased from 56 per cent for the larger properties to 82 per cent for the smaller, largest loans going to first-time buyers (Sheffield City Council, 1989). This expansion of private housing is in contrast to the part played by Sheffield in pioneering public housing in the past.

Even before 1926 when Sheffield became the first major city in the country to elect a Labour city council, the city's persistent policy of building working-class garden suburbs on the hills around the town was initiated by the Lib–Lab coalitions which had previously dominated local politics. In 1907, for instance, Sheffield hosted a national model cottage estate exhibition. During the inter-war period large amounts of public housing were built, largely constructed as suburban houses when other city councils were building city centre flats. After the Second World War, which further enlarged the city's population, Sheffield built 12 000 dwellings by 1955, most of them solid, three-bedroomed, semi-detached houses with gardens on suburban estates.

> From the end of the 1950s Sheffield was mainly engaged in redevelopment, replacing the remaining inner-city terraces with new estates, some suburban and some inner-city. These contained an increasing number of flats and maisonettes and also discernible was the trend towards the use of industrialised and systems building techniques. As these methods declined, at the beginning of the 1970s, the third phase of smaller-scale 'infill' developments began using mainly traditional techniques. (Dickens *et al.*, 1985, pp. 166–7)

However, Sheffield remained one of the largest builders of council houses in the country, erecting 43 000 between 1955 and 1978. As this brief summary shows, one legacy of half a century of almost uninterrupted Labour local government is that, despite recent losses through the right-to-buy schemes for council tenants (11 000 of the better council properties since 1980), Sheffield currently has roughly equal numbers of homes in owner occupation and renting and a lower proportion of owner occupiers than the national average of around two out of three households (Sheffield City Council, 1989).

Sheffield in the early 1950s was a 'boom town', Dickens *et al.* record (op. cit., p. 109).

> The steel industry was amongst the first to rationalise its national post-war development plans, around major new investments in established steel making areas. In Sheffield this created a special demand for skilled workers living in the area, so much so that in 1952 a shortage of skilled labour was reported to be threatening the growth of the industry.

Michael Carter wrote a classic account, *Home, School and Work* (1962), of young people growing up in these boom conditions when up to a third of male school leavers entered the steel industry, often in the same factories that employed their fathers. Since then employment in the steel industry in Sheffield and Rotherham has declined from 60 000 in 1971 to just 16 000 in 1989. Major redundancies and closures emerged from a series of 'corporate plans' introduced by BSC; from the private sector; and, increasingly, from the joint public–private ventures known as the Phoenix companies. 'South Yorkshire', notes the Council's Employment Department in a report entitled *The Uncertain Future of Special Steels*, 'is exceptional in suffering so many redundancies under all three forms of ownership.' Between 1971 and 1988 total job loss in Sheffield is estimated at 60 000, equivalent to 20 per cent of the employed labour force in 1971. Employment growth came from business services, public and private.

> This dramatic change in the industrial structure of the Sheffield economy is associated with a major change in the occupational structure, with a fall in the proportion of semi-skilled and skilled manual workers from 32% at the beginning of the period to 20% in 1996. Professional/managerial and other non-manual will have risen from 44% to 53% over the period. (PA Cambridge, 1989, p. 2)

The city has equally obviously not been unaffected by developments in 'Loseland', not just to the extent of an interaction with them as the economy polarized throughout the 1980s, but by an attempt to participate in them. After an initial reaction, epitomized by the council's media-dubbed 'Socialist Republic of South Yorkshire' phase, the city has attempted to share in the new wealth of services and administration for a reorganized corporate and global capitalism. 'Plans to hold the 1991 World Student Games in Sheffield, for a local airport, and the determination to attract businesses to the area reflect the City's commitment to release itself from industrial obsolescence,' states one characteristic council communication (1989b). But despite the arteries of motorway and rail and the new nerves of computerized telecommunication, Sheffield is a long way from the heartland of the new Europe. The result has been a decline in traditional industry comparable to the loss of the railway works in Swindon but, until a low point in 1986, without the same replacement by the offices and services of the Golden Triangle/Crescent/Corridor.

According to *Westside*, the business-orientated glossy distributed free to homes in the wealthier side of the city, 'Over the next few years the steady thud of drop hammers will be a distant memory as they are replaced with the sound of computer keyboards and booming retail, leisure and service industries.' In a less glossy but hardly less enthusiastic report entitled *Sheffield's Information Revolution?*, Wellington and Hockey claim: 'With a shift in its economic base from manufacturing to service industries, Sheffield is now undergoing a social, cultural and financial resurgence, unequalled since the Industrial Revolution.' But the shift to a service-based economy has arguably been less the result of growth in services and due more to the faster rate of decline of manufacturing. The fact that a quarter of all jobs are part-time indicates the growing casualization and flexibility in work organization that has taken place, and the interviews undertaken with young movers alone reveal how much unemployment persists. 'The Council', states a Housing Department publication, 'is well aware of the City's continuing high levels of poverty – 40% of all households and 63% of Council tenants were in receipt of Housing Benefit in March 1989.' And 'The Housing Committee is still facing an increasing backlog of serious disrepair, loss of stock and increasing homelessness' (1989, pp. 4–5). People are also leaving the city at the rate of about 7000 a year so that its population is expected to decrease from 534 400 now to 514 700 by 2001 (still making it officially, thanks to Merseyside's faster-falling population, England's fourth largest city). In September 1988 the unemployment rate for Sheffield was 12.8 per cent (15.8 for men, 8.9 for women) so that there were 32 unemployed people to each registered unfilled vacancy (Sheffield City Council Department of Employment, 1988). For young people, according to another '16–19' associated study (Riseborough, 1988, p. 5).

> Only 9 percent of 16–19-year-olds had a full-time job, 47 percent were on a variety of YTS schemes, 32 percent were in other full-time education or training, and a further 13 percent were not in full-time work or education/training.

YOUNG HOME-BUYERS IN SHEFFIELD

Crystal Peaks was where Michelle (20) and her husband had bought a two-bedroomed house with lounge–kitchen–diner downstairs when they married nearly three years earlier. When she received the first 16–19 Initiative newsletter telling the young people involved what had been found out so far, Michelle was concerned to learn that there were so few like herself who had married at 17 and had a two-and-a-half year old child already. But, even though her friends were only just getting round to buying their houses, she would 'not really' have preferred to have done things differently. She thought she ought to have done more studying, and described herself as 'a student housewife – a sort of frustrated career woman'. She had had to give up the office job she got from her YTS after school because she became pregnant. So

Michelle had followed the stereotypically feminine pattern of stopping work when she married and moved. However, a year ago she had returned to college for one day a week to complete the BTEC office course she had begun on YTS, and recently had started nursery nursing for two days a week. Her parents were both teachers and she was their only child until, in Michelle's last year at school, her mother had twins. 'They'd told her she couldn't have any more. She was in the paper and everything. It didn't affect my leaving though.' For Michelle had met her husband-to-be some time before at the youth club she attended, where he worked as a leader. He was five years older than she was, and they went out for a year before getting married, moving to an uncle's house for a month while the sale of the house they had bought came through. With her parents' two infants and her husband and herself expecting their own baby, the three-bedroomed private house Michelle had grown up in was suddenly too small: 'I couldn't have stayed at home but my parents were very good letting me go – they gave me a lot of independence.' In fact they helped with furniture and were generally 'very positive'. With their help, finding a house seemed 'quite easy'. 'This was the first place we looked at.'

Now they were struggling on Michelle's husband's wage of £103 a week to pay a mortgage that had risen to £182 a month and more since. They had lost Housing Benefit but got a rate rebate and were applying for family credit. 'But I would rather not get the mortgage rescheduled – it just gets you into more debt.' Instead,

> 'We'll probably have to move to a smaller house the way things are going. At the moment things are very hard. We haven't got any money for anything. It's a good job we've got my mum to back us up now and then. Due to them maybe we won't have to move house. We've got nothing for clothes and things but mum helps us out.'

Now that she had stopped working to look after her new family, Michelle's mother drove the five miles out of town every day her daughter was not at college. 'So I go there to help with the twins and on Sunday for lunch. Sometimes they come here but not so often, not for a meal or anything.' That was why Michelle said, 'I don't think I want a bigger family – one's enough. I look after my mum's two every day; it's like having two of your own.' Her hope was that she and her husband could hang on as they were until she completed her course and her child was at school. 'I'll have a job teaching by then hopefully so we'll have a higher standard of living.' She anticipated however that with interest rate rises, things would get worse before they got better.

Finances were easier for the 20-year-old young man earning £350 a week living with a fiancée four years older than himself who previously had her own flat. Still, with a year-old child and having bought their own home after nearly two years of moving backwards and forwards between his girlfriend and his parents, they found that 'Money is the big thing at the moment.' It would be easier when his fiancée went back to her work as a secretary but, thanks to the peculiar local practice of unseen bidding when house-buying, the price of their new two-bedroomed house had risen during the sale from £26 000 to £34 000. They would have been unable to buy it without the loan for the deposit from his father with whom he worked as a self-employed carpenter. But this interviewee shared the feeling of young house-buyers in Swindon that it was now or never before prices rose beyond their range. However, his main motivation for moving had been the birth of his son nine months before: 'If he hadn't've come along I'd still be living at home.'

The other interviewee who had bought in Sheffield had lost her house and returned home, not because she had been unable to keep up the payments, like those who had lost their homes in Swindon (which then led to the temporary breakdown of their partnerships), but because of the breakdown of her engagement. She and her fiancé had also been gazumped so that they paid £120 a month for a two-bedroomed house out of her wages of £90.50 a week as a sewing machinist and his of £130 as a wood machinist. They had been going out for four years and moved when she was 18 and he was 20, first temporarily into his parents' privately owned house. After three months there they got engaged and moved to their own home. 'It didn't work out' and after ten months they had a four-month 'trial separation' when 'I kept seeing him but I wasn't sure what I was going to do'. During this time she shared a friend's council flat and he went back to his parents. Then she 'got caught' [pregnant], lost the child and returned to her parents' to recover. Even though she was again sharing a bedroom with her sisters in her parents' small terraced house, this interviewee felt she was now treated differently by her parents: 'They treat me as an adult 'cos I've had that relationship so they know I'm not a baby anymore. Before, it was all, "What time are you coming in tonight?" but now they're not bothered 'cos they think as you've run a house you're responsible for yourself. To put it shortly, they're not so protective.' Her parents had been supportive throughout and even though she had moved ten miles away she had seen them so often that 'It weren't like being away really'. Even so she was now saving to buy another house, on her own this time.

ON THE MANOR

The Manor Estate was built after the First World War under the slogan of 'homes fit for heroes'. As one of the interviewees in this sample wrote in the local *Manor Matters* newspaper, 'The Manor is a far cry from this now but the Manor is home to those who make it home.' She was responding to a television documentary which, she wrote, 'portrayed us as low life' and 'didn't get across the point the Manor people were trying to make'. Many of the residents seemed to share her opinion; one man she talked to told her, 'They tried to stereotype you as working class because you came from the Manor.' Another said similarly, 'At job interviews they seem reluctant to give you the job because of where you come from.' The writer herself recorded, 'When I first moved here two years ago I didn't give the place much credit. I thought I was doomed to unemployment and being branded second class.' Now, 'In *Manor Matters* we try to paint a real picture of the community. We want people to know we aren't all second class, thieves and down and outs as they portray us in the press' (Gilliver, 1989). On the other hand, she did not close her eyes to the level to which many people had been reduced on the estate; as she said in interview, 'A lot of people round here will tell you they don't look at themselves as a person; they look at themselves as a thing, something that switches on and off.' As a result, she explained, 'A lot of opinions are the same around here 'cos we're all in the same situation.'

Lorraine (18) was born on the Manor and, like the girl who had bought and lost her own house (p. 40), she left school early.

'When I got towards the end of my fourth year I never bothered wi' school. I don't know what it is, a lot of kids get like that. It's not as if they're stupid. I mean, I were in the top sets until I started mucking about and missing school. It got to the stage with me my mum had to take me to school when I was 15. It were ridiculous! But after you soon regret it. I told my little sister not to start missing odd lessons and at least she got her exams, even though she's only on a Y[outh] T[raining] S[cheme] now. If I'd've done that in the first place I wouldn't be in the situation I'm in now. I wouldn't've worked in the market and met Big Ed or anything.'

Big Ed worked on his father's stall just round the corner from the shop where Lorraine worked on Saturdays and then full-time at 16 for £40 a week. She left after a year-and-a-half when she was eight months pregnant. 'I stayed at mum's till I had the baby and then moved two weeks after having made the place fit to move into.' Her fiancé, as he had become a year before, had already moved in with her parents

"cos his mum and dad weren't very pleased either. I had to go on the homeless list to get a place. I wasn't really homeless but it was impossible to stay where I was. They wouldn't give me one for overcrowding; they said I could share, especially as my sister was leaving, so I had to get out another way. I went to the council and told them that I weren't getting on with my dad so it would be better if I just left. It were true really 'cos I got pregnant and my dad's always been overprotective with us girls in the family. When my sister got pregnant it were like the end of the world and then when I got pregnant so young I thought he'd kill me. He wouldn't speak to me and you could cut the atmosphere wi' a knife.

'Mum were fine all the way through. She helped wi' a lot of things, especially before I got money off the S[ocial] S[ecurity]. She bought the cooker and kitchen unit so she really helped out. When we talked it over with them they agreed it was just too much us all living there together. They were pleased I was getting a house on my own 'cos when my sister left, her husband left her on her own and I think my dad thought the same thing would happen to me but it hasn't so I think he was quite pleased. I never got on wi' my dad for a bit but after I had little Ed he came round and he's been quite good. I'm very lucky: if I really need money for anything I can turn to my dad if I'm desperate. Now I see mum most 'cos dad works away, driving. If I know he's home I make an effort to go up and show him the baby. I go shopping on Saturdays with mum and pop up once or twice in the week and mum sometimes calls, if she's doing home-helps round here she'll come in for her dinner or a cup of tea. My younger sister comes down a couple of times a week, usually to borrow something and my big sister calls sometimes or I go to see her but my brothers work away so I don't see them as much.

'When Big Ed's family first found out I was expecting they weren't very interested in me or him but once I had the baby seeing him must have brought them round. Now we spend one day in the week with them and they spoil Little Ed rotten. They buy all his nappies plus the video and stereo as house-warming presents. Anything he wants he has off them. Big Ed works for his father's fruit and flower stall. I don't know how much he earns. I haven't got a clue but it varies; on average about £50. The last few months he's only been working half days, so half that. We only pay £2.61 rent for this house but if I told them Big Ed was living with me we would have to pay full rent – £25 plus. I'd be ten times worse off than I am now. That's how I got this house because I'm so young having a child I wanted to be near my mum and they think I'm on my own. The social worker at the hospital told me to tell them I didn't want a flat, I wanted a house near my parents being only 16 and having a child. You have to watch out for snoopers and what you tell people. They've already done Ed for maintenance. I get £57.05 S[ocial] S[ecurity] but the electricity meter alone takes £7–10, another £5 for the gas, then you've got £20–30 to live on so it doesn't leave much for clothes. We can just barely afford to live on the money I get and the money Ed gets. Luckily I got all my furniture and that before everything changed and I didn't have to pay them back the £400 or so off them.

'There's quite a few girls my age who've got children and houses on the estate. I mean, a girl on her own it's really hard. I were lucky, especially when everything started to change 'cos a lot of girls are getting pregnant and trying to leave and they can't get places anywhere. Compared to my two older brothers, they've bought their own homes and brand new things whereas I had to buy all second-hand things. They don't realize how hard it is to get money and keep it nice. I would've preferred to have done things different. I don't regret having Little Ed but I just wish it had been a few years later so me and Big Ed could've saved to buy our own home and have a car and holidays every year and everything, but these things happen and you just have to make the best of it.

'At the moment I'm a housewife but hopefully when the baby starts at nursery I'll go back to work, maybe help on the stall or anything. I miss not being at work. I'll work part-time at first and then later full-time. If I can't find a job I'd consider going back to college to take English and maths or maybe night-school and learn something – floristry, typing or computers or anything. . . . Ed is going to start working with my dad as a labourer and he'll get a lot more money, so we've decided we'll put that away and save just to have money to buy our own house and not just scrimp and save and have things on weekly payments 'cos that's the only way you can afford it. We wouldn't think of buying this house. I'd maybe consider having another child in about ten years' time. I want to live my life a bit more having missed out because of having children so young.'

Two other young women in similar circumstances were interviewed on this or another estate. They were in the older cohort of the sample and so were 20 but, like Lorraine, they had left school without qualifications and hardly been employed. They had also been rehoused near to their parents' council homes, one after a five-month interval living with her unemployed boyfriend of 24 in private rented accommodation, the other when her 27-year-old husband who had had his name on the council list for some time was given the tenancy of a house in the same street as his mother and his wife's mother. They each had two children and did not plan any more. Neither considered buying but one wanted an exchange from her flat. She thought she would never be able to afford to buy. For the other, her council tenancy represented her security because when she first moved in her husband had been unemployed. If he lost his job again, she feared she would not be able to keep up the payments and would lose her home. This attitude contrasted with the security which private ownership represented to many others, especially in Swindon.

Like Beverley in private accommodation in Swindon (p. 22) and Michelle in Crystal Peaks (p. 39), these three young women had followed the traditional but minority female stereotype of giving up work on moving and marrying – whether or not they were formally 'engaged'/married or not. The only difference was that they had done so some years younger than others and after working for a shorter time. In the absence of what they regarded as prospects and point for them in prolonging their education or of worthwhile employment they had therefore, as it were, skipped a stage. Again following the stereotyped pattern, they would return to part-time work when their children were old enough to be looked after by someone else at school or nursery. In the area in which they grew up and among their contemporaries such a progression seemed to them entirely 'normal', as one said. They were in addition supported by their parents, especially their mothers, whom they visited and who visited them regularly, even if they had been initially disapproving. At least their daughters were 'doing the right thing' even if at the 'wrong' time.

If they compared themselves with others who were working, they were not missing very much: 'Girls I know, they're mostly still at home. They stay at home and they go out to work, then weekends they go out and about spending it all.' If they sometimes missed not going 'out and about', there was the compensation of having their own home where 'I don't have to answer to anybody'. 'Sometimes I wish I'd waited a bit having children. Other times I'm not bothered.' Their contemporaries would soon catch up with them and their early start might then turn out to be an advantage. As the situation worsened, 'with all the rules they're bringing in, Poll Tax and all that crap', later starters might not get the housing they wanted. In the meantime the young women were caught up in their own immediate concerns of saving money and getting by which made long-term plans, like buying their own home, unthinkable so that, as one said, 'You never know how you're going to be from one week to the next.' This insecurity led to fatalism and fantasy, with which they made the best of their situation. The effort at self-justification was not great because their expectations were so limited: 'Plans? I've got none. We're happy as we are. Go to work part-time when the children grow up.' For the rest, 'I don't know what else I'd really like to do. I haven't really thought. I would like to work part-time, just for the extra money. But cars and that. . . . It's just dreaming, isn't it?'

For young women on their own with children the situation was even harder.

TWO YOUNG WOMEN ON THEIR OWN

The local office of the Commission for Racial Equality estimated the ethnic minority population of Sheffield in 1986 at 4.2 per cent of the total population. This is slightly below the UK average 4.5 per cent black population (equalled 2 162 000 in 1981). Unlike the rest of Britain, in which Indians are the largest group amongst black and Asian people, in Sheffield West Indians and Pakistanis constitute the two largest groups with approximately 10 000 each. Chinese, Indians, Yemenis, Bangladeshis and Somalis, in declining order, make up the remaining numbers of settled communities. The age structure of the black population means that in the younger age groups they are a larger percentage of the whole population of that age than 4.2 per cent, though this varies by minority group. For instance, 'The more settled West Indian population has fewer young people than the Pakistani population in which almost half are under 15 years of age' (Bussue and Drew, 1985, p. 14). Since the total '16–19' sample in Sheffield drew at random upon one in ten school leavers, at least five per cent of them should have been black or Asian but they were far fewer than this. For the 20 young movers interviewed in Sheffield there should have been at least one black or Asian, presuming that they moved no more and no less than their white counterparts, which is quite a presupposition. While it might be supposed that more extended family patterns among some minority communities might lead youngsters from these communities to move from their parents to stay with other relatives more than the norm, it also emerged in Liverpool that while black young people might want to move out of the L8 area where most of them lived, racism made it difficult for them to do so. Thornton asserted (1990, p. 27) that when in urgent housing need black people are more likely to turn to relatives and friends within their own communities rather than 'white' welfare agencies, so that their accommodation problems often remain hidden.

As it turned out there was only one young black man who could have been interviewed but he was 'too busy'. This was a pity because, as a long conversation with his Ghanaian grandfather made plain, his case might have made an illuminating contrast with the mainstream English and Scots youngsters, throwing light upon what otherwise could be taken for granted. For, as his grandfather said,

'We Ghanaians don't believe like English people do that when you get married that is your new family. No, when you get married that is like a companion because anything can happen. Your number one family is your parents. So you have two homes but one family.'

However, as a member of the third generation in the United Kingdom the young man's experience could well have reflected only some conflict between English norms and these traditional mores and not the culture clash facing several second-generation Asian girls (see below). In his absence it seemed justifiable to go outside the sample to find at least one minority youngster to interview. This was done by what is sometimes portentously called networking – finding a friend of one of the other interviewees.

The underrepresentation of blacks and Asians in the whole sample could have been due in part to the self-ascription in terms of nationality which the original questionnaires offered respondents, possibly confusing citizenship with nationality and minority identification. This made it difficult if not impossible to interpret the numbers of ethnic minority youth from the data. However, their underrepresentation was undoubtedly mainly due to the technique of random sampling and demonstrates, once again, that in a population that is not evenly dispersed a random sample is not necessarily representative, or, in other words, a colour-blind approach does not take account of ethnic reality. In a small area like Swindon, where the sample had been one in four school-leavers, this did not matter. But in Sheffield the black and Asian population is concentrated in five or six main areas, though in none of them does it amount to more than a quarter of the whole population of the area. In most other parts of the city the black and Asian population is under three per cent. The result is that black and Asian pupils are disproportionately represented in just a few of Sheffield's schools. So, if the sample were to have been representative, it should have been weighted towards sampling more leavers from those schools, or a special study undertaken as in Liverpool (see Connolly and Torkington, 1990). The drop-out rate from the sample, which was high and was compensated for by a boost sample, can also be anticipated to have been higher among ethnic minority young people, since all the available statistics show the social disadvantages of Sheffield's black population (e.g. Sheffield City Council, 1988). An additional factor that may have played a part in the underrepresentation of black and Asian young people in the 16–19 Initiative was that some Asian girls may have gone to the Subcontinent in their last year at school in order to get married and would therefore have failed to receive a questionnaire at all if they were in the younger cohort. On their return they could well be living at a different address from their original one and so relatives would have to be relied upon to send on the questionnaires, something they might not always be willing to do. The Sheffield Careers Office confirmed that this was a declining practice, although it was the case for Nazreen in Swindon and for the one Asian girl who was interviewed in Sheffield but whose reaction to her experiences was very different from Nazreen's.

Halimah (20) left school at Christmas 1984.

'Well, I didn't leave school. My dad took me to Bangladesh before that. I knew what were going to happen and I argued before I went back to Bangladesh. I told my dad, "I'm not going 'cos I know you're going to get me married" but he lied and said he weren't. Mum thought it were a good idea. She's one of those people who married in Muslim law and had to vow to do what she were told. She says now if she'd known better she'd never have let me go, and she's not going to let my sister go. My dad's divorced her but he still seems to think he owns us. Like me, he seemed to think I was an object; like I found out he got money for me getting married. Asian men seem to think they own the girls. He doesn't care about the grandson he's got. If he had his way I'd be in the house 24 hours a day. For six months I were arguing wi' him. I even packed my bags to leave at one time but I had nowhere to go. He threatened to take my young brother instead and it's not a country to have little kids in. I couldn't even speak the language when I went there.'

In Bangladesh, like Nazreen in Pakistan, Halimah lived first with her father's relatives and then, once her marriage was arranged, moved after the ceremony to her husband's home.

'One minute I were single, next minute I were married. When I were pregnant I were thinking, "I hope to God this isn't a girl inside me or she'll just go through what I've been through." They weren't going to let me over but I said I weren't going to stay there and have a baby. My dad were in two minds 'cos he knew I wouldn't come back but eventually I talked my husband's family into letting me come back to have the baby. I came back in a right state, six months pregnant and I'd jaundice as well as everything else.

'I wrote to the baby's dad and told him I wanted a divorce. He came once and gave me a lot of crap about wanting to see the baby but he didn't want to see the baby. I says, "On yer bike". But I can't get a divorce 'cos he won't agree to one so I've got to wait five years.'

When she first returned it was to her mother's three-bedroomed council house, which Halimah shared with her two older and three younger brothers and younger sister. After a year,

'I got a letter from my dad saying if he came back to mum's and found me there he'd kill me so I moved in a week 'cos I were in a right state when I got that letter 'cos I know what my dad's like. He would've killed me 'cos he's that kind of person. A friend told me about the housing association that they have a scheme to help people out in difficult situations. I borrowed some money from mum when I moved in and she hasn't asked for it back. She gave me a couple of carpets as well. I'm there, at mum's, every day. I think I would be even if I were ten miles away. It's only ten or fifteen minutes' walk so I go every day, unless it's chucking it down. If I see one of my brothers and he says "Are you going home?" that gets me in a muddle. This is my house and that's my home . . . "our house" meaning my mum's. At one point I thought of going back to my mum's but I thought, "No, I've come this far, I've got to stick it."

'The housing association are very bad for repairs. They don't want to know. You have to go down and threaten them wi' the authorities before they do owt. When I moved in they used to come straight away. I'm trying to get an exchange but as soon as people find out I'm on the top floor they don't want to know. I'm also trying to get a council house. The baby keeps falling down the stairs here and unless I take him down my mum's there's nowhere for him to play. The flats are rubbish really. The bins are at the bottom of the stairs and I have to take him wi' me to go down there. I'm on edge all the time 'cos of the windows. It's right hard to get your shopping up and the baby in a pram and we're not near the shops.

'Compared to other people I know, most of my friends are still at home and I would've preferred to have had a job and saved up before having a baby. That was my idea from the start but I had to have a father who went spoiling it all. Now my education days are over. I can't put my mind to it. It just goes in one ear and out the other. I suppose jobswise if they force us to go on ET I'd have to go. I've thought about a part-time job if I can find one to earn the £15 extra I'm allowed to. It'd be something to do in the day.

'I've got a boyfriend. He works in a bakery. I don't think it's a relationship that'll last though 'cos he's all wrapped up in his mum. Whenever he earns any money he runs home to show his mum and gives her what she wants. She's grabbing everything she can out of him. He's so immature – that's the top and bottom of it. The way I see it, men have ruled my life up to now and I'm not having it any more. It's our mothers who brought us into this world and we can't jack it in for them. They [men] don't do owt for us. I mean, look at him, that holiday I went on [for a week abroad with a friend who paid for her], he dared me to go on it and I said, "There's the door". So I won't get married. I prefer a single life. I'm definitely not a housewife or wife – I'm nobody's wife; that's one mistake I'll never make again. Even if I have a boyfriend, I don't want him to move in wi' me. I won't even have to chuck his clothes out then. It depends if I meet the right person who treats my son the same as their own but I don't think I'll meet anyone like that.

'I were brought up as a Moslem but I don't care now. I wear anything and talk to anybody. I mean, I didn't know what a pork sausage tasted like 'til I moved in here; now I never stop eating them. I cancelled the appointment to have my baby circumcised. My brothers are always asking when I'm going to have him chopped. They used to take my dad's side but now they agree wi' me; I've shown them a route and they're following me. I've no use for the baby learning Bengali. As far as I'm concerned he's my baby. I've made him on my own. I brought him up. I carried him. I wiped his arse. I don't think I'd have any more kids, not unless I were really certain in a relationship. It's just me and my baby.'

The experiences of the other single mother interviewed in Sheffield had led her to a similar view of her situation. Glennis (18) also left school early at Christmas but under her own volition, having, like Lorraine and others, lost interest in an institution that seemed to offer nothing to her.

'I never went to school anyway so I didn't know the proper leaving date. I got behind with GCSE coursework and I'd never catch up so there weren't any point. When I left school there was nowt for me. It were in between computers and skilled labour so I thought I might as well have a baby and settle down to that. I went to the council and they said they could give me a hostel place. I was down at the housing office constantly. I was offered a house on the other side of Sheffield which was falling down, literally. You couldn't take a baby there. Then they offered me a house on the Manor near my parents' but then they said I couldn't have it 'cos they'd offered me the other place and I weren't homeless, but after a fight with them I got it. It were more my idea than anybody else but it were a mutual decision because of overcrowding. Mum didn't want me to move and have responsibilities myself but she knew I had to live my own life and respected my decision and let me go. I didn't want my parents influencing my decisions. I wanted to make my own decisions and run my own life the way I wanted to.'

In a van her father borrowed Glennis moved the two miles from her mother's three-bedroomed council house which she had shared with her older brother, three older and one younger sisters. One brother and one sister were unemployed, like her father and herself. 'At first when I moved I used to see them nearly every day. Then it were a lot harder trying to get down there wi' the baby so I see them less now.' In her two-bedroomed house she sees her baby's father 'after a fashion'.

'He helps with the baby's clothing but that's all. He bought me a stereo but I had to sell it when I was broke. His mum didn't know about the baby for three or four months. I had to get a photo to put through his mum's door. When he came home she said, "Who's this girl then?" but she weren't bothered about it; she were just angry he hadn't told her and he still didn't take us down there. His sister took the baby round and when his mum saw it she were crying 'cos she's never had a baby granddaughter, so she sees the baby now.'

Like Halimah, Glennis set little store by this or any other relationship that she could foresee with men: 'They're immature. They don't think about your needs just about themselves.' So, 'I'm not planning to have any more kids.'

Instead,

'I'm planning to do a bit more training to get qualifications for a job and eventually get a job as a journalist. I went to the *Sheffield Daily Star* once and chatted to the editor and he told me to get to college and get A-levels and to do the course and come and see him again. I hope to do that eventually. I'll build up more credits through the Open College and get on an access course to college.'

At the local Training and Resource Centre, which is part of the South Yorkshire Open College Federation, Glennis had begun accumulating credits on an office skills course.

> 'It opens a few doors for you. But if the Social get to hear about me studying part-time, they'll say I'm available for work and cut me off benefit. It would be literally impossible for me to work at the moment. I only just virtually exist as it is. It's like the lasses round here are all in the same situation. They're on about getting a crèche up and getting part-time jobs but the Social's going to say they're available for full-time work. They expect you to leave your kids with any stranger.'

Glennis regretted getting herself into a situation in which she seemed to be trapped and from which the education she had previously rejected now offered a way out: 'I'd have preferred it if I had another chance to stay at school and get qualifications and get a decent job. I'd turn the clock back if I could.' However, she was determined, ambitious and saw herself as 'a creative person'. Nevertheless Glennis was in a vulnerable position living alone with her child. Her house had already been broken into a number of times and this continuing harassment by young males could drive her back to her family or to try to rely upon some other man whom she did not really want. 'I can't tell what's going to happen. I mean, I might get pregnant again and that might hold me back.' Compared with other girls her age, she asked, 'How many 16–18 year olds are there with their own house and a kid? I know some people who are in the same position as me, like my sisters, but to answer that question generally, it's not normal, is it?'

RETURNING HOME

Out of the 1600 total Sheffield sample 131 were indicated in the first trawl through the data as living at a different address from their parents. However, after the experience in Swindon of knocking on doors to find that the young people had not moved at all, before sending out letters to the Sheffield 'movers' a double-check showed that 30 were still living with their mother or father, even if their coded interview return indicated they had moved to their 'own home' (see p. 13). In addition, as in Swindon, psychologists in Sheffield were also extremely busy interviewing the young people in the sample so that, as well as 14 identified as moving who were also in the core interview sample, 32 others were also part of special studies and could not be interviewed. That left 55, of whom 19 were interviewed, plus one from outside the sample: 12 girls and 8 boys.

Thirty-six were also contacted, six of whom were students outside Sheffield. One girl was in the army. One boy had gone to Pakistan. One girl's mother said that her daughter was working abroad, but 'preferred not to say where'. (The briefcase factor should be recalled here, which in Sheffield had a different significance to carrying a briefcase around Swindon; in the North debt-collectors rather than salespersons are associated with briefcases.) The neighbour of one respondent 'hadn't seen her for months'. Another empty-looking flat was tried repeatedly with no success while one house, which was the last known address of another respondent, had been demolished completely. Another five sample members had moved without trace, including one rehoused but whom the housing department was unable to locate because she had then left her subsequent tenancy. In fact, the amount of rebuilding and refurbishment of the 1960s system-built high-rise flats in the centre of the City, including the notorious Park Hill and Hyde Park, in preparation for the 1991 World Student Games and by the council, in partnership with the UK Housing Trust, made it additionally difficult to trace these mobile young people – particularly as the council had rehoused a number of young tenants in short-life properties and later rehoused them again. A substantial, though reduced, private rented sector (eight per cent of all housing tenure) also made it difficult to trace any youngster who had been living there. Hope could be abandoned of ever finding any of the sample upon the thresholds of bed-sit houses whose occupants came and went, often without knowing one another.

One young person in the survey who had moved from his original residence wrote saying he wanted no part in any further questionnaires or interviews 'as it was getting too personal'. Another was 'not interested any more. She only filled it in for something to do,' her mother reported. Another's mother similarly relayed the message that 'She said she weren't going to bother, she were that busy'. As seen, the only black person in the original list of movers also said he was 'too busy', while someone else said he was 'not interested any more'. Two on the list of movers were in hospital. Another had moved, her mother did not know where. Another could not be contacted even through her local vicar. Still another did not answer a message to ring back and one letter was returned as 'not known at this address'. Despite the double-check, eight more were still found to be living with their parents and denied that they had ever left home though in one case this seemed unlikely to have been true.

Unlike the other areas, more of the Sheffield young movers who were interviewed were unemployed than the average for the Sheffield sample as a whole, even if this was taken as the average of those who had ever reported being unemployed, although they perhaps no longer were. This lends credence to the idea that unemployed youngsters are more likely to move to look for work and also because 'push' factors may compel them to leave home (see Introduction). There was not in Sheffield the exodus that became apparent in Liverpool and Scotland, although three young women and one young man who were interviewed had left Sheffield to work and subsequently returned home. One of these young people illustrated another North–South factor in that, although she was well qualified, having stayed in the sixth form to take A-levels, and then entered a Civil Service job in London, she returned to Sheffield after two years for a better quality of life. Here, with a temporary secretarial job paying only £95 a week, she saved more than out of double that money in London. Even though her hours of work were now longer, she had spent more time and money in London travelling. Rental accommodation in London had cost between £30 a week at a hostel to £50-plus for shared flats far from the centre where she worked. As with George, the student in London from Swindon, these were often short-contract lets, or sharing with others meant that if one person quit for any reason the others were left to pay an increased rent, find a new flatmate or move on. Back in Sheffield, she rented a two-bedroom house for £44 a week which she might share. Working on Friday and Saturday nights in a bar for £15 a night, she was saving money, although she would not buy her own house, as she planned to do on her own, until she had secured a better paid job with prospects.

This case also illustrated another critical consideration for a young person leaving home and then returning to the area, for she had the option of going back to her parents' three-bedroom privately owned house where she still had her own room. It was suggested (p. 36) that students studying away face the same dilemma on completion of their course, especially if they then return to their home town. For this interviewee the possibility was closed because of her cats, to which her father was allergic. These pets therefore became a mutually agreed reason for retaining her independence. This is just one example of the construction of justifications for children leaving and sometimes returning to their parents. Such justifications were crucial to the continuous negotiation between parents and children. For instance, although this interviewee's parents had been continuously supportive, regularly visiting and communicating by phone and letter, it did not seem they would be able to accept their daughter back on new terms, unlike the parents mentioned on p. 41. As the interviewee herself put it, 'I think I would find it really difficult if I had to live back home now . . . [because] I get on much better with my parents if I don't see them so often.'

Two other young people in the Sheffield sample had returned to the city after moving to work. During the last year of her further education City and Guilds catering course one, aged 21, had undertaken a placement at a Scottish hotel. There she met the young man (23) to whom she became engaged before returning to Sheffield to complete her course. He was a trainee manager at the hotel where she was subsequently employed. She had since moved with her fiancé, first, after eight months, to live in together at a hotel in Gloucester for six months, then for another six months to Stratford-upon-Avon, followed by five months in Coventry. For both of them these jobs represented improvements in their wages and responsibilities. In all of them they lived rent-free in the hotels or in accommodation provided for staff.

While away she felt she had not 'left home' but was just 'living away'. 'I knew I'd always come back. If I'd've had the same opportunities in Sheffield, I wouldn't've gone.' Now they had both found hotel/restaurant management work and were living in her parents' four-bedroomed private house until they could move into the three-bedroomed house they had found to buy. Within three years of being married they wanted two children. Optimistically, the interviewee imagined this would not interfere with her plans for joint hotel management and, unusually, she specified that she would go on to have more children 'if I don't have one of each'. They did not plan to move again.

A youth of 20 had also worked away and returned to Sheffield. He was an Easter leaver from school whose only further education/training was on a Youth Training Scheme in brass-foundry work and catering. Unusually, he completed it and then, after four months on the dole, took a job as a bakery van boy for £55 a week until he was laid off after more than a year. He had been unemployed since save for two months in the South stripping asbestos. This dangerous work was well paid at £250 a week and he was waiting for more work away dismantling a nuclear power station for, supposedly, £650 a week. He did not think of staying South but caught what the *New Statesman* (8.12.89) called 'the Tebbit Express', the trains at the beginning and end of the week carrying people from the towns of the North to work in 'Loseland' (see also p. 68). However, it was not because he had lived away in Brighton, staying in bed and breakfast in the week and returning to Sheffield at weekends, that he was on the list of those in the sample who had moved. It was because he had left his parents' three-bedroomed council house twice whilst unemployed. The first time he moved 200 yards to his sister's house on the same estate 'for a change'. However, even though he did not pay his sister for his keep, whereas he paid his parents £13 a week out of his giro, he returned a month later because it was just as 'boring' at his sister's. Also, with her two daughters and her husband (with whom he later went asbestos stripping), there was not enough room. He moved again after five months when he became engaged to his girlfriend, whom he had met fifteen months before. This stay was even shorter – one week – because 'We were arguing all the time – me and her mother and me and her. My girlfriend dragged me into it and then she changed her mind so I came back again.' Now he planned that when his girlfriend (19 and a machinist) got her own council flat he would move in with her.

One other person in the Sheffield sample had lived out of Sheffield for a year and returned to her retired grandfather's council flat which he had bought and where she had been brought up. She had continued living there since her mother moved out to remarry when her daughter was 18. Having completed sixth-form study, she went for a year to Australia with a friend. This was not really 'leaving home' but only 'living away' – 'It was like a year out of my life.' Now that she was back in Sheffield, she had taken work in a gym, similar to what she had been doing before she left but at a lower wage (£60 a week instead of £100 and a lot less than she had earned in Australia, although the cost of living there was higher). She was applying for jobs in teleselling, which she had done in Australia. She was not sure whether she would return to Australia next year to visit her boyfriend there – 'If I don't go, or when I come back, perhaps I'll get a flat.' Her parents would buy it for her and she would pay them a nominal rent. Her stepfather was a landlord with a number of properties. Therefore 'I wouldn't buy, not me personally, because I don't really need to.' Beyond that she had few plans: 'I'm still only a kid really. I just do what takes my fancy.'

Like her, another interviewee, a young man of 20 who had not moved out of the area but had returned to his first home, had reverted to the carefree stage of life when plans for the future are hardly considered. 'I've gone back to my being young stage now. I don't give a damn about anything, just having a good time and enjoying myself.' Like the girl above, his free time was taken up with the immediate concerns of an active social life that revolved around pubs and clubs in Sheffield and environs. Earning £140 a week as an auto-electrician, having completed a YTS cum three-year apprenticeship, he paid his self-employed electrician father and school-help mother £15 a week for a self-contained bed-sit in their three-bedroomed privately owned house where his two younger sisters were still at home. The self-contained bed-sit arrangement had been arrived at on his return from fourteen months' living away in his girlfriend's one-bedroom privately owned flat two miles away. She was 26 and a quality assurance manager and he had moved there gradually from the age of 18 when they met (as p. 40). He 'settled down' there but 'It weren't really my home. It was her place. I suppose it was like lodging really but with a lass you don't think of it as lodging, though I suppose it were as it turned out.' They shared her mortgage payments on the flat, so that he was paying £65 a month while he was away plus half of all the bills and food. They had also been on a couple of holidays together to Crete and to the West Indies. He looked back on his experience as a time away when he had to watch his money.

> 'But I suppose my outlook was different 'cos I were living wi' a girl and you're thinking what could happen and things like that, although we never made any plans. I suppose when I first moved I was only 19 and people were saying, "You're stupid, you're young, go and enjoy yourself", but I felt I was doing what I wanted to do so sod everybody else.'

Now that he was home again, 'My lifestyle's a lot better, but given the chance I'd move back tomorrow.'

Another of the sample, like the girl above and one in Swindon, had been brought up by his grandparents. 'Mum' for him was his grandmother, even though he had gone to live with his 'mother', as he carefully called her, when he was 14 and she had bought a house a few doors away. Similarly, he thought of his aunts and uncles, with whom he had been brought up, as his brothers and sisters, his mother being the oldest of the family who had had him young. It seemed his grandparents had undertaken to look after him so that she could continue with her career as a teacher. His mother felt he resented her for having allowed his grandparents to bring him up and that this contributed to his leaving home. He felt there were 'personal differences' between his mother and himself and he did not see her for a month when he first moved but then visited weekly. Other differences with the people with whom he had shared a privately rented flat made him move back after fourteen months. He resented being back: 'It's sort of inhibiting living here. It's like being a child again. I'm 20, I ought to be doing things myself.' He feared becoming 'like the guy next door, still living with his parents in his forties' and planned to move again soon. He had now decided, following sixth-form college and being unemployed, labouring and part-time bar work, that he wanted to become an actor. He was a student at a local college from where he hoped to go on to drama school. Like George in Swindon, he realized this was a very uncertain career. '"How will I be living in five or ten years' time?" – Do I have to answer that? I'd rather not. You can't look, you just don't know.'

'THE OTHER PEOPLE'

'This house is a sort of drop-in centre – well, more of a drop-out centre actually,' mused Ken (20), as he attempted to count the people with whom he shared a privately rented four-bedroom house in Sheffield's 'Muesli Valley'. They included the four members of a band called 'The Other People', all unemployed young men like himself aged between 20 and 23, and a succession of their friends and visitors, including 'the near permanent Captain Windscale, so called because he's a national disaster'. For these young men uncertainty was a way of life to be embraced in a seemingly continuous parody of 'The Young Ones'. Ken, for instance, claimed that before he came to this house he had 'wandered about a bit, a vagrant, you get the picture, but I didn't mind sleeping on people's floors and in their beds!' He claimed that he would go to a nightclub if homeless and pick up a girl in order to get somewhere to sleep – 'down the University, hanging around there's pretty good.' He had rented a room in another house in Sheffield for some time, although he was rather hazy about dates – 'But I like this interview. It reminds me of what I've been doing for the last three or four years.' He had also rented a bedsit after he first left his great-aunt. 'Technically she's not a relative so I could still claim housing benefit.' Presumably it was his mother who had told him this, since she was a social worker 'and one of Sheffield's leading feminists', as Ken described her.

> 'Even though my aunt is pretty mellow and I always got on with her better than my parents, I left because she was getting a bit old for noisy teenagers coming in late at night. It wasn't fair really and I wanted a place of my own where I could make a lot of noise and take boys and girls when I wanted.'

He had left his parents two years before because 'I wasn't getting on with them'. They separated a year later; 'I imagine it would be a fair assumption to say that I wasn't getting on very well with them because they weren't getting on with each other.' Since then, he added without any apparent regret, 'I wouldn't say I had a home 'cos there's nowhere I could go now my mum and dad are divorced.' However, 'I visited mum regularly when I first moved from my aunt's, plus more after she got divorced. Now I see her about once a fortnight either at home or at her work. I just pop round to have a cup of tea or a meal and raid the cupboards or to wind up her feminist friends. I used to phone as well but they've taken it off us, the bastards.' As for his father, 'he's got a bit of a funny attitude towards me these days, wants me to get a proper job and stuff like that. Also, I owe him some money.' Ken did have an uncle who was 'a bit of a pal and lends me his car' and he still saw his great-aunt once or twice a week. Friends had helped him to move from place to place and a landlord had helped him to move his piano into one house – 'The only trouble was he didn't move it out again!' Compared to other people his age, despite his disagreements with his parents, 'I imagine my leaving home was a lot more smooth, a lot less hassle and bad feeling.' He would 'not really' have preferred to have done things differently, 'You've no choice when you've got no money.'

Ken had decided upon a career as a musician, leaving FE business studies after less than a year and now playing occasionally and practising regularly at studios rented cheaply from the council. His plans were 'to get some cash together, bugger off down to London and become a session musician if I can't find a band.' So his period in the drop-out centre would be coming to an end ''cos I have actually got my act together, although I know it doesn't look like it.' And he added: 'I wasn't interested in money until a few weeks ago. Suddenly seeing other people with money, it makes you think.' His confidence that 'you always land on your feet, you just do' could be attributed to his middle-class background or, in addition, it could be that he would soon move out of that phase of his life, which was characterized by not planning ahead and was deliberately absorbed in the present (as p. 51). The 'other people' whom he would leave behind in Sheffield were from a mixture of what would conventionally be called working and middle-class families. The fathers of two of them were manual workers, one from Sheffield the other from Consett, while the third was apprehensive that the research was connected with Sheffield University since his father was a professor there.

Not everyone who had been sent before their time into this breathing world relished their situation as Ken apparently did. For a girl like Janet (20) the prospect was daunting and had come at a time when 'I didn't know what I was doing and I was really unhappy with myself'. She had split up with the boyfriend she had been with throughout sixth form and because of this failed her A-levels. At the same time matters were coming to a head in her grandparent's three-bedroomed privately owned house where she had been living with her mother since she was six and her parents divorced.

> 'When I left home I was getting fed up with us all living under one roof. There was no privacy there, that was it really. I didn't get on with my gran and she didn't approve of my new boyfriend and it was time for me to move 'cos I'd caused a lot of upset in the house and it wasn't fair. I was frightened to go but my mum was encouraging me because my gran is mentally ill and there were more and more rows and they were basically fed up with me being at home.'

She had left sixth form and started work in a series of shop and office jobs, which she hated, working up from £36 to £105 a week in her present administration officer post

with the Civil Service. After a year Janet moved into the private rented accommodation her mother found for her, paying first £21 and then £24 a week. Her mother
also moved out a few months later. Rows with her flatmates had caused her to move
after six months, and now Janet was attempting to make a home for herself in the
house she had moved to: 'I'm in the attic; it's lovely, my little attic, but I'm not
settled down because I'm not happy there. I don't like sharing with strangers. I just
want my own little kitchen really. I'd love to own my own house but I can't afford to
buy.' She was applying for council and, more hopefully, housing association accommodation. She had been going out with a new boyfriend since she moved to the new
house and he stayed there when he was not away playing football for Leicester City
or when he and Janet were not with his family in Sheffield. In contrast to her own
family, 'They're really large and they're really close. It's nice there.'

In common with others who had left their parents on bad terms, 'When I first
moved I didn't see them for about a month. I thought everybody had disowned me
and wanted me out and I felt awful. I wouldn't speak to them although mum used to
come and visit me.' Now that her mother had also moved and 'lives around the
corner', Janet visited her about twice a week, sometimes staying the night. She also
saw her grandparents on Sundays. 'They're all behind me now. It was for the best
really, although I turned against mum at the time.'

Compared to her contemporaries at sixth form, many of whom had gone on to
higher education, Janet felt a failure. She wanted to go back to college and try her
A-levels again 'but it's really money now. I couldn't live without a wage.' Considering
how hard these academically constricted examinations were to pass, her experience
must be shared by many thousands of others and they represent a considerable
national wastage. Certainly Janet was left feeling,

> 'I'm capable of doing more than I'm doing at the moment even though I don't think of
> myself as a career person. I don't feel I've found out what I want to do yet. I'd like to
> settle down and have a family but I don't want to feel I haven't done anything else
> before I have one. I'd like to be married really and have lots of children but I'd also like
> to prove to myself that I could get at least one A-level so I'd like to do more education
> which I will do after Christmas when I've packed in my pub job. I'll do evening courses
> – RSA typing and business studies to improve my job prospects – but I'd like to do my
> A-levels so I don't know what I'll do.
>
> 'Compared to the majority of girls my age, they're still at home. People tend to move
> when they're getting engaged or married or moving in with their boyfriends but in my
> case there was no reason to move.'

She had no plans to get married, although

> 'I think I'd like to be married for security but I'm not old enough within myself. My
> boyfriend has asked me but I think he's forgotten about it now. It seems to be the in-
> thing to do – you get engaged after you've been out with someone for a while but I think
> it's silly to get engaged for the sake of it. A lot of my friends have done that but they'll
> end up throwing the ring back.'

Now she had to consider whether to move with her boyfriend to Leicester, where he
was earning £1000 a month, so that,

> 'If I stop with him I'll probably have a few luxuries, if not I can see myself struggling.
> He's asked me to pack my job in and go down there to live with him but I won't until
> we've got like some security in the line of getting engaged and married and getting a

house together. I don't want him to say "Right, I don't want to see you any more" 'cos then I'm stuck.'

It was difficult if not impossible for a male interviewer to appreciate the niceties of these calculations. They illustrate the dependence of women upon men in cohabitation and the importance for them of obtaining the commitment represented by marriage or more or less formal engagement. The boot could sometimes be on the other foot when the woman had her own accommodation (as on p. 51).

Among the remaining young movers interviewed in Sheffield, one was fostered and the other had moved from care. Fostering or adoption is usually regarded as preferable to remaining in care and young people who move from care at 16 or 17 are a subject of special concern because of their vulnerability, often without the family support that has been seen to be vital for most young people leaving home. Indeed they were the subject of a special study being undertaken by Sheffield Housing Department (Pittard, 1991). The girl with foster-parents had moved, like the cases on pp. 29 and 52, initially to her grandparents. When her grandmother died social workers moved her to different foster families, including at first some relatives with whom she did not get on. She was now 20 and a student in Sheffield with a family she did get on with. She had recently re-established contact with her mother in Nottingham and regularly saw her father, who worked in London. Her experiences had given her a different perspective from that of most of the other interviewees on what constituted a home and a family. These perceptions were partly affected by her distance from the rest of her family in Sheffield, whom she regarded as very traditionally working class whereas she had her own view of the world.

Only 2 in all 86 cases had moved from care and the one in Sheffield was surely atypical in that after two years in a community home he had moved in the company of one of the workers there. She had helped him to get the tenancy of the council flat in Hyde Park they now shared and from which they hoped to be rehoused soon. She was self-employed as a writer on an Enterprise Allowance scheme while he was unemployed.

In addition to these two cases there was also a young man of 20 who had not moved at all but who, because of this, illustrated clearly what was becoming apparent as a feature in some of the biographies of the young movers identified by the sample whose parents' movements had been influential if not determinant in their own home-leaving. In this case the mother had moved to start a new family, leaving her two sons as tenants of the council house where she had brought them up on her own since being divorced eight years previously. Now that they were in their twenties she presumably considered they were old enough to look after themselves and indeed their domestic arrangements corresponded closely to those of many who had actually moved. For they lived independently and, to avoid any disagreements over what belonged to whom, they had even invested in two refrigerators where each stored his own food. 'I were a bit reluctant for mum to move at first', the interviewee said but, although he recognized that it was 'unusual', he stated that he would not have preferred to have done things differently and planned to remain where he was in the foreseeable future as he had no job and no prospects of getting anywhere else. He also visited his mother and her new family a mile and a half away once or twice a week although he did not spend a full day over there 'except at Christmas'.

Finally, the remaining case in Sheffield will be related in some detail because it shows clearly the influence that peers can have upon a young person's decision to leave home and on life generally. The frankness with which it was told indicates how much some people will tell a complete stranger, perhaps partly because he or she comes into their life for only a couple of hours to listen to anything they say and is someone whom they will never see again. The interview took place in the kitchen of Stan's parents' council house on another of the large estates in the hills above Sheffield city. His parents were sitting in the next room with his girlfriend and 1½-year-old child. He had never discussed his drug problem with them even though 'that's what caused all the arguments in the first place' and led to them throwing him out – 'It were just sort of "Get out and don't come back".' Stan said that he would 'like to sit down and have a conversation with my parents about it but that never seems to happen between me and them . . .'. His girlfriend's family knew about it 'and they accept me for what I am' but he had never tried to get any professional help, not considering that he needed it.

'I would've preferred to have lived my younger life more happily 'cos between 15 and 18 I had everything against me and it were my own fault through glue sniffing and the way I reacted to people and treated people.' After he left school Stan went on YTS for two years 'doing all different things – gardening, printing, catering'. Since then he had been two years unemployed ('with a lot of fiddling here and there'), except for three months when his father got him a temporary job at the factory where he worked as a toolmaker. During this time

> 'I got involved wi' drugs through little gangs that used to go around and I suppose we just wanted to see what it were like and just liked it and carried on doing it. One of them [in the gang] is still sniffing but it's right daft doing it that long.'

This corresponded to the attitude of other interviewees to 'stages' in their life that they passed through and that were more or less appropriate at different ages. It also resembled the demarcations between drugs, especially hard drugs:

> 'I never inject drugs and I wouldn't knock about with a person who was. I'd class him as endangering our lives by doing it in front of us. I have taken other things but I couldn't get into it seriously. I'm a mellow acid and reggae person. I suppose it means I like my drugs 'cos acid and reggae that means it comes under those drugs [LSD and marijuana]. I smoke draw every day although I have started to cut down. I've sat in with friends and just smoked a little bit instead of everything that comes past so I suppose that's a step in the right direction. It's not hard to give it up, only at first, but when you realize what's happened you sort of come to your senses. My girlfriend helped me to do that. I were thinking about giving it up anyway but she like pushed me to stop it. If you take drugs then you don't want to work so I've got to start cutting down.'

He had met his girlfriend three months before his parents threw him out and so he then moved into her mother's council house a couple of miles away. He did not stay there longer than three months, however, because 'Her mum had a boyfriend and he kept causing problems wi' the girlfriend so her mum told her to leave so I took her where she should've gone.' This was to Sheffield's Homeless Families Unit who put them in a hostel since Stan's girlfriend was now seven months pregnant. Their child was born there before they were rehoused after a further three months. Like Janet (above),

> 'I didn't see my parents at all after I first left. I started seeing them now and again just before my girlfriend had the baby. While we were at the hostel we used to go to her mum's sometimes but it was mostly out to the chippy, not like proper meals.'

Now that they had moved back nearby 'I see them every week for Sunday dinner and the girlfriend comes down during the week and I sometimes come during the day with her and the baby or by myself.' Like Janet, Stan seemed to accept that it had all been for the best:

> 'I mean, when you get to my age you start thinking about moving but I did it when I was younger. I didn't want to move but, saying that, if I hadn't moved I think I would've got into a worse situation than I am now wi' my family. I'd've had them all against me, instead of listening to what my dad were saying.'

Not that he and his girlfriend were happy where they were because 'We had to take the first place they offered us 'cos the housing said if you don't take the first offer you won't get a place at all.' So they were trying to get a transfer: 'I'm very hopeful of getting an exchange but my dad is not so hopeful for us 'cos we've got a lot of arrears.' For Stan, 'The first thing is to get this house sorted out. I think after that I'll find myself a nice steady job and just try to make it run as smoothly as I can.'

Chapter 4

Liverpool

IMAGE AND REALITY

Swindon in summer, Sheffield in autumn, Liverpool in winter – perception of place is surely altered by weather as by landscape (p. 17). But the effects of cold, sleet and leaden skies cannot alter the facts of a once great city decayed into what should be a national scandal. Half of an ageing population of near half a million live on or below the official poverty line. Half the city's children receive free school meals. A third of the population are retired, sick or unemployed. A third of the male and a quarter of the total workforce is registered unemployed and over half of them have not worked for a year (1988 figures). Only 13 per cent of 16–19-year-old Liverpool school leavers found employment that year. There are associated problems of addiction, disease and crime. Six and a half thousand of its youngest and ablest citizens quit the city each year and the population is projected to fall to half of its 1931 peak of 855 688 by 2001. Without exception Liverpool appears at or near the top of the deprivation league of any study of UK and even European urban decline and poverty. Social polarization concentrates the working class within the city boundaries while the professionals and administrators spread out around the countryside. Streets of fine buildings fall into dereliction, shops are boarded up, businesses have fled.

Confronted with these impressions of an itinerant Southerner, Liverpudlians typically leap to their city's defence – 'You should have seen it ten years ago!'; 'Have you seen Manchester?' They resent their national image; as one of the interviewees put it, 'A lot of Southerners seem to think we all sit in our little terraced "Bread"-like houses and talk about "Our Mam".' Yet they also enjoy their notoriety, as a young man who, like many others had for a time been working down South, said, 'I was the first real Scouser they'd met who wasn't on the telly.' The media image of Liverpool's folksy charms have been cultivated by a generation of programme makers whose idea of the English working class stood still when they left it two and more decades ago; then, as they remember it, the population everywhere was predominantly white and lived in terraced housing. With few tower blocks and its six per cent black population long confined to one postal area, Liverpool, like Newcastle, that other favourite haunt of television series about 'ordinary people', adds the virtues of a scenic location, sea and city brooded over by twin cathedral towers.

It is true that there have been improvements in Liverpool, like the Council House building with which the previous Labour administration tried to regenerate the local economy, even if only, as has been said, to replace high-rise by low-rise slums. Unemployment has also fallen but it is still relatively high, although eased somewhat for young people by the demographic downturn. Even some services and offices have relocated to the area, and the usual gloss has been put upon the central dock/marina by refurbishing old buildings as offices, by a new shopping centre, business and technology parks, a Task Force, Enterprise Zone and Development Corporation. However, Liverpool remains blighted not only by its image but by the more substantial realities of regional economics.

As analysts agree, Liverpool overdepended upon the port to which it owed its original wealth as the gateway to England's first colony, Ireland, and then as harbour to the slave and colonial trade upon which Britain built its empire. Even though Liverpool is still Britain's second largest port, like both islands peopled by four nations, it now stands on the sidelines of world trade. The handful of firms dominating what manufacturing industry remains owe their origins to the port. Similarly, many of the service sector companies provide broking, banking and insurance to port-related activities. The skills profile of the workforce, with 19 per cent in the unskilled and 'undefined' categories compared with 11 per cent nationally, reflects the tradition of casual, cyclical and seasonal dock-working and its associated industries. (Conversely, employers/managers/professionals represent 9 per cent, compared with 15 per cent nationally.) With the decline of the port, the food, drink and tobacco industries that were the city's most important manufactures no longer needed to remain. In addition, the many branch plants locally were vulnerable to closure during restructuring. Those that stayed introduced new technology to survive, only contributing to job loss. There was a consequent underrepresentation of growth industries and increasing reliance upon the service sector, especially the public sector with a low level of private investment. Even so, white-collar occupations have also been falling since the 1970s and retailing is now the most buoyant part of the local economy with the port contracted around its container depot.

The political consequences of this decline are detailed in Michael Parkinson's story of 'one city's struggle against government cuts'. Published in 1985, this chronicle leaves 'Liverpool on the Brink', as its title indicates. It details the record of the Labour council that was elected on a programme of no cuts in jobs or services in 1980. Labour in Liverpool thus entered later upon the political evolution that occurred earlier in Swindon and then Sheffield but without any recovery from what Parkinson calls 'municipal Stalinism' (p. 125) or 'socialism in one city' (p. 149). Indeed, the return of problems that refuse to go away prompted the author, who is Liverpool University's director of Urban Studies, to tell the *Independent* (19.7.90): 'I have given up predicting the day when Liverpool will have its financial crisis. Liverpool will run and run.' Since then, however, the Poll Tax bid fair to be the last straw to break the back of the city's budget deficit. Despite, or perhaps because of, what Parkinson calls 'the pleasures and perversities of Liverpool politics' (op. cit., p. 35), 'During the 1980s Liverpool had become a Labour city' (Roberts and Parsell, 1988b, p. 6). Parkinson commented on the basis of his surveys at the time that 'The explanation of the extraordinary public willingness to resist the government lay in the depth of the pro-City, anti-Government sentiment which ran through voters in all the political parties' (ibid., p. 66). His findings are echoed by the one in seven 1985 and 1987 school leavers in the '16–19' survey, particularly what Parkinson called 'Perhaps the most extraordinary feature of the responses . . . the general optimism about the City's long-term future. . . . This was', he adds, 'an unrealistic view . . .' (p. 67). He predicts,

> Liverpool's economy will continue to deteriorate during the 1990s. There will be increasing inequality and social polarisation with the poorest in an economic ghetto. Already there are two parallel labour markets – the core employed and the marginal and unemployed. The gap between the two will inevitably widen. The social consequences hardly need underlining. (p. 183)

The local economic background of the Liverpool sample of young home leavers has been underlined here because local factors have already been seen to exert so much influence upon young people starting out early in Swindon and Sheffield. Indeed, analysis of the whole sample showed that 16–19-year-olds in Liverpool were less likely to leave home unless to move out of the area for or in search of employment (pp. 4 and 14). Different housing situations locally have also been seen to offer different possibilities to young people leaving home and in this respect Liverpool's housing market is as peculiar as its labour market. Like Sheffield, 'the proportion of people in public housing is higher in Liverpool than the national average and estimates are that demand for private housing in the city is 10 per cent lower than the national figure' (Parkinson, p. 182). Like everywhere else, there has been loss of the best public stock through 'right to buy' so that the proportion of council dwellings declined from 39 per cent in 1971 to 33 per cent in 1986. Conversely, owner occupation has increased to 50 per cent while housing associations have taken up some of the slack and now account for 10 per cent of all tenures (Liverpool City Council, 1987, p. 3). With a specialist housing association catering exclusively for the needs of young people and others offering sheltered accommodation in partnership with council social services, the associations are an important housing resource for young people.

The council makes 10 per cent of its permanent lettings available to homeless families annually (equalling 441 in 1988/9) and there were only 35 families in bed and breakfast in January 1990 (regarded as exceptional by council officers). However, the 13 000 council waiting list includes applicants for transfers who are unwilling to take any of the 21 000 post-war systems-built dwellings identified as hard to let or to be demolished, while 10 000 inter-war houses have still to be modernized. Similarly, although 232 lettings went to single people under 25 in 1988/9, numbers of single young people accepted by Housing Aid Centres as homeless and in priority need increased by 16 per cent to 599 in 1988/9, 324 women and 275 men. 'The main reasons given for homelessness among singles were: 1. parents, relatives and friends unable to accommodate any longer (45%), 2. prison discharge (6%), 3. marital violence or dispute (29%)' (Bolton, 1989). Homelessness came third after financial/social security and accommodation enquiries made by over a thousand young people to a city centre Young Person's Advisory Service (q.v., 1989).

Private renting, as everywhere else, has declined to under 10 per cent of all tenures and is concentrated in just two or three areas. However, thanks to the activities of estate agents using business expansion grants to buy up, convert and rent out empty properties vacated by owners who either could not sell them or whose homes were repossessed after they could not afford to buy them, Liverpool may be the only area of the country where the private rented sector is actually expanding. While rents are rising locally, they are still comparatively low, as are house prices, terraced houses being available for around £12 000 each. However, of the seventy-eight young people contacted in Liverpool only three had bought their own houses (though others hoped to) and one of them had subsequently moved out to rent privately.

Only 78 out of the original 140 identified as living at a different address from their parents/guardians were contacted because, again after double checking, 30 were found to be also shown as living with their parent(s). Twenty-seven were part of the Anglo-German comparison and five were in the Liverpool core sample and unavailable for interview. Twenty-three out of the 78 were interviewed, 16 girls and 7 boys. Of the remainder, nine boys and four girls were found to be still with their mother or father, plus one girl who had moved with her mother and another who had moved with her father. Six boys and five girls had moved out of the area and not returned (two boys and two girls to London, one boy each to Birmingham, Telford, Whitehaven and Torquay, two girls to marry/cohabit in St Helens, and one girl, whose mother was Japanese, to live with relatives in Japan). There were four male students and one male trainee chef out of the area, plus one boy in prison. One boy was 'too busy', and another did not wish to take part 'unless you have to'; a third said, 'It makes me feel like a guinea pig'. Another had only thought about moving – 'I thought I would so I wrote it down', but was still at his parental home. Another had had the questionnaire forwarded to him while he was away for three weeks, 'staying with friends'. One boy could not be traced because he took turns staying with different sisters as well as returning to his girlfriend and child, while from another there was no answer, and a wrong address for a third. Although only one girl was unwilling to take part in the interview because she was 'too busy working nights', the girls were harder to trace than the boys: one was lost track of in bed-sit land, another had 'gone away', the address of a third was found to be derelict, while one letter was returned 'address not known'. There was no answer from one, and two more did not reply to messages left for them. An interview was twice arranged with one girl but she did not turn up. Another was tried repeatedly to no effect (her child was sick). The parents of two girls in the sample did not know their daughters' address: 'We had a fall-out,' as one father explained; 'She's just up and gone. That's how they are these kids,' said the other. One foster-mother did not know where her foster-daughter had moved to and nor did the foster-home of the one girl in care in the sample. One girl had moved to Chinatown but the new occupants of her parents' old fish and chip shop could not say where in Chinatown exactly.

How much of this difficulty was due to the new dimensions that the briefcase factor (pp. 21 and 48) took on in Liverpool is obscure. Certainly people had to be more cautious about opening their doors after dark – 'Who are you?', 'What's he done like?', 'Who wants her?' – but in addition the interviewer was warned repeatedly that a briefcase, bike and car were all targets for theft: 'I wouldn't carry a nice briefcase like that around here if I were you!' One interviewee was amazed that a car parked outside her mother's flats was still in one piece five minutes later. Although such expectations, like the tale of a taxi losing its hub caps while stopped at a traffic light, were perhaps related as compensation for living in so notorious a place, as Londoners talk about traffic, Scots about weather and New Yorkers about crime, there were also serious aspects to this side of Liverpool life which exerted their influence upon whether young people wished to remain or to leave (see p. 105 et seq.).

RETURNING HOME FROM THE SOUTH

Thirteen out of 23 young movers interviewed in Liverpool had returned to their parental home after periods away of from four months to two-and-a-half years. Three of them had moved back to their parents' twice and one of these had then left for a third time. Nine had returned from out of the area, including one boy medically discharged from the army, one injured apprentice footballer and one girl twice employed as a nanny by the same family in London. Hotel and catering work needing 'live-in' employees was seen in Sheffield to be another area of work requiring young people to move. In Liverpool one girl in the younger cohort had worked in hotels after completing a FE diploma in reception skills. She had moved back to her teacher and educational welfare officer parents with her fiancé (26), whom she had met in the South. They now occupied a self-contained flat (as p. 51) within her parents' privately owned house, which the fiancé had converted and for which they paid her parents £25 a week. They hoped to move out and buy when he had established his painting and decorating business locally. She had meantime found a receptionist job in Liverpool's prestigious Adelphi Hotel for £107 a week. While away they had lived during the summer in a mobile home her parents brought down and rented to them for £25 a week when the cost of renting (£50 a week in winter) in Worcestershire rose prohibitively. It was too expensive for them to buy or rent permanently in the South.

Kathy (20) had also worked in hotel and catering in the South where, as she put it, 'I was living with a bloke for a while'. Her story combines economic reasons for moving to work with personal ones related to her own family background. She also had gone to FE for a year to do a legal secretary's course but did not like the work experience. Then, after a period trying different jobs, including telesales – 'diabolical' – and shop work – 'I left that because the manager had different ideas about my job description; he thought it included out of work duties, like sleeping with him' – she became assistant manager of a roadside restaurant for £77 a week plus accommodation. She was joined there by her younger brother 'after he didn't get on with where he was working in London' but when there was no longer room for both of them Kathy returned to Liverpool. She then paid her parents £15 a week ('and any cooking and cleaning that had to be done obviously') to stay in their privately owned house but not for long, moving after two months and temporary clerical work to another live-in job in a pub in Cornwall. It was less the lack of job opportunities locally than her relations with her father that caused her to move.

> 'He drinks a lot and that makes it worse. Plus, he's a bit cocky with his hands. [So] I wanted to get my own independence 'cos it wasn't getting any easier. I was never allowed out to play from the age of 13 with me being the only girl out of the three of us and him being a policeman as well, he expected me to stay home and look after him. I remember my older brother coming home with all his mates and saying, "We're taking our kid out to the pub" and my dad said, "No". So my brother said, "She's 18, you can't stop her." I left the first time soon after that.'

Like her elder brother, 'who was actually kicked out when he was 19', and her younger brother who had also left, 'We'd all got a taste of our own independence and we couldn't go back to live under his rules'.

All the same, Kathy did come back a second time when her parents had a fire in their house and asked her for help. This time she stayed with her older brother: 'I didn't pay any rent; I just cooked and washed up for him. I was his housewife.' Even when she was with her brother, 'My father had too much say over my life. I had to go round at seven everyday and sit with them 'til eleven.' After another two months she left for a third time because relations with her father and her brother had deteriorated and because she had met a new boyfriend. 'I met him on the Monday and I was living with him on the Wednesday.' Later, 'We just went out one Saturday and bought a ring.' He was a lorry driver aged 26 living in a council flat in Rochdale and earning £250 a week. 'When I first met him he was heavily in debt but he isn't now, obviously.' She had found temporary secretarial work in Rochdale for £170 a week and together they were saving to go on holiday to Florida – 'It was either buy a house or go on this holiday so we'll buy a house later. There's plenty of time.' As she saw it, 'I've had my five years of fun and now I'm ready to settle down. . . . Up to eight months ago I was chasing after something I couldn't have. I've found it now. I wanted somewhere to settle down and call it my home.'

Ray (21) was the third returnee who had cohabited whilst away, although like Kathy, but unlike many other movers in Swindon particularly, he had not moved for that purpose. He moved for work: 'Because you're young you think money rules so if you can just get a better salary down there it'll sort all your problems out.' Although he went on a YTS in business accounts, Ray had been working part-time for £40 a week in his parents' pub since he left school. Then in the summer when he was 19 he took the coach with his girlfriend to Plymouth, staying at first on the sofa of an uncle of hers there. During these first two weeks, 'I was never out of the pub and the money my parents gave me to go down was straight into the pub.' Then his girlfriend's uncle found them a flat for £60 a week 'which was a bit too luxurious for the first time', especially as the job in a butcher's that Ray found paid only £90 a week. Even so,

> If the girlfriend had got a job we might have made it but she wasn't interested. She had the habit of smoking and drinking and just sitting on her arse but what put me off her was her sister had a baby and she was always going on about babies. Then she got homesick – the bug to go home. I think she lost interest in the whole thing. [Whereas] after three or four weeks I was quite enjoying it down there; I felt quite settled.

Nevertheless Ray returned with his girlfriend to Liverpool although he no longer sees her: 'Once you live with someone you see the other side of them', an experience that had been shared by many of the movers.

> 'I think it was a mistake really but that's the way things happened. Looking back I can't see the point of taking on that much responsibility for a house and bills to pay. Maybe I picked the wrong spot. Maybe I should've picked London.'

Ray regretted having gone to Plymouth instead of joining the army, which he had applied to do – 'That was going to be my life at one time instead of all this.' For now that he was back in Liverpool Ray was with his brother sharing his parents' house as they had moved to a new pub where he was again helping them out part-time. 'I don't have to pay nothing but what I normally do is say to my mum I'll do an extra Saturday for them, looking after the pub.' Like the two brothers left on their own in Sheffield (p. 55), Ray and his brother had arranged their shared accommodation separately to avoid any disagreements:

> 'We live our own lives. We had an argument when my parents first moved away. We pay the bills together but he's in debt so he's finding it hard but we've agreed about doing our own washing and I won't clean up nothing of his. We always argue.'

Ray had a new girlfriend he planned to marry 'but not formally. Once I have the money in a couple of years I'll buy her a ring. A good age is about the age I am now – 21. That's the time to get serious. Just because of circumstances I can't now but maybe I will by the time I'm 25.' He still hoped to go into a skilled trade, which was the reason he had wanted to join the army:

> 'There's lots of things I could do, like I was a jobber on the buildings but I want to aim for one specific thing. I wanted to go to college to do joinery but it's too late to apply for this year. Perhaps it's taken this time for me to realize what I want to do.'

For three others interviewed who had returned to their parents' homes in Liverpool their time away had also helped them to realize what they really wanted to do. They had moved to work and were not cohabiting while away. Two of them had completed two years of sixth form and had decided to resume their studies after two years away in one case and five months in the other. The third had decided not to continue studying as he had originally planned.

The first of the two former sixth-formers had a job at Christie's in London starting at £144 a week but after a year and a half decided this was not what she wanted to do. She had not returned to Liverpool because of the difficulties of living in London (unlike the Sheffield returnee p. 49); she had been lucky in having first a brother and then friends to stay with in the suburbs so that travel was her major expense. Rather, 'I knew ultimately I would go back to Liverpool if I could get the course I wanted.' This was a course in performance technology for record production in which a Liverpool college specialized owing to the place of the city in the music industry. And she might have gone straight to HE from sixth form as many of her friends had done if she had not been under pressure from her family to look after her mother:

> 'There'd only been my mum and I in the house since my father died and my [older] brothers and sisters were saying "You can't go off and leave mum on her own." They didn't come right out with it. They were rather sly and subtle about it because I don't think they wanted the responsibility of coming round to look after her.'

Even though she had now returned to her mother, her move away had established her independence. It had also confirmed her in her intended vocation because 'I don't think at 18 you really know what you want to do with the rest of your life.'

This view was shared by the other sixth-former, who was in the younger rather than older cohort. He had moved North instead of South and worked as a waiter in a hotel in the Lake District for three weeks before joining a friend who was a student in Newcastle and working for three months in a warehouse for £75 a week – 'and that was like the worst job ever as well'. After a few weeks on the floor of his friend's flat he had rented his own for £27 a week. His parents had visited him there once on his birthday and he had kept in regular contact with them.

> 'They were very worried, mainly my mum, she was just fearing for my life basically. When I first went my plans were to make a go of it, like settle down there and get a good job but after a while I needed money and then I just took the first job that came along but at the time I didn't have any goals like I do now. A lot of people were lucky at school and had clear goals for what they wanted to do, like study medicine for instance, but I wasn't very pleased with how I did in school; I'd got sick of art and didn't want to do the foundation course any more.'

He had, however, found a media arts course in Newcastle and had applied for it. Back in Liverpool he was paying his parents £10 a week to live in their four-bedroomed private house with his grandmother while getting a portfolio together to support his application. Meanwhile he helped out part-time in his father's butcher's shop as he had while he was still at school. He had not been away long enough or established himself well enough to change his previous relationship with them: 'My parents say I've matured a lot but they still treat me like a little kid – being the only child. I appreciated it at first but now it's getting like it used to be – suffocating.'

The third case among those who had worked away for a time and had decided upon what to do before returning was the lad known to all involved in the Liverpool research as 'the yuppie'. Although only 19, Steve was self-employed as a financial consultant earning £230 a week, having worked for over a year with an insurance company in Liverpool starting as a clerk on £77 a week. He had not stayed in the sixth form but with five O-levels had been accepted on to a photography course at FE. However, he had taken a summer job at Tesco's in London for £60 a week and 'I did so well that the college was knocked on the head and I got used to having the money.' As a stock controller he was earning £105 a week 'with a lot of overtime' and might have progressed further if his living arrangements in his brother's flat for £15 a week had not broken down so badly that his manager at work had taken him into his own home for a couple of weeks. Steve could not afford to live anywhere else in London so his parents brought him back to Liverpool, as they had taken him, in their car.

> 'On my return to my parents I didn't have the same sort of relation with them because before I was a schoolboy but when I came back I was a worker and they treated me as more mature. I was more at ease with them because they were working as well. I'm like their financial adviser. I've sorted out my father's early retirement. I've insured their car for instance.'

He was also buying his own two-bedroom house on a £280 a month mortgage he had arranged for himself. 'I've got no reason to move now but I will have to eventually and there's a house available and I'm getting it at a good price fully furnished and everything so I might as well.' His father and mother (a brewery inspector and a chief cashier who owned their own house) were 'very pleased', 'unlike when I moved, I was only 17 and mum was very upset'. Steve was confident he would settle down in his new home and that his business would continue to prosper. In fact, rising interest rates kept him busier than ever rescheduling mortgages. His social life revolved around the people he worked with – 'The girlfriends I go out with are nothing serious. You've got to have variety!' He anticipated moving house again when he married in three or four years' time. Meanwhile he felt he had stolen a march on his school contemporaries: 'They're all at college on grants and I'm in an F-reg car with a car phone. They look at me and think I'm doing really well but all that's happening to me will happen to them in three or four years' time.'

RETURNING HOME AFTER LIVING LOCALLY

Apart from some temporary factory work one Christmas, Angela (21) had never worked since leaving school at 16. Although she had twice started a tailoring course at FE she had had to leave it. The first time she could not get an educational maintenance grant and next year the grant she managed to get ran out, partly because she was by then living away from home. Instead of moving to work or cohabit, she left home to establish her independence. 'I felt it was time to make a move.' It was also, she said, 'a novelty', like the long-term unemployed youth in Sheffield who had moved to his sister's 'for a change' (p. 50). She recognized that it was unusual to leave for no particular reason: 'There were girls my age leaving but they were married or had children or they were kicked out but I went of my own accord.'

Angela heard about a bedsit 'down the road' to rent for £25 a week 'but the Social [Security] paid it'. 'My mother and father both said, "You won't last. You'll be back in a few months" but they didn't try to stop me.' She stayed nearly a year but then moved back because

> 'I wasn't old enough. I thought I was more grown up than I was. I thought I'd left for good but I wasn't really old enough in the end to, you know, put money in the 'lecky, make your money work and that. [Also] it got boring and lonely. I missed my family – just having someone to sit with.' [Even though she visited her parents for three or four hours every day.]

Angela stayed at home for five months before she moved again, this time because 'I was going with someone at the time. He never moved in but we needed time to ourselves.' She was a mile or two further away but 'I was more or less here [at her father's house]. I was really half way in and out of the house. I was sleeping here and having meals here.' Her parents had started their divorce 'so they had their own problems. But it wasn't because of that I left. I was thinking about it before then.' After another seven months Angela moved back to look after her father, who was now on his own in the school-keeper's house where she had been brought up with her younger sister, who had now also left home. 'I do the tidying up and the cooking and that', compared with the flat, where 'I got lazy because you didn't have to get up, just lie in bed all day.' She also moved because of her boyfriend: 'He wanted to move in but I didn't want him to but he wouldn't go home and that. We broke up at the time but got back together after – not now though.' Angela did not plan to move again for a while but she had her name down with the Council and wanted to buy a house in a few years time. She had no plans for marriage or a family, which she thought could wait until her late twenties.

> 'I'm looking for a job but for what I want to do in tailoring it's hard because I'm too old now. They like to get kids straight from school. Really I don't want to stay in Liverpool. I'd like to open my own shop somewhere else but that's a dream really.'

Like Angela, another of the girls who had returned after living away for a time had kept her own key to her parents' house and came in and out as she pleased while away. She had shared a flat with a friend for five months and then worked for four months over the summer at Butlin's in Wales. She had left because of arguments with her father but, like Steve and others, found she had established a new relationship with her parents on her return.

Another interviewee who later returned walked out of her home on her eighteenth birthday: 'It was very dramatic – brilliant! "I'm going. Bye! I'll pack my stuff later."' She was unemployed at the time, having gone on YTS after school and then to a temporary clerical job with the council for £90 a week. She moved into a bedsit for £12 a week – 'a dump basically' – with her boyfriend who was a year older than she and an apprentice technician. Together they wrote off to five or six housing associations:

'It's easy if you've got your head screwed on – just tell a few white lies about how long you've been there. That's the only way you can do it. We did the council as well but they were more used to it and the woman sussed us out when she came round to interview us. She was like an old hag and she wasn't very impressed.'

After six months when the boyfriend got a housing association flat, 'I gave him all my money and he paid the bills and gave me some back – bad move.' Another mistake was letting her boyfriend have the tenancy in his name so that when after two years they split up she had nowhere else to go but back to her parents' three-bedroomed private house, which she shared with two brothers. 'It's more or less the same as before but because I'm older the reins aren't so tight. I just go out every night now. I tend not to stay in too much.' The strain in relations with her parents was evident when her father came back from his work in the docks towards the end of the interview. His daughter was saying she had not decided what she would do next but she was certainly not going to stay in a shop for the rest of her life.

'I don't think of settling down 'cos I haven't got my life in order. I'd be really like disillusioned if I got married and had a baby now and found I'd wasted my life. And I wouldn't buy a house. You've got to get your head sorted before you buy a house.'

Her father asked, 'What happens if me and your mother thought like that?' 'Well, we're different, aren't we?' answered his daughter, but it did not seem her father could accept this.

Karen (21) was similar in that she had had a succession of temporary Youth Training and Community Project jobs since leaving school. She left her parents' three-bedroomed private house, which they shared with her brother and uncle, when she was 19, partly because she was not getting on with her mother and father, and moved in with a friend. Like Ray with his girlfriend in Plymouth (p. 63), Karen found it different living with someone. Also, the two-bedroom house the two young women rented was expensive (£50 a week each) and they were both constantly in debt. So after six months Karen moved out when her then boyfriend (30 and a musician) offered her a room in the house he owned. She paid him £10 a week at first but when she lost her job stopped paying. After a year she split up with him and tried at first to continue living there until she realized 'it wasn't fair'. Also, her mother was ill. Even though her father was now redundant, Karen came home to help and paid no rent. She used her Income Support to get out of the house as much as possible because 'we're all getting under each other's feet again'.

'I know mum doesn't want me to go but soon I'll have to because we're not getting on again. When I moved out, it was a kind of moonlight flit; my best friend came and helped me bundle everything in her car. I had told them I was looking for a place but when it actually came to it I just left early in the morning. I said I'd visit them but I wouldn't give them my address because I didn't want them to visit me. At first I'd come about three times a week plus phone every day. In the end I gave them my address but mum never came because she thought it would upset her. I never gave them my boyfriend's address because they're strict Catholics. I told them he was my landlord. When they found I was living with him and they'd been through the "Oh, how could you?" and all that, I began to get on a bit better with them and he could come and visit them. I saw them less when I was with him and after my uncle died I didn't go so often. For a time at my boyfriend's I wanted to marry him and everything but at the back of my mind I knew it wouldn't last. From the moment I walked in I was threatening to walk out and eventually I did.'

STILL LIVING LOCALLY

Home buyers

Only 8 out of the 23 interviewed in Liverpool were still living away from their parental home at the time of interview and had never returned to stay with their parents. One of these had at first remained in her parents' house when they moved out but was unable on a nurse's salary to keep up the mortgage payments on it and so moved with her husband (also a nurse) to rent. 'The yuppie', Steve, was in the process of buying his own house but, apart from these two, Nick was the only other person interviewed who had bought.

Nick was not the stereotypical home-buyer. For a start, he was only 18. Like Kathy, who had decided to go on holiday with her fiancé and buy later, it had been a toss-up for Nick whether to go on an expensive holiday or use the money to put down on a house. He had wanted to go to the West Indies but his mother persuaded him to buy while prices were low. Also, as with Steve, the chance to buy what seemed a good deal had presented itself and so Nick was taking out a mortgage for £18 000 on a newly built two-bedroom house that cost £15 000. This would give him £3000 in his hand, which he intended to use for furniture and carpets. He would pay a mortgage of £180 a month on his average weekly take-home pay of £170 for £3 an hour, seven days a week, as a trainee pipe-fitter/welder. This job, which his father had got for him six months before with the small company he worked for, was not regular employment nor was the training recognized, although Nick was confident he could stay because his father had been there for ten years. He would also be able to move once trained and thought of going to Germany or Saudi Arabia. As Nick said, he was the only one of all his mates, most of whom lived at home with their parents, who was working and he lived 'quite well' compared to them. His parents were 'made up' (pleased) about his buying a house because they had always rented from a housing association. However, since applying for a mortgage the rate had risen from 13.9 to 15.5 per cent (and higher since) but if the worst came to the worst Nick figured he could sell his house at a profit since prices were rising as well. He envisaged that his endowment mortgage would also give him a cash bonus when he completed it.

Nick and his 17-year-old unemployed girlfriend had met a year before they moved to share the one-bedroom flat literally across the road from Nick's parents', where they had been for the last four months. It had no bath or toilet so 'We have to run round to me ma's'. Since the toilet had broken two weeks ago they had not paid the £32 a week rent, nor did Nick intend to pay any more before they left – 'They can keep the £100 deposit'. Nick had wanted to move when he first met his girlfriend but he was then unemployed and his parents stopped him 'because I was under 18'. He had left school when he was 14 – 'I got a job so I didn't go in.' He worked in a newsagent's over the road for £12 a day – 'a lot of money when you're only 15'. When the shop closed Nick went on a garage mechanic YTS 'but I was palmed off on a showroom washing cars'. He also had 'a bit of trouble with a Ferrari' which he test-drove into a lamp-post – 'That was another reason I left'. He then 'lived off me ma for a year until I could get the dole when I was 18. A couple of weeks after I was on the dole me ol' fella got me a job.' If he had not got a job Nick would have gone to London but not to work: 'I've been offered jobs down there on building sites and that but I don't fancy it.' Instead, he would have travelled down on 'the dole express' day-saver to collect social security once a fortnight from an address in the capital while also signing on in Liverpool. He claimed many of his mates did this 'and good luck to them'. 'The whole system's a shambles' so anything was justifiable. Only radical action would ever sort it out – 'Where is it that's having a revolution now? Romania. I'm telling you, it'll be like that here soon and bloody good too!'

Others

Of the other young movers who were still living away when interviewed, two young women were cohabiting in rented accommodation. One had moved from her parents' Chinese take-away and chip shop to the one her fiancé was renting on the other side of town. She had failed her A-levels at college and been on Employment Training but was now unemployed, just helping her fiancé in his shop and, since she was living with her parents, paying no rent. She had become engaged only recently, eight months after moving. Her parents did not mind and she saw them and her younger brother and sister fortnightly and on special occasions like birthdays and Chinese festivals when the whole family went out to restaurants. She planned to marry later in the year but not to have children – 'That's far off.' She hoped to stay on in the shop and get to know the customers. She would work there if her fiancé offered her a job but at present he did not need her so she thought she might go and work in another shop instead.

A girl of 19 lived with the boyfriend of 25 she met while on YTS, after leaving school at 16. She had been placed in an office of the local Territorial Army and he was a part-time sergeant instructor there. After completing YTS she joined up herself and this was now her occupation. Although it was only part-time, she earned £100 a week and more during camps. They had been living for the past three years in a privately rented flat which they found through a friend of her family; they paid him £11 a week each. Her parents did not want her to leave their three-bedroom council home so early but left the decision to her. Her two younger brothers and sister there were still at school. She saw her family regularly during the week and went shopping with her mother at weekends, staying over odd nights when her boyfriend was at camp. She planned to stay where she was 'for now' but hoped to buy 'eventually'. Her boyfriend was hoping to be taken on permanently when he completed Employment Training and she had started floristry at FE one day a week with the aim of having her own shop one day. She had no plans to marry and was 'too young to think about a family'. Whatever they did, they would both keep on with the Army part-time.

Only one single mother was interviewed and she lived with her year-old child in a housing association flat having moved from her grandparents' house in the next street. They had brought her up since her parents divorced, when she was very young, but they were retired and their privately owned two-bedroomed house was too small for a baby as well. Theresa (20) had tried living with her mother and her new family for a couple of weeks but they did not get on. Before she became pregnant her only occupation had been on YTS catering after she left school but she quit after nine months because she did not like her placement in an old people's home.

'So what did you do then?'

'I had a baby.'

'What about the father? Do you see him?'

'He's unemployed. He'll buy things for the baby but he doesn't do anything for her, take her so many days a week or anything like that. I wouldn't let him. He still comes here now and again. I see him sometimes but . . .'

'Everyone I know has left home and lives on their own, all my mates like, all except the sensible ones who live with their mothers. I'm not sensible 'cos I shouldn't't've had a baby and I should've stayed there. You can't do your own thing when you've got a baby. I spend all my life clearing up after the baby. I never stop. I do it of a morning before I go out to Nan's and then back again before I go to bed. I'd like a job but I've got no one to mind the baby. When she starts school I will but I don't know what. I'd like to work in a shop but I'll take whatever jobs they offer me. I'll never have any more children. You're stuck down for ever. If I met a fella and he had loads of money I'd get married but I don't think that's likely so I don't plan to at the moment – I'm too young.'

Theresa's immediate problem seemed to be hanging on where she was, like Halimah and Glennis on their own in Sheffield.

I want to go home. When my gas gets cut off then I'll have to go. I'm supposed to be getting evicted 'cos the Social [Security] won't pay my rent. [But] If I can stick it out I'll get a council place in June after a year on the waiting list. I'd rather be on my own with my own freedom. It's just the fella upstairs, he frightens me of a night when I'm on my own. He's just weird looking and walks around at night. He hasn't actually bothered me but I suppose what it is I've never had to be on my own but now I am.'

As well as her grandparents, Theresa's mother came round in a car every weekday to take her out. She also had 'loads of friends' who came round nearly every night until late 'and I go to them'. With their help she might stick it out until June.

ALTERNATIVES AND OTHERS

With the exception of 'The Other People' in Sheffield, most interviewees, even Nick, were strikingly conventional in their aspirations and intentions. These were framed in the moderate terms of the 'good life': a steady job, house and family, with a car and annual holidays abroad as extras mentioned by some. As the 1982 Study Commission on the Family found, 'whether they think about it or not, the "happy" family is, for most people, the pinnacle of interpersonal achievement'. 'Mr and Mrs Wonderfully Happy Average', as one young married woman put it. Even those who had chosen uncertain and unconventional careers as musicians or actors also took this predominant ideology of 'familialism', as Donzelot (1980) called it, for granted. They hoped to attain the same 'one day'; 'I don't think about the details – how many children and so forth – it's just a general sort of idea' (George, Swindon). For a few interviewees council housing represented the security for the future to which they aspired but for most their ideal was to own their own home. Others, like Theresa, recognized this whole package as a dream for them, but Dominic (19) was the only interviewee in the whole sample who rejected it.

'I hate the idea of buying a house and placing myself in a little box. My idea of hell is working on a dingy little conveyor belt putting things together then retiring – tacky. I just want to do something creative with my life, something spiritually fulfilling. I don't care about money. I'm quite happy to be on the dole as long as I'm doing things I enjoy. . . . One day last summer – it was a sunny day and I started thinking about why are people so horrible to each other. I just started to think about what's wrong and right and why people are what they are like and why I was what I was like. It's hard to explain. It was just the day. I felt like I could change the world by being myself and being honest and respecting people. It's a start anyway but it's a bit difficult. I'm not a materialist but you need some security. It's a bit of a dilemma.'

Dominic first left his mother's three-bedroom housing association house when he was 14 and for the last time when he was 16 during his last year at school.

'Before that I was in and out of care with two months at most at home. I'd always worked towards going home but the situation blew up again and the last time I decided not to work towards going back home but to get my own place. We just don't get on, me and mum, or my brother at the time. It's just a personality clash and we're still the same really. I love the thought of her but when I see her. . . . She had a boyfriend at the time and he was telling her to like put me into care and because of that I was really depressed so I used to sag school and things.'

At first he was in an admissions unit for younger children and then in a community home.

'At the home it was more like a prison 'cos the people were on remand and they had to lock the doors. While in care I was going to my dad's a few weekends 'cos I hadn't seen him for 13 years and I decided to write to him but that didn't work out either. I was visiting with the intention of living permanently after a trial period but I was a virtual stranger to him and he was remarried and everything.'

Instead, Dominic was helped to live on his own:

'For a month I had a flat with two others to sort of prepare you for moving out but that didn't work either 'cos of the people I was with – one of them was dead messy and the other was a smackhead. I didn't fancy having all these experts helping me but I was prioritized to get a place so they helped me in that respect.'

The last time Dominic had seen his family was at Christmas:

'I went there with the intention of staying a week but we had a big argument on Boxing Day and I came back. I'd love to have stayed and had a family life but I suppose my mum would have to be a different person.'

While in community care Dominic was placed on YTS working with handicapped people. After completing his two years he collected glasses in a pub for two nights a week but was better off on the dole, although he did not sign on at first ''cos I felt bad about it'. He had applied for jobs in the creative and artistic areas he was interested in 'but nobody would have me 'cos I've got no experience'. So he was attending an adult education course in photography and was considering going to college.

'One thing I regret is not going on with my education. I had no encouragement; in the third year at school I used to come first in everything and I'd come back and tell my mum and she'd say, "Yeah, only tell me later" – watching "Crossroads" or something.'

'I'd love to get out of this housing association place. It's claustrophobic. I haven't got any friends here, not friends friends. I want to move where there are more sympathetic people, like a warehouse or studio. There was an old factory building I liked the look of. I wouldn't think of getting married and having children. I'm bisexual anyway. (I hope my mum doesn't see this by the way!) My ideal state would be to find a man and a woman to share my life with. I just feel like it's going to happen eventually but just now I don't know if I'll get through this week without a court summons. I'm scared to open the door at the moment cos the 'lecky's on my back. I'm just terrible with money. . . . I don't like to think what I'll be doing in ten years' time. I like to go with the flow. I'll still be confused probably but still honest and trying to do what you've written down there.'

Of course Dominic's idealism could be dismissed as the product of a passing phase, although it has been seen how for several of the young people interviewed their time away from home had enabled them to sort out their ideas, try out different alternatives and realize what it was that they really wanted to do. But the comforting notion that they would change could never apply to those who really were different. Thus the rationalization by the brothers of the one gay girl interviewed that 'It's just a phase she's going through', in fact for her applied to them – they would have to go through that phase of rationalization and then finally accept her as she was. She herself recognized that ideas of a family future were for her 'just wishful thinking'.

Lynne (21) lived with her girlfriend (25) and a young man the same age with whom her girlfriend shared the joint mortgage of a new three-bedroomed house. It was on a small estate resembling the nearby real Brookside Close, where the television soap opera is made. In fact they identified with a character in this series because 'When we first moved here we thought we'd get bricks through our windows because that's what happened to this gay character in "Brookside" but nothing like that happened. Everyone's been great.' Lynne had moved in gradually over some six months and had been living at the house permanently for more than a year when interviewed. During that time her friends had given her confidence to apply for work because she had been unemployed for three years since leaving school. Lynne first worked part-time in a factory for £43 and then full-time as a care assistant in an old people's home for £94. She now intended to study to become a nurse. 'I'd love to do that because my school days were wasted. I sagged off too much. I used to be a terrible scally but I'm not now.' She had been brought up on one of the three most notorious Liverpool estates, whereas of the suburb where her friends had grown up as neighbours she said: 'It's a different world, like where you can walk past boys without having names called at you and chips thrown at you'. These two also had very different occupations from hers, in the Civil Service and an insurance company. But Lynne still missed her family and felt guilty about leaving her mother, who was ill. She paid no rent at her new address but had gone on paying her mother £10 out of her Social Security payment for months after she had virtually gone. Even now, 'I hate saying that I've left home because I love to go back there sometimes.' She visited on her day off and phoned every night. She would like to leave Liverpool one day but could not imagine it because 'my family keeps me here. I think every Scouse person is the same – they wouldn't stay but for their family.'

It has been seen how large a part their families played in the lives of the young people interviewed and how the absence of family support left someone like Dominic very vulnerable. Most interviewees were still in regular contact with their parents, however strained relations had been when they moved, even to the point of being broken off for a time. Not only parents but other members of the wider, extended family and particularly grandparents were important. In Liverpool, Theresa had been brought up by her grandparents, and another young woman who was interviewed had moved from her parents' council house to her grandmother's to look after her when she became ill. This had begun as a temporary arrangement but became permanent. Although the granddaughter feared that one day she would return from her office job in town to find that her grandmother had died, her move had the advantages that she had, as she put it, walked straight from one home into another, the tenancy of which would soon pass to her.

Similarly, a young woman whose mother had moved out was able, after a tussle with the council, to gain the tenancy of the council house in which she had been brought up. After her father died when she was 17, her elder brother (38) had come back to look after mother and daughter but when a year later the mother moved out to a new relationship, if not to start a new family, as p. 55 in Sheffield, brother and sister could not get on and he left. She was never alone in the house, however, because in the meantime her boyfriend had moved in and she now described herself as his common-law wife and mother to his seven-year-old son.

The council also agreed to give a tenancy to the one girl in the survey both of whose parents had died. Her mother died when she was 12 and her father when she was 17 so, as above, her older brother (26) returned to become her guardian. He went after a year leaving her on her own, which she preferred. The council wanted to rehouse her into a one-bedroom flat but she persuaded them to let her remain where she had friends and near her relatives. She was studying beauty therapy at FE and expected to leave Liverpool to find work when she completed her course. She said she would go 'wherever the wind takes me', explaining that 'I've got no ties you see and, although I'll be sorry to leave the house, the future's exciting.'

Chapter 5

Kirkcaldy

KIRKCALDY DISTRICT AND 'THE LANG TOON'

Fife in spring – snow on the ground. The Kirkcaldy District of the Fife region of Scotland is different from the other areas of the '16–19' survey not only because it is in another country. Unlike Swindon, Sheffield and Liverpool, Kirkcaldy (population 49 000 and falling), while it is the largest town in Fife, is not the centre of a distinct travel-to-work area. Although at the time of the previous ESRC 'Economic Life' study in 1981 (see p. 3) only 13 per cent of residents worked outwith the District while 10 per cent of those employed within it travelled in from outside, these numbers have undoubtedly increased with the booming of Edinburgh and the extension of the East Fife regional road. This taps into Scotland's motorway system and will bring commuters seeking relief from the capital's rising house prices into the area, while workers from the area will be within half an hour's drive of Edinburgh. It will also enhance the claim of Glenrothes new town (population 37 000 and rising) to represent 'the new industrial heart of Fife', as its own publicity puts it. Glenrothes is already the seat of the Regional Council, managing education, transport and social services. In Kirkcaldy the District Council administers housing, planning and other services, and the District includes the towns strung along its coast as well as Glenrothes and other towns and villages inland, a total population of 147 000. Its political complexion has always been Labour and, though Fife returned a Communist MP after the Second World War, the main opposition now comes from the Nationalists. Such was the grip of Scottish Labourism that there was no development towards and away from resistance to accommodation with the English Conservative government equivalent to that which occurred in Swindon, Sheffield and Liverpool.

The coastal towns include the holiday resorts of Burntisland and Kinghorn, south of Kirkcaldy. From here many residents travel to work towards Rosyth Dockyards and the other industries clustered around the north end of the Forth Bridges, though one interviewee explained, 'In Burntisland the main employer is the aluminium but ye hae tae be a Mason tae get in there.' Further up the coast, north of Kirkcaldy, depressed former coal-mining communities stretch to Levenmouth, before giving way to the fishing villages that dot the shore of East Fife all the way around to St Andrews. Thus, although all these interconnected towns and villages are within twenty minutes' drive of Kirkcaldy, they are divided into at least four discrete areas. Nearly three-quarters of the District includes agricultural land, moorland and woodland. (Only one of the young movers actually lived on a farm, however, and he had moved out of the district to another farm nearby. For the distinctive character-istics of rural youth see Wallace (forthcoming) and Jones, 1990, who claimed, 'Young people brought up in rural areas of Scotland appear to marry and become parents and to leave home earlier than those living in towns.')

Kirkcaldy District cannot really be presented as a microcosm of Scotland. Fife has higher than the national average unemployment, for instance, but more private home ownership than Scotland as a whole. Nor is Kirkcaldy a hybrid of Liverpool and Swindon, as it sometimes appears in the generalizations born of the '16–19' study. The latter characterization rests upon the decline of traditional industry, largely coal-mining, on the one hand and the creation of what could fancifully be called a 'silicon glen' at Glenrothes on the other. 'Wee silicon glen' might be more accurate, although the new town's largest employer is a high-technology/microelectronics company and Mitsubishi's acquisition of Apricot Computers' manufacturing operation marks Glenrothes as a base for that Japanese company's penetration of European markets. This is typical of the strategy of such multinational companies; as Morgan and Sayer indicate, 'Within the chosen advanced countries, fabrication and assembly plants tend to be located in peripheral regions . . . while "front-end" activities like marketing, design centres and development are located in or near metropolitan regions' (1988, p. 61). So the district is linked to Swindon in the South by the very differences which separate and divide them. Another similarity in the development of the computer industry in the two areas is that they both arose from government sponsorship originating in the relocation of electronics companies during the Second World War, Marconis' having moved across the Firth of Forth for security reasons. Kirkcaldy was also a centre for the manufacture of equipment for the (formerly) state-owned telephone network, and the UK computer firm Amstrad has contracted the town's GEC Plessey to manufacture computers there instead of, as previously, in the Third World.

As well as expanding this 'hi-tech' base, the Glenrothes new town corporation was also confident of attracting offices relocating from Edinburgh (see the paper prepared for it by planning consultants Pieda, 1990). It has, however, lost its assisted area status and faced an uncertain future as its new town designation and the central government support that that brought have also come to an end. Indeed, uncertainty seems to have surrounded Glenrothes since its inception as a new town founded after the war to rehouse and reoccupy miners displaced by pit closures. This was hailed by the local MP as 'another revolution – without bloodshed – in which Man is taking control of his environment from the day the first brick was laid' (quoted in Wood, 1989, p. 39). However, building was halted for a time in 1955. Even the name of the new town was in doubt and the subject of a long correspondence in *The Scotsman* – the indigenous Auchmuty only narrowly rejected against the synthetic Glenrothes because of possible confusion with nearby Auchtermuchty. Now a fragile recovery is endangered by recession and whether the new town has generated the investment to lift it into independent industrial take-off seems doubtful.

In Kirkcaldy District as a whole the loss of mining, which in 1981 occupied one male worker in ten, was traumatic. Associated industries, like linoleum manufacture, have also virtually disappeared. For young people the picture is depressingly familiar: as the Colleges and Careers Sub-Committee of Fife Education Authority reported in

March 1990, 'While there has been a reduction in the number of unemployed from 440 to 392 young people, throughout the period from December 169 young people have entered employment, 779 have entered YTS and 90 have transferred to Job Centres.' The news of this fall in youth unemployment was greeted by one regional councillor reported in the *Glenrothes Courier and Advertiser* (5.4.90) as 'Lies and more damned lies on the part of the government, which has cooked the books . . . the reality of the situation is that many of the 3551 youngsters on so-called "special schemes", such as YTS, are still without a decent wage.' Certainly in the towns around Levenmouth unemployment approached Liverpool levels. One interviewee related how he had unsuccessfully applied for a place youth training for carpentry in competition with hundreds of applicants. Until the opening of an oil-rig construction yard, which in any case reportedly brought in 700 out of its 1000 total workforce from out of the area, the largest employer in one of the worst hit towns was the parish church. 'The God Squad wi' a direct line no tae God but tae the EEC coffers', as the father of another interviewee remarked, seemed to own much of the vacant property, ran YTS, Employment Training and Community Industry locally. Large posters advertised its presence and the arrival of 'Hope for Buckhaven'.

Partly because of this depressing employment outlook more of the young people surveyed had remained in education than in the other areas of the study. (This unemployment effect upon education retention rates was also noticeable in Liverpool, although it should be noted that, there as well as elsewhere, more females than males remain in education, at least initially, despite better employment opportunities for them overall.) However, more Scottish young people have always remained in education than their English and Welsh peers, even though some of them can leave a year earlier. More have also gone on to higher education. In part this is due to different school-leaving regulations which mean that around a third of a school year group are ineligible to leave until Christmas of the first post-compulsory year. This staggered school leaving encourages many 16-year-olds to remain at school. Also, post-compulsory schooling is organized on a yearly basis, instead of the two-year sixth form to A-levels. As a result, the 'highers' qualifications for entry to higher education are broader and less specialized than A-levels, and higher education courses last for four years instead of three.

Non-advanced further education has also been completely revised in Scotland following a 1983 Action Plan. All NAFE courses now consist of modules of forty hours each covered by a single National Certificate. There are no grades of pass; assessment is continuous and criterion referenced. They may be taken in any combination full- or part-time at school, college or at work. Some interviewees had a jaundiced view of this modular system, however; gaining modular credits had done nothing for them and so were not seen as 'real qualifications'. Yet the system has the potential, and to some extent the effect, of rendering relations between education and training more flexible so that students/trainees can switch subject areas to collect modules to suit the requirements of their employment or their own interest. Integration of education and training is increased by the possibility of combining vocational modules with academic subjects. There is no institution of higher education in Kirkcaldy but three of Fife's four technical colleges are situated in the District, plus an Information Technology Centre in Levenmouth.

The housing situation also appeared to be better in Kirkcaldy District than in the other areas of the survey. Even though there had been no further new council house building since 1989, and despite a loss of 20 per cent through tenants' right to buy, the tenure balance in the District was still 50.5:49.5 public:private (cf. 55:45 for Scotland as a whole). There were only a few housing association and private rented homes. Consequently most single homeless applicants to Kirkcaldy's housing list were still with their parents. The 1712 single homeless were the largest category amongst the 5000 on the council's waiting list, plus another 5000 seeking transfers. However, the council did not have any bed and breakfast accommodation for homeless families, although it had one temporary accommodation unit for eight families and were building another. House prices were below those in other parts of the central belt of Scotland but rising. This was blamed by one or two respondents on English people coming in and buying up houses and pubs. One had even bought himself a decaying castle for £100 000, along with the title of local laird. The complaint about English publicans, buying up pubs with the proceeds of house sales in the South much as retired boxers used to do on the proceeds of their winnings, was complemented by more definitely racist resentment of Asian shopkeepers. As elsewhere, corner shops had become less profitable in competition with the new drive-in 'supastores' and 'shopping worlds' owned by the four or five large retailing chains so that only Asian families were prepared to run them (see Aldrich *et al.*, 1981).

The other major difference with the other survey areas was that at the time of interviews the Poll Tax had been in operation in Scotland for a year before it had been introduced south of the border. There was much dispute locally between protesters against the tax and the Regional Council charged with collecting it. The situation was complicated by the District Council's joining with neighbouring Dunfermline to refuse to cooperate with collection of the tax. However, in the first year of collection it appeared that 87 per cent of what would have been gathered from the rates had been taken in, leaving 6000 new non-payers out of Fife's total 280 000. Whether or not because of this shortfall, the tax was raised in its second year from £295 to £316.

There was no 'Poll-Tax effect' showing up as an increase in the numbers of young people in the Scottish sample indicated from their questionnaire returns as having moved house (see pp. 89–91). The total of 150 living at an address different from that of their parents/guardians was in line with the other areas. As usual though this was an overestimation and 17 were shown by double check not to have moved at all. Another 13 were found on contact to be with their mother/father, including four who had moved with their parents; one was 'only awa' a couple o' weeks', another had lived with a relative for a month and a third had 'only been awa' a few days whilst on YTS'. One girl had always lived with her grandmother and one boy, whose parents were divorced, was with his mother in Glasgow but moved backwards and forwards between her and his father in Glenrothes. There were 18 male students (at Aberdeen 6, Edinburgh 4, Dundee 2, Luton 1, Cambridge 1) and 4 female (at Edinburgh 2, Dundee 1, Glasgow 1). Thirteen boys had moved out of the area (4 in England, 1 in Anstruther, 2 in Aberdeen, 2 in Edinburgh, 1 'with his girlfriend in Dundee', 2 'married and moved', 1 in the USA). Twelve girls had also left the locality (2 to Surrey, where one was nannying, 3 to Dundee, 2 to Glasgow, 1 to Dunfermline, 1 to Grantoun-on-Spey, 1 to Perth, 1 to Australia and 1 as a commuter to college in Edinburgh and later to work in Dunfermline). In addition, 5 boys were in the army and 2 in the navy. Three were 'not interested any more', one 'would rather not' and three were left a message to phone but did not reply. Two were wrong addresses, another's flat was empty and a neighbour said he had 'flitted a while ago'. One no answer and new address not known; one moved, present occupants did not know where; two letters returned 'not known at this address'. One lad was ill with 'flu. Two girls were left a message to phone but did not reply; one had moved to a new address but did not reply; three had moved to addresses that could not be located; one had moved 'who knows where?' (neighbour). Four letters were returned marked 'not known at this address' and one letter was returned marked 'gone away'. Four were wrongly addressed. Two girls were too far away to interview in the time available (one of these was the one Chinese name in the sample of Kirkcaldy movers). Two addresses were empty properties, one flat was being done up and at another there was no answer, despite repeated calling. One missed two appointments owing to mutual misunderstandings and another because she did not really want to take part. Another wrote that she had 'nothing further to say'; another was 'too busy'; one no longer wished to take part; another stated, 'Ah've got a lot o' personal problems just noo an' Ah don't need this.'

In the end 23 young movers were interviewed, 12 girls and 11 boys. They included two who were actually homeless at the time of interview, it being possible to locate such people in a smaller area where 'everybody knows everybody else'. Also, following salesman's lore, the further north you go the more helpful people are – even though with the Poll Tax they very often had more to conceal. Greeted by such warmth and friendliness, the interviewer's briefcase was finally abandoned! Another peculiarity of the Scots, who tend to be friendly but not garrulous, was that the interviews, which in Liverpool had tended to become longer and longer, became shorter so that interviewees said more in fewer words. This might have been an interviewer effect, growing increasingly familiar with the semistructured question-naire to know which questions to ask for the answers required. Whatever the case may be, selected interviews are again presented as representative of different types of move in the life courses of the interviewees.

FOUR HOME BUYERS

Only four of the young movers interviewed in Kirkcaldy District had bought their own homes, all in Kirkcaldy town itself. One 21-year-old woman was already in her second privately owned ex-council house in a large estate on the edge of town. Like some of the young buyers in Swindon and elsewhere, she felt under pressure to buy before prices rose further. This had not been her motivation for moving, however – 'We just wanted tae live on oor ain' – and the second time, 'Just tae get a bigger hoose'. Her fiancé (23) was an engineer at Rosyth, earning about £200 a week, while she described herself as 'a gofa' – Ah go fa' this an' Ah go fa' that'. In fact she was a wages clerk on £119 a week, though she started on only £40, at 16, after two months on a dental reception YTS, straight after leaving school. She and her fiancé's mortgage payments were £320 a month for their two-bedroomed house, £200 for the previous one-bedroom one. They had been 'school sweethearts', becoming engaged in the year after she left school. They moved two years after that. Her father, a foreman, and her mother, 'a school-crossing patrol officer, equals a lollipop lady', who lived in a two-bedroom council property, were pleased their only child had bought her own home, and that she was planning to marry in a few months' time. As her new home was closer to where her parents lived ('just across the road'), she now saw them more often than when she first moved, once every two days instead of once or twice a week. She also saw her fiancé's family as regularly because 'They stay quite near as well.' She did not plan to move again and saw herself still in the same situation in ten years' time, except with the two 'screamin' kids' which she planned to have at the age of 25.

The other buyers in Kirkcaldy were all young men, also in the older cohort and so aged between 20 and 21. One paid £200 a month mortgage for a two-bedroomed flat. He had a four-month-old baby, though no plans to marry his girlfriend of 19. They had met a year and a half before they bought an ex-council flat together. She was no longer working (she had been on YTS) but he had been in the the the same employment since completing a one-year YTS after school and now earned £154 a week with Kirkcaldy District Council. He saw his parents ('a marine surgeon, means he fillets fish' and a social worker) 'regularly' – twice a week, 'a bit too regularly maybe', especially since the baby had been born. They were council tenants and also pleased their only child had bought his own flat. He and his girlfriend planned one other child after buying a house in a year's time. He hoped to buy a two-bedroomed ex-council house and would then 'do it up'. This was where he too saw himself living in ten years' time.

Another young man who had bought also had no plans to marry, though he had become engaged a year before moving into a one-bedroom flat, for £197 per month joint mortgage, with his fiancée, who was a 19-year-old computer operator earning £110 a week. He had refused to go on YTS when he left school and had been unemployed for two years before gaining his present job in a wood yard, first as a labourer and then as a machine operator for £165 a week. His parents, who owned their own three-bedroom house, were also 'quite chuffed' he had bought. His father and younger brother worked on the roads for the regional transport department and his mother was a housewife. They also were not far away and he saw them regularly. Like the last couple mentioned, he and his fiancée planned to buy a two-bedroomed house after a couple of years. Unlike the others though, they were not planning a family because 'we've got oor jobs tae think aboot; she's got a great job in Glenrothes wi' a career' and he hoped to open his own business. Still, 25 seemed to him a good age to start having the two children he wanted.

Like the others, the last of the young men who had bought found his (one-bedroom) flat easily through an advertisement in the local paper. He moved in with his fiancée of three months whom he had met one year before they bought, but he was now left with paying the £180 a month mortgage since they had called off their engagement five months after moving in. He earned £102 a week as a clerk with the health board in Edinburgh (less £12 for travel). He had previously earned the same in a shop after a year of FE but got 'fed up wi' shop work'. His parents, who owned their own five-bedroomed house (his father a manager with the council and his stepmother running her own business), were 'happy if Ah'm happy'. He saw them regularly two or three times a week and had his tea with them at weekends. He would not go back though, he was too settled, but could go to them if he were 'strugglin' financially'. As it was, 'Ah survive but things could be easier if Ah had a better-paid job.' He was looking for one but, unlike the other buyers, had no plans to move on. He said he could not make any plans beyond his summer holidays in June, when he was going to Italy for the World Cup. All the same he thought that in five or ten years' time he would be married 'wi' a couple o' kids as well. Ye know, the usual – two up an' two doon.'

SEVEN TENANTS

In Kirkcaldy the most usual form of tenure among those interviewed was council renting. However, as in Swindon, this was regarded by many as a step on the way to buying, and council houses were seen as quite acceptable buys. In terms of their life course, only one of those interviewed corresponded to the traditional stages of engagement, marriage and simultaneous moving. This was a young man of 20 who had moved four doors down the terrace from his father's cottage into another cottage owned by the brickworks that employed them both. He had been working there as a labourer (for £150 a week, with overtime) after a year on YTS, following school leaving. Although he explained that he would not lose the two-bedroomed house (for which he paid £25 a week rent) if he left his job, these tied cottages that made up the small village lined along the road represented a relic of an older form of tenure. This still survived in Fife, mostly in the shape of National Coal Board cottages that had not yet been sold off following the pit closures. The lad had been trying to get another job and hoped to buy in a few years' time. His wife (19), also from the village, stayed at home looking after their baby, born six months after they married and moved, which had been a year and a half previously. They had their names down on the council list in case they decided to have another child and would then consider buying their council house.

Another interviewee of 20 had also become engaged when she knew she was pregnant, although she had not married until two years after the child was born and then it seemed largely because her husband had joined the army and they would then get army accommodation in Germany. When they moved into their own council flat from their parents' respective council houses, she had stopped 'working' for 'the God Squad' (p. 76), after leaving school to a year on YTS, followed by Community Industry. They had been treated as a priority case by the council and so were rehoused quickly into an estate they considered 'rough' and from which they managed to make an exchange for another two-bedroomed flat after a year and a half. Like her father, her husband had been unemployed when they moved and they saw his joining the army as giving them 'a new start'. He hoped to learn a trade and they hoped to come back and buy locally after his service was completed in six years' time. Then they might have another child. One unconsidered consequence of the ending of the Cold War and the disbandment of the armed forces, if this 'peace dividend' ever occurs, is that it will close off one of the few remaining access routes to trade training for young men in Scotland and the North, places from which the Services have traditionally drawn their manpower. Leaving the armed forces also gives access to council housing if you have not saved enough to buy. The hoped-for trade training did not always materialize, however, and service life was a hard way to get it, as the young man medically discharged from the army who had returned to his parents in Liverpool after a year in barracks had realized and decided it was not for him (p. 62).

Another female interviewee in the older cohort had become engaged, in her case three months after she moved into her one-bedroom council flat, two minutes' walk from her parents' three-bedroomed ex-council house. When she was on a clerical YTS after school all her friends were putting in applications to the council and so she did likewise, being offered her flat three years later on condition she accepted it in the dilapidated condition in which it had been left by the previous tenant. So, supported by her parents (docker, telephonist), she and her fiancé, a trainee plasterer of 23, also from Burntisland, spent a month making the flat habitable before they moved in. They would have bought a house straight away but did not have the money. As it was, they hoped to buy locally in a couple of years when they married, though they had not set a date. When this was and how many children they then had depended upon their circumstances – whether her fiancé got a job and whether she got a rise or another job. She described her present occupation as that of 'skivvy', secretary to the manager of a travel agent, earning £73 a week. She also peeled potatoes in a local café for half an hour every night on her way home but, despite this extra £14 a week, did not manage to save. 'We're skimpin' every month.'

Four other young women interviewed, all in the older cohort and living with or engaged to boyfriends/fiancés, had moved into council or (Glenrothes) corporation flats. (Typically Kirkcaldy semi-detached council houses with gardens were divided between tenancies upstairs and down, while Glenrothes corporation housing was smaller and newer.) One interviewee had a year-old child and described herself as a housewife. She had previously worked at 'YTS jobs' and in a Wimpy Bar for £60 a week. Another was a laboratory assistant earning £131 a week; she had remained at school one year to take highers. Another worked part-time in a market while studying nursery nursing at FE. The fourth was unemployed/sick (see below). Boyfriends/fiancés (31 and divorced/separated, 27, 26 and 24) were an engineer, self-employed window cleaner, fork-lift truck driver and unemployed. All four interviewees had moved within half a mile of their parents, who were also council/corporation tenants. Also, except for the case related below, all saw their parents regularly, at least two or three times a week. While parents had been 'a bit upset', they had left the decision to move to their daughters. Relations were eased if, as in one case here and in several others already interviewed, the move was a gradual one: 'They knew we were seein' each other an' Ah wis stayin' here odd nights an' that so it wis OK.' None of the interviewees could afford to buy but two hoped to do so, especially with house prices in Glenrothes as low as £10 000 and if, as one said, 'Ah wis in a braw cooncil hoose'. She hoped to be transferred, as did another, into cottage-type accommodation. For another, 'We'll stop here. This is us.' All regarded their progress as fairly usual since all their friends had also got 'their ain hooses'.

One of these cases will be related in detail since Helen's route to her 'ain hoose' had not been a direct one. Also, it illustrates the importance that has already been seen to attach to parental support, which in her case was lacking but which was, luckily for her, supplemented by other relatives, especially grandparents, who have already been seen often to play such an important part in young people's lives. Helen (21) lived in a village outside Glenrothes that, like the other settlements round about, had become a satellite to the new town. She had already left her parents' council house for her grandparents' council cottage at the other end of the village when she was still at school:

'Ah used tae stay there when Ah wis younger, when ma dad had a bad accident an' Ah stayed wi' them a few years. Ah thought o' ma gran's as ma home an' ma gran as ma maither [as p. 52]. She was mair o' a mum than ma ain mum wis. She used tae buy ma claes an' ma shoes e'en when Ah stayed wi' ma ain mum an' dad. Then Ah wis goin oot wi' somebody mum an' dad didnae like so they said tae choose between him or them so ma gran took me in 'cos she didnae want tae see me oot on the street but then she left ma grandfaither 'cos he's an alcoholic.'

They went to a hostel in Glenrothes and Helen stayed on there, even after her grandmother was rehoused out of it after six months. By this time she had left school, completed a one-year YTS (catering) and started an apprenticeship as a baker. Although she was also working in a market on Saturdays and at another job packing, so that she was earning about £100 a week, it cost £35 for bed and board sharing a room, first with her grandmother and then with another girl. As Helen had an aunt and uncle in Dunfermline she moved there, paying them £10 a week for her keep while in a temporary job that paid £80 a week. After nine months she had outstayed her welcome and moved again, becoming a live-in nanny in Dunfermline looking after two infants while their parents tried to start a business on an Enterprise Allowance scheme. Here there was a familiar conflict: 'The folk were takin' a lend o' me. Ah wis only gettin £40 a week an' they werenae geein' me ony days off. Plus the bairns were spoiled. Ah wis teachin' them one thing an' their ma wis teachin' them another.' After six months Helen returned to her home village and rejoined her grandmother in her own flat. She found a new job as a barmaid/cook for £90 a week and a new boyfriend. Then her grandmother died.

Helen was left alone in the two-bedroomed apartment but was soon joined by her younger brother and by her fiancé, to whom she became engaged when he moved in. He was 27 and a fork-lift truck driver. Having 'fought' the council to be allowed to keep the house, Helen had no more plans for work: 'Ah just plan tae get married an' have a family – a boy an' a lass, that'll dae. Ah dinnae think Ah could cope wi' ony mair.' This despite the fact that 'him leavin' me' was the greatest difficulty that she thought she now faced. 'Ah dinnae trust him but Ah'm definitely gettin' married' because 'Ah've got security noo. Naebody can put me oot. Ah can make ma ain decisions.' Her husband-to-be was therefore in a sense superfluous: 'Even if we have a joint tenancy it'll be ma hoose 'cos Ah was here first.' She would go back to work when her children were older and so hoped to become 'an auld married hag!' (cf. p. 33).

Her parents were now divorced and Helen never saw her mother.

> 'Ah speak tae ma dad but no tae ma mum. He just stays across the street so Ah see him three or four days a week dependin' on what shift he's on. Ah didnae see him when Ah wis awa' at Glenrothes or Dunfermline 'cos he wis wi' her at the time. They thought Ah'd be back but Ah never have been. Ah knew Ah wis never goin' back. Ah just wanted a change tae dae what Ah wanted. Ah'd dae what Ah want tae dae an' that's it. Ah think Ah wis lucky Ah had places tae go everytime Ah wanted tae move 'cos a lot o' folk – young lassies who're no gettin' on wi' their mums an' dads – want tae move but they've nowhere tae go like Ah've had.'

RETURNING HOME

As in the north of England, and particularly in Liverpool, many of those interviewed in Kirkcaldy District had returned to their parental home after periods of living away that varied in length from two months to over two years. However, unlike Liverpool and Sheffield where people had come back from the South, these returnees had not moved far out of the area, with the exception of one young woman who had been to live with her grandparents in Belfast. While many young Scots had moved out of the district, they had not, unlike those young people interviewed in Sheffield and Liverpool, come back again. It can be supposed that the reason for this was that, while some had gone to England to find work, many others had moved the much shorter distance to Edinburgh and Glasgow, or north to Dundee and Aberdeen, where there was also more work to be had than in Fife (see the list of destinations on

p. 77 and Appendix 5). In addition it has been noted that the larger number of higher-education students from Kirkcaldy than the other areas had to move out of the area because there were no institutions of higher education within it, as students did in Swindon for the same reason.

One lad had been employed since taking highers in sixth form by an oil company in Aberdeen to train as a multidisciplinary engineer at college there. He rented digs in Aberdeen for which the company covered the costs and he returned to his parents' at weekends. Similarly, a nursing student since taking highers in sixth form had alternated for six months at a time between a nurses' home in Dunfermline and her parents' house in Buckhaven whilst training in the hospital in Kirkcaldy. She enjoyed, as she said, 'the best o' both worlds'. She also returned home on alternate weekends whilst away.

The only interviewee who had moved whilst a student had done so during the last year of ONC/HNC business studies at the technical college in Kirkcaldy. He had rented a two-bedroomed flat in town for £150 a month between three friends, including the girl next door, who was also at the college. He supplemented his grant with part-time bar work. It was only a few miles from his parents' privately owned five-bedroomed house, where he and his two younger brothers each had their own room, but he wanted a change and was not getting on with his parents at the time. Still, he remained in regular contact with them, his mother visiting once a week when she went to town and he, like many others, telephoning whenever he needed something. He would have stayed when he completed his study but the lease ran out and he could not afford to rent elsewhere on full-time wages of £65 a week as a barman–waiter in Kirkcaldy and next as a salesman in Glenrothes for the same, plus commission. He also became ill with a life-threatening disease and returned home. Although he was now 20 this placed him in a unique relationship to his parents, at once younger because partially an invalid needing nursing and simultaneously older because facing the possible end of his life. He had certainly noticed their different attitude towards him and now that it was hoped he had recovered he got on better with them. He helped his father with his television repair business, saving money to go to America visiting relatives on a working holiday with a friend. Apart from this planned trip, if he moved again he would like to save and buy but he could see no immediate prospect of this.

Translation to Belfast for eight months seemed to have made little difference to a girl of 18 who went there because she was bored with Glenrothes and had visited Belfast before on holiday. She had completed a year on an office YTS, after leaving school, and in Belfast joined the Youth Training Programme for the second year doing painting and decorating, gardening, photography 'an' just everythin''. She had her own bedroom in her grandparents' privately owned house whereas she had to share with her sisters in the three-bedroomed house her parents had bought from the Glenrothes corporation. However, she had not intended to stay and returned because she missed everybody she knew, although she had kept in regular contact by phone and letter with her parents who visited her once, and she had come to them at New Year. Her parents had left to her the decision to leave or return and she did not consider that her relationship with them was any different now she had returned. She paid them more 'digs' money, that was all: £15 a week out of her wages of £91 for assembling electronic components in Glenrothes. This compared with the £7 a week she used to pay out of her YTS allowance of £27.50 and the £10 she gave her grandparents from the £35 for second-year YTP. She had no plans to move again until she left to get married, which she thought she would do at the usual estimate of 25 or 26. She did not think her time away when she was 17 was unusual: 'A lot o' folk do it, stay wi' boyfriends an' that, stay wi' onybody.'

Claire (20), who had moved at 18 to Livingston with her boyfriend, had intended to start a new life and thought she would get a council house with him there since they were expecting a baby. Instead she stayed first with her grandmother for three months and then, when she got a pensioner's flat, Claire move in with her baby's father and his family. After two overcrowded months she left with her baby to go to another relative in Livingston, staying for eight months with her aunt and uncle's family. When her cousin was rehoused with her child, Claire moved with her for a further eight months. She could not get her own tenancy because the Livingston housing authorities would not accept someone from out of the area, so eventually she abandoned the effort to settle there and returned with another boyfriend to her parents' in Kinghorn, hoping to be rehoused by Kirkcaldy. All her moves had been within the council sector and she had not worked since leaving school, save for three months part-time, in a dry cleaners in Livingston, for £30 a week. Her parents had not wanted her to go and were glad she was back. They had kept in regular touch by phone and visits while she was away. But with an older sister and her husband also in her parents' three-bedroomed house as well as a younger sister, herself, baby and boyfriend, they were overcrowded again with no hope of being rehoused for at least nine months since Claire had put her name down with Kirkcaldy only when she got back. The nineteen months away had thus been wasted: 'Ah dinnae seem tae be gettin' onywhere. Nothin's happenin' for me, just wastin' ma time.'

Like others interviewed who had returned to their parents', Frank (20), who had spent ten months with a girlfriend in Cupar, found himself treated differently by his parents on his return. This more adult relationship might have developed anyway as a result of his growing older and now bringing in £145 a week from his apprenticeship as a multiskilled craftsman in a Glenrothes paper-making factory. Again his parents had not wanted him to go, were glad he was back and had helped him to move to and fro. They had been in daily contact as he used to call in for his tea after work in Glenrothes before going back to Cupar. When he left, aged 17, he had thought, 'That's it, that's me made the move' but as the months went by he realized 'This isnae goin' tae last.' The tenancy of the council flat he shared in Cupar had been left to his girlfriend, also 17 and a trainee chef, when her mother went South. They had become 'engaged' when he moved in but, like others, he referred to her as his girlfriend rather than fiancée. Now that he was back in his parents' corporation house sharing the second bedroom with his younger brother, also an apprentice, Frank reckoned that he would move again but not until he had completed his five-year apprenticeship. 'Ah'll rent at first an' dependin' on the hoose Ah'd think aboot buyin' off the cooncil.' He did not think his experience unusual: 'People at that age tend tae go through a bad time wi' their parents an' some o' them break awa' Ah wid say.' In retrospect, however, he would have done things differently, not in such a rush and with more planning beforehand. He now thought he would get married 'sometime between 23 an' 26', but his experience had taught him that the greatest difficulty he faced was 'Gettin' a lass that's goin' tae put up wi' me for the rest o' her life!'

Pat's six-month move away when she was 19 to live with a boyfriend (26) in Leven seemed a more desperate assertion of independence. She had been unemployed and then was kept on part-time, for £61 a week, by the shop in which she did a year's YTS. Her parents were also 'no very pleased' when she left, though she reported that her relationship with them now she was back was unchanged. She had her own room in the three-bedroomed former Coal Board cottage where her younger sister, who was still at school, also lived, and she gave her mother £20 a week for board. In her boyfriend's one-bedroom privately rented flat she had not paid rent, just done the shopping, although as a butcher he would bring home meat. She did not really want to go to begin with but he had asked her and she thought she would move out and settle down there as her new home. Now that she was back she thought that she would prefer to have her own place to rent before moving in with someone else again. Unless she applied to the council, however, she could not afford to move without a full-time job and, as she said in a phrase echoed by many of the Kirkcaldy interviewees, 'There's no many o' them goin' aboot'.

Three other interviewees, all male in the older cohort, had moved within the area and returned to their parents once, twice and three times.

Gavin (21) had moved from his mother's housing-association-rented three-bedroomed house, where his younger sister also lived, to marry a girl he had met while on YTS, after leaving school. She was two years older than he was and they had a child before they moved. His father was in England and they could not stay with his mother for the familiar reason that 'She didnae like the wife and Ah had a tiff wi' her: Ah said, "If ye'll no accept her ye'll no accept me" an' I walked oot the door an' asked ma auntie tae put us up.' Typically again, 'Through time when we told her we were gettin' married she got tae grips wi' hersel an' decided she wisnae wantin' tae lose a son an' noo she an' the wife get on fine.' So initially they paid his aunt £20 a week for the four months until they got their own two-bedroomed council house. Their overcrowding in a two-bedroom housing association flat with his aunt and uncle, both unemployed, and their younger daughter, plus a visit to the local MP's surgery, helped their relatively speedy rehousing. By this time Gavin was labouring for the council for £105–£230 a week, after being unemployed for some months following YTS, but they had another child and, after less than a year in their new house, his wife left to go back to her mother. Gavin hung on in the council house for nearly a year but then went back to his mother. He was by then unemployed again because, as he said, 'marital breakdoon affected ma work'. Meanwhile his wife had got herself rehoused from her mother's with the two children, and Gavin began seeing her again at the four-bedroomed flat the council had given her. They were now attempting a reconciliation and sharing the tenancy. 'Ma pal wid come up wi' me an' take the children oot the way so we sorted it oot oorsels.' Gavin was on ET gardening, which was what he really wanted to do; he spent most of his time gardening for his grandmother while unemployed. His wife was a couple of years older than he was and, although the story is one that must be all too familiar to housing and social workers, perhaps the reconciliation, as Gavin himself called it, would succeed. He was certainly hopeful of getting rehoused to a better estate and of going on an Enterprise Allowance scheme to finance his own landscape gardening business, eventually to buy their own house. If he did not get work, however, he was considering going to England to join his father.

Although Rob (20) had returned twice to his parents' after renting with friends for nearly a year and with a girlfriend and other friends for four months, his movements were irregular even now he was back: 'Sometimes Ah'll not be home for a couple o' days an' other days Ah'll just dander in at eight in the mornin'.' However, in his perpetual effort to get bookings for the thrash metal band he led, he used his parents' home as an office and was described by his mother as 'born wi' a phone in his ear'.

They seemed unusually forbearing, even though Rob was 'at the moment' unable to pay them any money for his keep or their telephone bill – 'It's grim survival as it is', he explained. Incidentally, although Rob's father had bought the two-bedroomed council house they lived in, he was one of the few people interviewed to express the view that he saw no necessity for private home ownership 'if the facilities are OK an' it's a fair rent'. Rob's father and his wife tolerated their only child's musical endeavours and his other plans to make a record, open a record shop in Leven, become an A and R man for a record company, etc., in favour of which he had dropped out of an FE computer programming course to become unemployed, after staying at school for a year to take highers. He was now on ET 'but Ah only go noo an' again 'cos Ah'm not gettin fuck all off it'. However, his parents must have been relieved when, at 19, Rob first moved with two friends into a rented three-bedroom flat with large attic, for £50 a week. He lined the attic with egg boxes to turn into a practice studio. 'They were quite happy tae get rid o' me.' Although, 'Ah didnae really leave home; Ah wis only doon the road.' When the lease on the flat ran out Rob came back again (in so far as he ever left and as far as he ever stayed once he was back). After seven months he moved with a mate to share a one-bedroom flat with two girls five miles away. All of them were unemployed and they took it in turns to use the bedroom or sleep on the sofa. During some of this time Rob was in Edinburgh on a placement from a 'promotions management and events organization' FE course working in a record shop when he would sleep on friends' floors. After four months he split up with his girlfriend, returned to his parents' for six months and was now planning to rent again with friends. 'But gettin' a place is no sae easy. Ye get a few combin' aw the papers aw the time but it's like gettin' a job, there's that many people lookin' for places.' As with jobs, word of mouth could be the best recommendation.

While Rob had returned because he had never really gone, he was keen to move and planned one day to have his own house (in California!), by contrast Jimmy (21) had not wanted to leave and for this reason kept returning. His mother had first thrown him out when he was only 16 because she could not accept the fact that he was gay. 'It'd been like that aw' the time before when Ah wis 14 or 15. Ah went tae ma dad's but it wis durin' the miners' strike so he wis never there.' When Rob came back, with two sisters also in his mother's two-bedroom flat, 'I slept in a cupboard – really.' He was on YTS after leaving school and went to an unemployed couple nearby, who sub-let him a room in their council flat, for £35 a week. Social security would not pay this, however, so after three months Jimmy had reason to come back to his mother but after only two months 'she just wanted me oot'. This time he went to friends of his father nearby, but 'It wis just too much folk in the hoose an' a lot o' bother wi' the police an' that'. So after a month he moved in with his eldest sister who had by now left home. This was equally unsatisfactory 'because o' her boyfriend' and Jimmy came back to his mother again. This time he stayed for two years until his application for rehousing came through 'but Ah still wisnae gettin' on wi' her'. He had been unemployed for eight months after completing two years of retailing YTS and then found part-time bar work for £50 a week. Even when he later moved over to full-time work packing vegetables on piece rate for £80 a week he could not keep up his own two-bedroomed flat:

'They were wantin' £20 a week, plus electricity an' that an' it wis a dive. Ah wis very rarely there; Ah wis aye roond here. Ah just ate oot at the chippy a' the time an' Ah never ever used tae shop for masel'. Ah used tae just come up here if Ah wanted onythin'.'

He was now back again and still not getting on with his mother. He had reluctantly applied for live-in bar work in the South, for which he would be paid £86 a week, but admitted he was 'scared' of the prospect.

'But there's no really onythin' goin' aboot here so Ah'm just goin' tae have tae really try an' dae ma best. It's just so far awa'. Ah'll have tae rely on just bein' masel' an' try tae look after masel' cos Ah've no done very well at it so far an' ma life's goin' tae have tae change.'

HOMELESS IN KIRKCALDY

If Jimmy was virtually homeless, as well as his many 'pals' he also had his mother's flat, unwelcoming though it was, to fall back upon. Those who were completely homeless had even less family support and their situation shows how crucial that support is to young people leaving home. To say this is not to endorse the prevalent government view that homelessness among young people is caused by the break-up of the family. Rather, as the government's own financial watchdog, the Audit Commission, reported (22.8.90), the underlying cause of homelessness is the lack of affordable accommodation. Given this condition, young people without family support are likely to become homeless. While in Swindon and Sheffield two young men admitted that they had been homeless for short periods (pp. 31, 32 and 52), it was possible to locate youngsters in the Kirkcaldy sample who were homeless still because, as mentioned, more people there were more helpful and knew, it seemed, everyone else. However, doubtless similar cases, who were not part of the '16–19' sample, could have been located in any of the areas by visiting hostels or through agencies dealing with the homeless young. As Hutson and Liddiard found in Wales,

homeless youngsters [who, they emphasized,] do not constitute a homogeneous group . . . appeared to be highly mobile, moving frequently within different types of insecure accommodation; this mobility generally occurred within the confines of their home town, or, at most, their home county. [So that] It was clear that young people normally become homeless initially in their home area. This is not surprising as the minimal resource these young people have is local knowledge and contacts. It is usually only when local resources dry up that a young person may move further afield. [They added,] This finding has clear implications for policy. (1990, p. 169)

Loss of family support began for Angus (21) when his parents divorced. Then his father and stepmother separated so that when Angus left school he lived with his father, 'like one o' the bairns, kinda thing, but it wis mair like livin' on ma ain 'cos he wis very seldom there'. Angus had started an accountancy course at FE but left after a year – 'mainly ma ain fault'. He was unemployed and then on a community programme before getting a temporary part-time clerical job for £50 a week. When he was 19 he moved, for three months, from his father's two-bedroomed council flat into a privately rented bed-sit, with his girlfriend of the same age, 'but Ah had tae move 'cos it wisnae big enough for the two o' us an' there wis nae bath.' He returned to his father's. Then,

'She came back an' told me she's pregnant. We got a hoose nae problem after that. Ah wish Ah could get pregnant! That wis me settled then – the nearest tae haime since Ah

left ma family but it just wisnae happenin'. It wis just two different minds, so Ah left an'
ever since then Ah've been homeless.'

Angus left his girlfriend and child after a year and, since his father had now moved
("cos he forgot tae pay the rent'), went to his sister and her husband's two-bedroom
council house. He and they were all unemployed and 'They had tae keep their
mooths shut aboot me livin' there or they'd lose their rent rebate. That's why Ah
hadtae say Ah wis wi' friends aw the time. That's typical o' the lies ye've got tae tell.
It wis crackin' me up wi' bein' ill an' everythin'.' He went into hospital with an ulcer
over Christmas. He thought he had arranged a private rent but when he came out
after ten days it had fallen through, so he went first to his father's new girlfriend in
their council house for a month. 'But Ah had tae share a room wi' her two children
an' they got pissed off.' Since then he had been 'just dottin' aboot frae place tae
place'.

The council did not regard him as a priority for rehousing.

'Ah'm just gettin' pushed frae pillar tae post, frae the cooncil tae the Social [Security] an
back again. When Ah wis on the street Ah just walked aboot aw night 'cos it wis too
cold tae sleep an' then Ah wid go intae a café when they opened an' fa' asleep over a
cup o' coffee an' miss ma appointment wi' the hoosin'. Ah've thought o' squattin' but
ye've got nae legal right tae it here like ye hae in England.'

Eventually he moved, with his Alsatian dog, into his father's cousin's one-bedroom
council flat, initially for the couple of weeks the cousin was away, but as he had not
come back Angus had been there for two months. 'But when he does come back
Ah'll havetae move 'cos he's allergic tae dugs but the dug's been roond everybody
an' Ah don't know where Ah can take him noo.' The problem was thus compounded
but was not unusual: 'When Ah've been up tae the cooncil Ah've seen guys wi' their
dugs an' Ah ken a few people that've been put oot their hooses wi' their dugs; their
wife's kicked them oot an' they're just goin' frae floor tae floor tryin' tae get by.' This
was his own situation and one result of it was that 'Ma stuff's dotted aw over the
places Ah've been'.

His position was certainly insecure. Even if his father's cousin did not return, as he
might any day, Angus faced the possibility of the gas and electricity being cut off
since they were in arrears when he moved in. He was applying for a crisis loan from
Social Security and he wanted to rent with a friend who was also homeless but faced
the usual problem of raising a deposit. 'Ah check the local paper every week for flats
tae let but they're aw "No DSS". Even if they take ye they hit ye wi' aw this deposit
an' stuff an' there's nae way ye can get that kinda money off the dole.' As he was still
sick he could not work but luckily found some undemanding research work for a
couple of days that gave him enough money to put down a deposit on a flat with his
mate.

He had a new girlfriend, but said, 'Ah'm not really intae settlin' doon wi' a lassie
noo like. Ah widnae dae that 'til Ah got masel' thegether.' He thought that he might
go back to college and continue with his course so that he could get a decent job.
Then in five or ten years' time,

'Ah'll no be so skint, definitely not, but Ah'm no sure where Ah'll be; there's just loads
o' ideas that it's goin' tae come. It's just sortin' it aw oot. If Ah havnae got it sussed in
that time Ah'll start worryin'. Ah think big aw the time; Ah'm quite ambitious.'

If Angus at least had some family and friends he could fall back on, for which reason of course the council did not regard him as sufficient priority for rehousing, another homeless interviewee had no one else in her family she could turn to. Moira was younger, however, only 18, and could thus get institutional support that was not available to Angus. Like him, her trouble started with her parents' divorce. She was then 16, living with her two older sisters and older brother in the five-bedroomed council house in Kirkcaldy in which they had been brought up. Her father was unemployed and her mother a housewife but despite their divorce he did not leave or he came back, it was not clear which. What is clear is that it was her mother who had to leave, taking her children with her to a women's refuge in Glenrothes. After six months there they were rehoused by the council into a three-bedroomed house but, after five months, Moira's mother gave up the tenancy and returned to her husband. Two years later this process was repeated but, by this time, Moira's brother and one of her sisters had left home and the other had become ill and gone into hospital. So Moira alone shared the refuge bedroom with her mother and when, after three months, her mother decided to return again to her husband, Moira refused to go with her. With the help of a social worker she got the YWCA in Kirkcaldy to take her in and had been there for a year when interviewed. This gave her the time to complete her studies at sixth form and gain a place at Glasgow University. This had always been a bone of contention with her father; she said, 'He's never been keen on me goin' tae college; he's always wanted me tae go straight tae work an' Ah've never got on wi' him.'

Moira was homeless in the real sense that, although she had a roof over her head, there was nowhere she could call her home: 'Ah don't even talk aboot home. Ah just talk aboot the Y[WCA].' She still faced the problem of where to go for summer when she would no longer be eligible to stay there; in the autumn she had to look for somewhere else to live in Glasgow. She might go to her sister in London, as she had done the previous summer for a working holiday. She also saw her brother and other sister in Kirkcaldy two or three times a week. 'But Ah have nothin' tae dae wi' onybody else, aunts or uncles or that.' She saw her mother about once a week, although when her mother first went back again to her father she did not see her for months. She was even on better terms with her father.

Moira was certainly unusual, as she herself recognized: 'The other girls at the hostel are aw a bit older than me. Ah mean, this aw happened tae me when Ah wis at school.' One effect of her experience, and perhaps her way out of it, had been her growing interest in psychology, which she was now going to study at university. 'Ah became interested in it just watchin' ma family an' wonderin' why they're like that.'

THE POLL TAX

In Kirkcaldy it was impossible to obtain any breakdown by age but it seems that, in line with indications from the two most populous regions (Strathclyde and Lothian), young people were disproportionately represented among non-payers of the Poll Tax in the first year of its collection (1989) and also among those moving around to avoid registration. As Corr, Jamieson and Tomes (1990) confirm for the '16–19' respondents they interviewed in Kirkcaldy during 1989, 'Most are in arrears with their payments, some by happenstance, but more commonly as a deliberate tactic and a form of protest.' There was no evidence that as one of their interviewees alleged, 'A lot of families now are trying to get their kids to move out 'cos of the Poll Tax.' Rather, as Corr *et al.* write, 'It seemed that parents were more likely to be concerned that their children should not get into debt.'

However, among the 23 young people interviewed in Kirkcaldy who were, or had been, living free of direct parental influence, only 7 had paid the tax since it was introduced in 1989, and one of these (p. 79) worked for the council and paid through his wages. Another home owner (p. 78) was also up to date on her monthly instalments but others in council tenancies and on income support had only to find a reduced Poll Tax and so could afford to pay £5 a month. As she had started paying when in this situation, one tenant had gone on to pay the full amount when her husband started work (p. 80). Another council tenant (pp. 80–1) had also paid but regretted doing so; 'Ah'm a mug,' she said. 'Ah wish Ah hadnae 'cos it's worse if ye start payin' an' then stop than if ye never start. So Ah'd better go on as Ah've got mair tae lose than other folk 'cos everythin' here is under ma roof in ma name, whereas at ma ma's there's nothin' o' mine.' She supported the campaign against the tax. The student nurse (p. 83) had also paid up to date but regarded it as unfair that she should pay the full rate while other students did not.

Others, like Moira (p. 89), had only become eligible for the tax at the time of interview. Similarly, while away in Northern Ireland the interviewee (p. 83) had not had to pay but accepted that she would have to now she was back. The student-trainee in Aberdeen (p. 83) paid a reduced rate 'but the Poll Tax department has buggered aboot tae that extent Ah havnae paid a penny. They got their wires crossed when Ah moved an' they've not sorted it oot yet.' He intended paying but added, 'Before Ah wis employed there wis no way Ah was goin' tae pay.' Frank (p. 84), who had been away from his parents' home when the tax was brought in, did not pay until 'they caught up wi' me'. It was all paid up now and he was starting on his second year. The council had also 'caught up with' the student (p. 83) after he also returned to his parents following a year away in Kirkcaldy. He had joined in the anti-Poll Tax campaign at college but was now resigned to the fact that 'Ah'll havetae pay eventually'.

The only Tory supporter among those interviewed in Kirkcaldy (p. 79) was four months behind with his payments. 'Ah'm goin' tae have tae put ma mind tae it an' pay it,' he said. While he liked Mrs Thatcher as Prime Minister, there were 'a couple o' things' he did not like and the Poll Tax was one of them. Similarly, one of the Kirkcaldy Council tenants was three months behind. She found it harder to pay because it was a separate payment that was no longer in with the rent as the rates had been. Like another of the council tenants (below), she objected to the way 'They took the rates off the rent an' then they put the rent up'. The tenant of the brickworks' cottage (p. 80) was also behind with his payments but did not now intend to pay, especially as he had no savings to do so. 'When it started,' he explained, 'we didnae hae the books for it an' so we got behind. Ah don't know what'll happen; maybe we'll get an arrest warrant tae stop ma wages. There's not many people payin' but ye've got no option: they take ye tae court an' charge ye for that as well.'

The rest had not paid, either because they could not afford to or because they had not yet received a demand and/or on principle. One of the four home owners was typical: 'Ah disagree wi' it so they get very little off me. They're still chasin' me for it.' One of the council tenants had 'not paid a penny' because 'Ah can't afford tae pay.' However, she was resigned to the fact that 'We'll havetae pay it in the long run off Income Support but it'll never be paid voluntarily.' Others who had not paid reassured themselves that there were many in the same position: 'Ye get letters aw the time but Ah'm just one o' millions. Ah don't believe in it.' All the same, 'Ah would pay this year 'cos Ah'm on the dole but they've taken the book noo' (Helen, pp. 81–2). Bureaucratic confusions had also given other interviewees further reason not to pay: 'Ah'm refusin' tae pay it 'cos they're askin' the full amount but Ah'm tellin' them Ah'm on unemployment benefit but they won't gie me a rebate. Ah've had seven books off them but Ah've just thrown them in the bucket' (Gavin, p. 85). Rob (pp. 85–6) characteristically was even more defiant:

> 'Ah've not paid the first year an' Ah'm no goin' tae pay this year. Eventually they'll probably get a warrant tae take ma stuff awa' but Ah'll suss that oot 'cos there'll be nothin' there but Ah've heard they've started takin' it oot o' your dole. Ah hope not 'cos Ah cannae afford tae pay it, apart frae Ah dinnae agree wi' it.'

Jimmy (p. 86) had never paid; 'Nothin' happened aboot it. Ma address changed so much Ah don't think they ever caught up wi' me.' Similarly, Pat (pp. 84–5) had not yet been asked to pay since she had moved away from her parents' home when the tax was introduced and was now back again so that 'they havnae caught up wi' me'. And Angus (pp. 87–8) added to his account that 'The only good thing aboot bein' homeless is they cannae hit ye wi' the Poll Tax 'cos they cannae find ye.'

Only one of the interviewees connected non-registration for the tax with eligibility to vote. Claire (p. 84) had voted once but could not remember who for. 'Ah don't know what'll happen again 'cos Ah'm no paying the Poll Tax so Ah'll no be registered tae vote. Ah don't pay it 'cos Ah dinnae agree wi' it.' They had caught up with her now she was back at her parents' but 'Ah'm no ready tae pay yet. If Ah had ma ain place Ah'd have tae pay it then but while Ah'm livin' in digs sort o' thing it disnae seem right so Ah'm no payin' it.' Her boyfriend added that 'It's the young folk that arenae payin' it. Your workin' class'll pay it 'cos they're benefitin' from it but for the unemployed they're no payin' it.' This was a use of the term 'working class' that echoed what others had said in Liverpool and Sheffield (see p. 99) and relates to the debate on the 'underclass' and to the role of the Poll Tax in a more or less deliberate government attempt to exclude whole sections of the population from effective participation in society.

In the other areas it was Liverpool youngsters who were most vociferous in their stated inability and/or determination not to pay the new tax whether they were back at their parents' home or not. In all likelihood this was due to the imminence of its introduction in Liverpool at the time of interviews and to the prominent part it played in local politics there (see p. 59). Already in early 1990, as the City's Basement Youth Project annual report stated, 'The impending Poll Tax has had the effect of "obliterating" large numbers of people from official statistics in Liverpool.' In Swindon, as seen (p. 20), a Homeless Families Officer thought that the introduction of the tax would make her job much harder and that the research ought to be repeated next year to take account of this.

Chapter 6

Comparing, Contrasting and Concluding

SUMMING-UP

'There ye are, hen,' said a Kirkcaldy interviewee to her younger friend as the interview ended with some questions on her part, 'Stay at school an' gan tae university an' then ye can gan aroond the place talkin' tae folk!' Rewarding though this may be, the most difficult part of any research is writing it up. Elation at completing the task quickly gives way to despair faced with the amount of information collected. Invariably there is too much, for at the time it was recorded every item had seemed significant, or at least worth keeping in case it turned out to be so. All the movers it had been possible to contact in the four '16–19' areas had been interviewed, less those lost to other studies, and a set of 86 cases collected. Important area differences had emerged, with 8 out of 20 being home-buyers in Swindon (really 8 out of 18 since two were students), compared with 4, 3 and 3 home-buyers in Kirkcaldy, Sheffield and Liverpool, out of 23, 20 and 23 respectively (whether they had subsequently lost their homes or not, as two had in Swindon and one each in the three other areas). In Kirkcaldy and Sheffield there were more council tenancies than elsewhere, whereas in Liverpool private renting and housing associations offered more opportunities to young people. In all the areas save Liverpool, there was an accepted route to private ownership through the 'right to buy' council tenancies. Also in Liverpool, there were more 'broken transitions', as Willis (1984) called them, returning home because of failure to establish themselves working in the South or living locally.

Moving out of the area to work was marked in Kirkcaldy and Liverpool, and interviewees had returned home from the South in Sheffield and Liverpool. However, returning to their parents' home after living away for a time, for whatever reason, was confirmed as part of a long, drawn-out process for many of those interviewed. Even apparently final departures could come to be seen as just a first step (e.g. p. 66) the better to recoil before setting out again, so that, as the bluesman says, 'Just because I'm leaving baby, it don't mean I'm gone'. Semi-formal links were often maintained, e.g. a key to the door, returning for meals and to wash clothes, even for baths. Nearly half the interviewees had returned, including some who had then gone again. It is reasonable to assume that those who leave younger are more likely to return than those who leave later, though there was less time available in which to record this for the older cohort. Leaving to marry/cohabit, which most will do later, is for the majority a more permanent move in any case.

Forty-nine interviewees (33 women) had moved to marry/cohabit and of these 15 had returned. Twenty-one interviewees had children (6 men; 15 women), including four single mothers rehoused with their children, plus one single mother who returned to her parents with her child. Twelve interviewees in total were married (six of them with children) and 12 engaged (four with children). The sequence of events had rarely been the traditional order of engagement, followed by simultaneous marriage and move, then children. Indeed, as has been seen, several of those cohabiting, with or without children, had no plans to get married and for many interviewees 'engagements' seemed more nominal than real and a mark of convention and intent rather than a definite commitment to marry. Nevertheless, only one married and one engaged cohabitee had returned to their first home and the married one was attempting a reconciliation with his wife (p. 85). There was evidence in the interviews that some young people had moved to marry/cohabit earlier than planned due to pregnancy, e.g. p. 40.

Moving to work was the next most common reason for moving and most common among the younger cohort, although only those who had returned could be interviewed. Fourteen interviewees had returned from working away – 8 female, 6 male, only one in Swindon who had worked for a time in London, plus two students in Swindon. (For the total contacted who had moved to work but could not be followed out of their areas, see pp. 21, 48–9, 61 and 77–8 plus summary in Appendix 5.) Jones (1990) inferred three reasons for moving (to marry/cohabit, for work and to study) from the Scottish Young People's Survey. The most common reason she found for leaving home by age 18 was to start a job, among young men, and to set up home, among young women. (As Kiernan, who also added 'friction at home'/'poor accommodation' and 'other negative reasons', 12 per cent men, 11 per cent women and 'to set up home', 9 per cent men, 8 per cent women, quoted in Roll, 1990, p. 38.) The reason that moving to work did not figure so largely in the '16–19' interviews was that those who had moved out of their area (usually to work) were not followed up. However, as Jones wrote (p. 15), leaving home to get a particular short-term job can be a temporary move, as was the case for the asbestos stripper from Sheffield for example (p. 50). Also, as noted (p. 36), for students the crunch between temporarily 'living away' during term time and 'leaving' permanently comes at the end of their course. In addition, interviews revealed a small group who moved mainly 'for a change' (e.g. p. 83) or to establish their independence (p. 66) and attempt to live a different sort of life (e.g. pp. 52–3). But even in interview where the reasons subjects gave for moving could be explored, it was often difficult to disentangle the main reason for a move. It was also sometimes unclear whether they were pushed out or had walked out (on threats to walk out by children and threats to kick them out by parents, see Hutson and Jenkins (1989, p. 57) and compare threats to walk out of cohabitation in Karen's interview, p. 67). Similarly, returning home, choice and constraint were often intertwined.

Of course, interviews with the young people rather than the parents revealed only one side of the story but, even so, events were seldom as clear as those admitted to by Stan in Sheffield who said, 'It were just sort of "Get out and don't come back!"' (p. 56), or Diane in Swindon who 'got fed up with my mum's boyfriend beating me up' (p. 32). Often feelings were mutual, for example: 'My mum said, "Get out!" and

I said, "I'm going anyhow!"' (p. 25). So only 9 cases out of the total 86 could be unambiguously attributed to parental eviction (and one of these in Swindon had had to tell the council he had been kicked out in order to get rehoused). Most interviewees had moved on their own initiative; it had been their idea to move, at most a joint decision with a partner or friend. Typically, even if they were worried or upset, parents left their children to decide what to do with their own lives. 'I think they thought if it was what I wanted to do then they would back me up.' At most, parents 'aired their views': 'At first they were telling me it wouldn't work and "you're too young" – all that saga but they didn't try to stop me and they were happy in the end.' Among those who had returned after being kicked out, like Jimmy in Kirkcaldy (p. 86), or after walking out (e.g. pp. 66–7), there was still palpable tension with their parent(s), as evidenced by the father of the Swindon interviewee (p. 31) who asked through the kitchen door, 'Has he told you, the sooner he goes the better I'll be pleased?' So for these interview subjects it was not the case that, as Jones stated of her large quantitative survey (1990, p. 12), returners were more likely than leavers to have left home originally because they did not get on with their families. Nor, for those for whom this was the case, did it necessarily imply that they just needed a 'cooling off period', valuable as this may have been. Rather, they often had literally nowhere else to go and so returned to the same situation they left (e.g. p. 65). Unless they can reach a new accommodation with their parents (sometimes literally, as in the self-contained flat arrangement, e.g. pp. 51 and 62), they are likely to leave again when an opportunity presents itself (e.g. pp. 52 and 86.) A gradual move, as of Lynne into her girlfriend's house (p. 72), can ease the pains of parting, though it requires somewhere else to move to. Yet however bad the circumstances in which they left, only two of those interviewed (both of whom had moved from being in care) were completely out of contact with their parents. Many others were again in regular contact with their parents, having left after seemingly terminal breakdowns in their relationships (e.g. Moira, p. 89). Most of those who had not moved to work had moved within a few miles of their parents, often in the same road or on the same estate, and they saw each other two, three or four times a week.

Because home leaving was only one of several different processes going on concurrently, it was invariably affected by other events in the young people's lives and those of their parents/families. For example Ken, whose parents divorced the year after he left home, very reasonably imagined: 'it would be a fair assumption to say that I wasn't getting on very well with them because they weren't getting on with each other' (p. 53). Even so, one perhaps surprising finding was the number of parents leaving their children, seven in all. This was clearest with the two sets of brothers left in possession of the houses in which they had been brought up when their parents/mother moved to work/remarry (pp. 55 and 63). One interviewee had also been left the council tenancy when her mother moved to remarry (p. 73) and another, also in Liverpool, had bought her parents' house when they could not sell it, though she subsequently moved on to rent when she and her husband could not keep up the payments (p. 68). In Sheffield Janet had also moved shortly before her mother left to remarry (p. 54) and Michelle moved to Crystal Peaks six months before her parents had twins (p. 40). Also in Sheffield, the girl who had spent a year in Australia returned to live with her grandfather now that her mother had moved to remarry (p. 51). In addition, one young woman in Liverpool was living alone after both her parents died (p. 73).

As expected, many of those whose relations with their parents were poor and had contributed to their leaving home were stepchildren. Twenty-seven in all (nearly a third) were the children of divorced/separated/deceased parents. This compared with the much-quoted and generally accepted average of one in five 16-year-olds who now live or have lived for some time in a single-parent family, rising to one in four if current trends continue into the next decade (a figure that seems to originate with Haskey, 1990). Tasker's 1990 study in Cambridge found the daughters of divorced parents more likely to have left home than the daughters of the non-divorced but there was no difference for sons in her sample. Thornton (1990, p. 8) referred to

> a major national survey for the Department of the Environment in 1977–80 [which found that] 41 per cent of single homeless persons under the age of 20 . . . left home due to family break-up, while a further 24 per cent stated their reason for homelessness to be 'parental dispute', a category including conflict with a step-parent. More recently, a study of 16- and 17-year-old hostel residents by Shelter in Scotland found that a majority cited family conflict, including marriage breakdown and arguments with step-parents, as a factor in their homelessness.

From Thornton's own 1989 survey of local authority housing departments:

> family breakdown was mentioned as a cause of young homelessness by several respondents. One reply stated, 'We are finding an increase in the number of single people presenting as homeless because their parents have remarried and the step parent is not prepared to accommodate them any longer once they reach the age of 16 or 17.'

Certainly conflict with step-parents (usually, as would be expected, between daughters and stepfathers but also between sons and stepfathers) was taken for granted as a reason for leaving home among many stepchild movers interviewed – e.g. p. 25: 'Say no more!'

The importance of support from members of the family other than the parents, especially from grandparents, has been shown repeatedly in the interviews. As *The Swindon Under-25 Survey* noted, 'The traditional image of young people fails to convey any recognition of how much they depend on their family' (Curphey and Grant, 1985, p. 23). Many parents had helped their children move – with transport, furniture and sometimes, to a limited extent, financially. However, the sample was too young and too weighted towards the 'working class' (as conventionally defined) to observe the financial flows between generations becoming characteristic of later-moving 'middle-class' generations. (Notably, according to Nissen (1987) between property-owning grandparents who, on their retirement to smaller dwellings, help their grandchildren to buy with proceeds from their sale.) Three interviewees had been brought up by their grandparents, plus one still living with her grandfather now that her mother had moved. Thirty-three (38 per cent of all cases) had lived with relatives other than their parents, even if only for a short time, thirteen with grandparents. This seemingly contradicts the general finding of Cunningham-Burley's 1985 and 1986 studies of grandparenting, which was that 'grandparents did not want full involvement in bringing up their grandchildren at all, but with the proviso "unless there was something wrong"' (personal communication). This lends support to the reasonable presupposition that children from families where 'something is wrong' are more likely to leave sooner than from 'normal' or 'intact' families, especially as leaving 'earlier' than average contributes to the conventional definition of 'abnormality'. Hence the evident feeling of some parents of social disapprobation that their children had left home younger than average, to the extent of concealing the fact from a prying researcher. In Australia, Young (1987) also noted the reluctance of parents to disclose their children's departures. This shared parental feeling could lend weight to their children's threats to walk out (above).

Other relatives stayed with were older brother/sister (10), in-laws (8), aunt/uncle (7), cousins (2), younger brother, father's cousin and great aunt (1 each). Two interviewees had also stayed with an employer or employer's family and two girls had been employed as live-in nannies. Living with kin (13 per cent of the 1981 NCDS sample of 23-year-olds for example) is typically associated with traditional working-class families, although Leonard (1980) noted another traditional pattern for working-class youngsters, namely to live in hostel accommodation. This and other forms of 'transitional' housing, especially the persistently dwindling private rented sector, have been severely squeezed since. Other relatives often represented a place to go, initially or temporarily, for children leaving because of differences with their parents. In traditional working-class communities they were, and often still are, never far away. Extended families, or what Harris calls 'extended kin relationships' (1983, p. 48) were certainly alive for the majority of young leavers interviewed. Indeed, it was noticeable that Halimah, for example (p. 45), talked of her relatives in exactly the same way as Lorraine (p. 42), who said that she would not have any more children because her sister had two and her brother one 'so that's enough babies in the family'. The only difference was that many of the relatives Halimah was talking about were in Bangladesh while Teresa's were living locally in Sheffield. As Harris said, 'there is no question as to the continued importance of extended kinship networks in industrial societies' (ibid., p. 91).

Finch has detailed family obligations in a time of social change, especially in the 1980s when 'the Conservative government has become increasingly explicit about its desire to encourage families to take care of their members' (1989, p. 3). Families unable to do this have been pathologized so that there is seen to be 'something wrong' with them. Respectable independence is lost by dependence upon the state and its agents – social security, social workers – or, increasingly, upon charity. An 'underclass' of the new rough is thus ideologically constructed beyond the pale of respectable society and blamed for its own situation. As with the discussion of homelessness (p. 87), the problem lies not with individuals or their families but with the circumstances in which they find themselves. Leaving home earlier than the average is not a problem in itself but in the situations in which it is likely to occur it can become problematic. The solution to the problem is then seen in the behaviour itself, also in the particular factors which contributed towards it and which are then supposed amenable to treatment in isolation from more general causes. This leads to theoretical approaches like those parodied by Kelman: 'Please allow us to conceptualise your problem, thus we attain a sensation of nourishment ergo that your problem, though not yet solved, has been conceptualized, which is tantamount to a solution of course' (1989, p. 86). The attempt in this study to situate description of leaving home by young people in the local contexts in which it occurs has deliberately avoided such approaches.

CLASS AND AGE

In a society divided principally by class and race as well as by age and gender (p. 1) some conceptualization along these lines is necessary since this is, as a Kelman character would say, 'how we find it'. It is one of the weaknesses of this study that it has been little concerned with black and Asian young people (see pp. 44–5), but as far as class is concerned the conventional division between non-manual = 'middle class' and manual = 'working class' is clearly inadequate, not only because of the difficulties of categorizing 'youth classes' (p. 11). This is evident in the responses to the self-assigned class question in the '16–19' questionnaires returned by the whole sample. Not having been fully reported elsewhere, they will be detailed here. Given a choice between 'upper-middle', 'middle' and 'working' four out of five respondents acknowledged social class, as against 22 per cent answering 'don't know' or 'no class'. (Scots, or rather Fifers, were most likely to reject the notion of social class – 25 per cent of them not assigning themselves to any class.) Sixty-four per cent of all those choosing one of the three class options called themselves 'working class' as against 34 per cent 'middle class'. As would be expected in a sample restricted to state school leavers, numbers assigning themselves to 'upper middle' were very low – less than 2 per cent. There were no differences in the self-assigned class of young men and women, despite there being many more woman than men in 'non-manual' employment. Girls and boys in all areas were equally likely to assign themselves to the middle class, except in Swindon where fewer girls did so. Swindon residents were most likely to call themselves middle class (39 per cent), while young Liverpudlians were most likely to put themselves in the working class (60 per cent, cf. Sheffield 45). Having a father in non-manual work increased the numbers of females and males calling themselves middle class but reduced the numbers not recognizing class by only a small amount. In the sample overall, 79 per cent of school leavers were in non-manual occupations yet 56 per cent of them called themselves working class. Since out of the 21 per cent in manual occupations 56 per cent also called themselves working class, being in manual/non-manual employment clearly made no difference to self-ascribed class affiliation or rejection.

There was a substantial area difference in self-assigned class, however. Of those in work, white-collar workers in Swindon were most likely to call themselves middle class (31 per cent), less likely to in Sheffield (26 per cent) and Kirkcaldy (19 per cent) and most unlikely so to describe themselves in Liverpool (10 per cent). Conversely, less than half Swindon's white-collar workers called themselves working class, but three-quarters of white-collar-occupied Liverpudlians called themselves working class. More white-collar workers in Swindon than elsewhere also rejected notions of class and Swindon manual workers were least likely to call themselves working class – only just over half did so, compared with 83 per cent of Liverpudlian manual workers. Manual workers everywhere were less likely than non-manual to reject notions of class, save in Fife, where manual workers were more apt than non-manual to reject class categorization. For these young people, therefore, class was not assigned in their questionnaire returns on the basis of conventional occupational distinctions between manual and non-manual work, distinctions which are breaking down with the latest applications of new technology. It also had little to do with class of origin – there was as little relation between self-assigned class and father's occupational class as between self-assigned class and own occupation. Locality was the most powerful influence upon self-assigned class. Living in Swindon was associated with a greater likelihood of middle-class self-assignment, whatever the respondents' objective class status. Liverpool, by contrast, was associated strongly with working-class self-assignment, even by those in white collar jobs. It is obvious from this that perceptions of class structure vary widely and that the sociological definition of class bears remarkably little resemblance to the image of the class structure held by those to whom the definition is applied.

How do these findings from the sample overall compare with the young home-leavers interviewed? As can be seen from the appendixed list of interviewees' parents' occupations, along with their own occupations and educational qualifications (often taken as a surrogate measure for social class, since education so effectively filters pupils/students for their future occupation), the sample was overwhelmingly 'working class'. There is clearly some association between parental occupation, educational qualifications and home ownership, though not in Swindon. There is also a link between whether parents owned their own homes and whether their children did (see below). However, such lists of occupations elicited from informants themselves are often misleading; they do not reveal whether a 'plumber', for example, is self-employed and owns her/his own business employing other people, or again, what exactly a 'trainee-' or 'assistant-manager' is, since the description can be applied to someone running a small shop part-time, for instance. 'Office' and 'secretarial' can also be camouflage words. With the expansion of offices and services more workers have been placed in the 'non-manual' category, for example in Sheffield, p. 39. Thus a Sheffield interviewee could state that in her opinion the class system locally and, by extension, nationally 'seems to have broken down completely except the really upper class'. More people work with other people, selling them goods and services, or handle pieces of paper, as opposed to manufacturing objects. Yet their autonomy and wages are not necessarily greater and are often less than they would have been on a factory floor. More 'flexible' working has increased autonomy and responsibility but often with less security, along with part-time and irregular or shift working. The few clearly 'middle-class' occupations in the list, e.g. teacher, social worker, often earn lower wages than many of those who would be placed in the skilled or semi-skilled worker category, and differences are therefore more often cultural than material. The numbers of unemployed tend to be underestimated also, since interviewees habitually gave their parents' occupations whether they were working at the time or not.

In a section of the interview called 'About Yourself' interviewees were asked directly, 'Would you describe yourself as working class, middle class, or would you describe yourself as belonging to some other class, or wouldn't you describe yourself like this?' (See Appendix 2 for the full interview schedule.) This followed questions on their identity: 'Do you prefer to be called a youth/teenager (if under 20), young person or young adult?' (Most preferred the latter two.) They were then asked whether they identified with their occupation or aspiration (what they wanted to be and/or were training/studying to become), i.e. thought of themselves as a 'computer operator', 'housewife', 'gofa', etc. (Most who had an employment or were training/studying for one identified with it but many distanced themselves from it – 'It's just a name'/'It doesn't mean anything'.) They were asked whether they followed any particular (subcultural) style, music or fashion. (Most claimed to be eclectic in their choice.) Following on from this, answers to the self-ascribed class question were very varied, sometimes resulting in long descriptions of the social system in which 'Everyone is working class, except the Queen', or 'Class is a superficial thing – it's just how you talk and the clothes you wear', or even 'They're aw bastards, just some are rich bastards'. This merely demonstrates the obvious fact that what people say in answer to an interview is different from which box they tick in a questionnaire, which is different again from what they really think and how they behave in situations where their actions can be predicted by the objective indicators of social class used by sociologists (e.g. income and housing tenure, to predict voting behaviour). Often in interview people will give the answer they think the interviewer wants to hear, which in part possibly explains the larger number describing themselves as 'middle class' to a briefcase-wielding interviewer than had returned this answer in their questionnaires. Perhaps, though, the differences between interview and questionnaire explain the variation with the overall '16–19' response and those of the young people in Ipswich interviewed by Marsden *et al.* (1990). Over three-quarters of his sample of YTS trainees rejected the notion of social class, 'some flatly refusing to respond because the idea smacked of snobbery, divisiveness and unequal worth' (p. 126).

Among the young movers there were a small number who used the opportunity of the interview to explain their choice of 'no class', meaning what has been called an underclass beneath the working population (p. 8). 'I would like to be working class if I could get a job', as one unemployed Sheffield man stated, or as an unemployed Kirkcaldy mother said, 'Ah'm definitely no' workin' class 'cos Ah'm no' workin'' (cf. p. 91). Others placed themselves in the 'middle class' by reference to this 'rough' class beneath them. For example, Theresa in Liverpool, who described herself as 'ordinary class, not posh and not scruffy' and Diane in Swindon, another unmarried mother, who gave the same answer: 'Common, like every other normal person, not a snob and not a tramp'. It was a comfortable place to be: 'Not rich, not poor, just happy as I am', as a young Swindon house-owner said. Incidentally, this gives a new twist to the meaning of 'middle class', originally intermediate between the workers and the aristocracy.

Marsden, whose trainees' most common self-definition was 'middle class', 'by which they seemed to mean the bulk of ordinary people who lay between a small and remote upper class and a disreputable but diminishing lower class' (ibid.), took their answers as proof of how completely working-class youngsters had absorbed the ethos of Thatcherism. However, for many of the Liverpool core interviews which were also examined, 'middle class' was not different from 'working class'. Both of them, as several Liverpudlian youngsters put it, have to work to live. Yet while defining themselves as being 'in the middle' between 'snobs' above and 'scallies' below, very few admitted in interview to being themselves in the scallywag class. Admittedly, if such an underclass existed, its members would be the hardest to trace even in a large sample. But the interview answers show that while many agree the rich have got richer and the poor poorer, most see themselves situated between these two poles. ('Snobs' also had an alternative meaning, of those who are really middle/working class but try to deny the fact – like most sociologists who maintain the distinction between the two groups!)

The effect of changed economic circumstances upon the allegiances and opinions of the young movers interviewed in Swindon has been seen in their shared aspiration, whatever their circumstances, to own their own home, if they did not own it already. However, a majority of Swindonians adhered to Labour in their political preference, though many were also attracted to the alternative politics represented by the Greens. (Cf. the '16–19' all-Swindon sample, 40 per cent of whom favoured the Conservatives in 1987; Roberts and Parsell, 1988b, p. 17.) Class affiliation in the Swindon interviews seemed unrelated to housing tenure or whether or not the subject's parents owned their own home but was generally uncertain. By comparison it has been seen how in the North not all those interviewed shared the aspiration to own their own home, although most agreed that it was desirable. For a minority a council tenancy rather than home ownership represented security (e.g. p. 43). For several young mothers in council or housing association accommodation, ownership did not represent a realistic alternative. The most they hoped for was an exchange to better premises or location. Several of the young men just did not plan that far ahead at this stage in their lives, e.g. p. 51. Some young women with children just followed the traditionally expected course of their lives without planning ahead at all – 'bimbling along', as a Swindon resident put it (p. 30). For others, moving into a new place to rent or being rehoused was the limit of their immediate intentions.

Contrary to expectation, class affiliation in the Sheffield interviews seemed as vague as in Swindon, though not in the Liverpool ones. However, a majority of the Sheffield sample also said that they had or intended to vote Labour, as in Liverpool; while in Scotland support for the Opposition was divided with the SNP. Only a minority in all areas supported the ruling Conservatives and such support again did not necessarily correlate with owner occupation or aspiration for home ownership. A minority were also prepared to justify their failure or refusal to vote with various pithy remarks that made it clear this was not due solely to so-called 'apathy' on their part.

There was, of course, an association between those young people whose parents owned their homes and those who aimed to buy or who had bought. Yet some interviewees had moved to private ownership from parental homes in the public rented or housing association sectors and many more had parents who had bought their own council homes. This is to be expected during a period when the share of owner-occupied dwellings is rising. Housing progression is generally from private rented 'transitional' housing through to private ownership, or to public renting and then to home ownership, as long as people can afford to take out mortgages and as long as private and public housing stock is available for sale. In Kirkcaldy and Swindon there was a generally accepted route to ownership through council tenancies and ex-council properties, which were not seen by the young people interviewed as inferior to other private properties available to them. It is a situation that will change when this period comes to an end and will be little affected by extension of right-to-buy pilot schemes to convert rents to mortgages. Predictably these would actually be available to very few council tenants, as in the Scottish Homes and Welsh pilots of the scheme (see Shelter 9–10.90). With 1.2 million council homes already sold through right to buy, the pattern of housing tenure in Britain has been fundamentally altered but selling council homes without building new ones is a characteristically short-run policy that inevitably exhausts the limited numbers of both saleable properties and people able to afford them. As Pickvance and Pickvance (1990) say, 'The reduction in availability of council housing due to privatization of the existing stock and a low level of new building means that early child rearing can no longer be guaranteed to give access to council housing' (p. 13). Indeed some of those inter-viewed were aware of these changes, e.g. p. 43. For others, not themselves in that situation, it did not seem a good way forward 'even if you're living at home and having family problems. . . . I know lots of people who've tried to get a flat but they can't get one, so they end up getting pregnant, and then they end up going round in circles waiting for their Monday books and up to their eyes in debt.' All the single mothers interviewed regretted getting into such a situation (see p. 70). Together with changes in the labour market that are bringing a relative improvement in employment possibilities for (young) women, the vexed group of young home leavers who are single mothers may thus become a still smaller minority.

The selection of cases was at too young an age and the section of their life course covered in interview too brief really to distinguish the emergence of what the Pickvances call 'housing strategies' (elsewhere 'trajectories' or 'careers', pp. 11–12) operating in the context of different housing supply conditions to which households and individuals have unequal access. Nor did it include students, save for the sake of comparison in Swindon and other students elsewhere who had coincidentally moved from their first homes. Enough has been said about students, however, for it (pp. 33–6) to be recognized that the 'institutionalized transition', simultaneously from school to work and from parental home to own home via 'living away' during term times, is increasingly problematic. Among the remaining cases, it is possible to distinguish a group of the especially disadvantaged who included the single mothers. Unemployed young people found it particularly hard to raise the deposit necessary for private renting. As Jones says, 'Whether or not young people return home under these circumstances appears to depend on the economic status of their parents. If the parents are unemployed, there is little to be gained from returning home in terms of labour market information and if parents receive housing benefit some of this would be withdrawn. It is in such circumstances that young people may become homeless' (1990, p. 65). This was the case with the homeless young man in Kirkcaldy. His father, as well as being unemployed, was also divorced and, as seen, it is those without family support who are most at risk (e.g. pp. 31, 87), and those leaving care, custody or mental hospital.

Between those groups of the un- and subemployed and those few youngsters (not represented in this sample) who enjoyed benefits such as those reported of some English student owner-occupiers in Edinburgh (p. 34), there was a range of such diversity in the cases interviewed as to confirm Anderson's speculation that 'we are returning to a situation of much greater diversity of experience' (quoted on p. 12). Jones's 1990 survey in Scotland agreed: 'Perhaps the main point which needs to be stressed is the extent to which young people differ from one another in their social and economic circumstances' (p. 94). This is not only because leaving home is related to the variety of other transitions to adulthood, both in terms of household and economic status, but also because of the varieties in timing when the young person embarks upon this course. As Jones also said, 'The housing needs of a seventeen-year old leaving home to start a course or take up a job are likely to be different from those of a nineteen-year old leaving home for the same reason' (ibid.). This led her to recommend a variety of housing provision for young people, a recommendation that can only be endorsed. Similarly, Thornton urged 'a variety of provision, including furnished as well as unfurnished properties, supported, semi-supported and shared units, and directed access emergency accommodation' as part of 'a major national programme of investment in public rented housing' (1990, p. 75). Her SHAC-sponsored report also recommended the more immediately effective restoration of young people's rights to full benefits, which have been lost to under-18-year-olds and reduced for under-25s. This would also help young people's position in the labour as well as the housing market.

The variety of experience which has been remarked and which is illustrated by the interviews in this book may also offer some explanation for the differences in class ascription which this section began by noting. The widening of differentials along a spectrum, the poles of which are growing further apart, may offer the illusion of equality, or at least of only minor quantitative variations, to those between the two extremes ('not posh but not scruffy'). Their position relative to others in the same intermediate position is also not fixed but grows more fluid with rapid changes in wages and employment status following the latest applications of new technology. This 'homogenization' of the centre cannot of course be comprehended within the confines of one country for, as Amin wrote, 'Social classes are not defined exclusively by their position in the local system but – and no less significantly – by their relationship to the range of forces operating on a world scale' (1990, p. 5). For the individuals concerned, the appreciation of a similarity behind apparently minor differences may emerge in interview, whereas conventional class ascriptions ticked in a questionnaire are affected by traditional notions (though not the traditional sociological distinction between 'manual' and 'non-manual'). In addition, people's perceptions are especially influenced by what Ashton, Maguire and Spilsbury call 'local labour market cultures' (1990, p. 193).

LIFESTYLES AND FINANCES

While variety of experience is clearly illustrated by the different interview cases that have been presented, these are a mere collection of individuals even though they were selected from a larger representative sample. Upon close examination they disintegrate into unique life histories, the immediate determinants of which are not directly social but psychological, e.g. p. 23. Broken down into their constituent variables and compared in such a way as to lose sight of individuals for the first time, they may be reconstituted in groups of the same type. This departs from the attempt made so far to preserve individual cases and compare them as configurations defined by the similarities of their life courses and/or housing tenure, following Ragin's 1990 prescription for Qualitative Comparative Analysis.

As well as the recent biography of their life course with regard especially to their education/training, employment, housing and relations to significant others, interviewees were also asked to estimate the amount of time per week they spent on various activities and, if they had returned to their parents, to compare this with their lifestyle while they were away. Abandoning individual cases and aggregating the quantities they gave for the amounts of time they spent on different activities, it is evident that, despite the variety of experience that has been noted, very broadly similar patterns of current lifestyle emerged. Graph 1 shows the average in hours per week of the leisure/non-work activities estimated by all interviewees. Like practically everyone else, except students – only 48 per cent of whom watch television daily according to a survey in *National Student* magazine (9.90) – most of the young people spent most of their 'free' time watching television, whether they devoted their full attention to it or not. This was the case for men and women (Graph 2), those with or without children (Graph 3), on Income Support or earning/on a grant (Graph 4), whether living at their parents' home or away (Graph 5) and across all areas (Graph 6). However, those on Income Support spent nearly twice as much time in front of the television as those earning or on a grant. Those with children and female (overlapping categories with Income Support) also spent more time watching than others. All those interviewed owned, rented or had access to a television and only one person (Stan, pp. 56–7) said he intended to get rid of it.

On average, housework/cooking took up the next most amount of time, but for young women twice as much time as for males, for whom it came second to time spent with friends and listening to or playing music. (Of course not all categories were mutually exclusive: you could spent time listening to music with friends, as many did, or while doing housework, or even – with bizarre effect – while watching television with the sound turned down (as 'The Other People' in Sheffield sometimes did!). Unsurprisingly, women also spent more time shopping (including window-shopping) than males, as did those with children and those on Income Support, who had to shop around. Those with children (who were mostly female) also spent more time doing housework and cooking. They also spent more time with their families, as did those on Income Support, showing once again the importance of help from relatives. As another single mother said, 'The only friend I go and see is my mum.' (If interviewees had returned to their parents' home, time spent 'with family' means only with other relatives or in-laws.) People on Income Support who had a boy/girlfriend also spent more time with that person if they were not living with them (in which cases their time was similarly discounted).

Young women, whether they had children or not, spent more time with friends than young men did. Males made up for this by spending more time in the pub, listening to music and playing/watching sports (see Appendix 6). Females and males living at their parents' home spent more time with friends and more time in pubs and clubs, being more sociable altogether because they had more money to spend, whether or not they were employed. They spent more time than when living away on every leisure activity except watching television, doing housework/cooking and shopping (not counting time spent with the families they were living with). If they paid board money or made a contribution working for their parents in or out of the house, this was considerably less than equivalent local rent levels (q.v. Jamieson and Corr). Not surprisingly the difference was most marked for those in the North who had lived and worked in the South; as one Liverpool girl who had been employed in London said, 'I spent more but did less.'

Nor will it surprise parents to learn that, even by their own sometimes generous estimations, those at home spent less time on housework than they did while away, even if, by the more candid admissions of some, while they lived away they also did 'as little as possible' with the result that 'It's like Chaos City' and 'We wouldn't care if the whole floor was covered with litter', to quote a few. Others, it should be said, though admittedly a minority, meticulously cleaned and tidied their accommodation whilst living away. Those living away also had to do their own cooking but often did not eat as well as at home: 'Ah just ate oot the chippy aw the time . . . canned food . . . It's just something simple . . . I didn't really eat properly . . . carry-oots, fish an' chips, crisps an' stuff', to quote a few. And 'Chinese take-aways tend to be popular among hotel staff 'cos you get sick of fancy cooking in the hotel.' On the other hand, living with friends could turn cooking into 'a social thing and we used to take turns cooking for each other'. Sharing with strangers or friends you no longer got on with could provide reasons for leaving private rented accommodation. Similarly, both sets of brothers left on their own by their parents lived as separately as possible to avoid arguments. Conflicts over the amount of housework parents expected interviewees to do were also cited as the occasion, if not the underlying reason, for leaving home. For those unemployed and living at home with their parents the pattern could be different again: 'While mum and dad are at work I clean the house up for them during the day and make my own dinner.' And different again for those whose parents were unemployed: 'We're under each other's feet all day long.' With relatives youngsters could be better off than at home: 'With nan it's like having a second mum. . . . She cooks for me all the time. . . . It's luxurious being looked after by a little old lady.' Thus you could have the best of both worlds: 'While you're with relatives you're away but you still feel part of the family.'

Moving from home often meant leaving behind not only services but facilities that had previously been taken for granted – washing machines, hi-fis, videos and computers. Computers were in any case very much a minority taste, a hobby left over from an earlier phase, like model car racing. Although many movers had videos, especially back at their parents' where there might also be satellite TV, theirs were not the 'electronic homes' inhabited by the younger age group surveyed by Willis in Wolverhampton (1985). 'I live on the Manor. I'm unemployed. What is a video?'

It needs no ghost come from the grave to reveal that the overlapping categories of living on Income Support, whether at home or away and having children, placed young people into a reduced pattern of leisure activity and expenditure. They were poor not only materially but also in Townsend's sense of 'relative deprivation'.

> People are relatively deprived if they cannot obtain, at all or sufficiently, the conditions of life – that is, the diets, amenities, standards and services – which allow them to play the roles, participate in the relationships and follow the customary behaviour which is expected of them by virtue of their membership of society. If they lack or are denied resources to obtain access to these conditions of life and so fulfil membership of society they may be said to be in poverty. (1987, p. 100)

As stated, they spent more time watching television, saw their relatives more and went out less, although shopping more. 'It's bare existence,' as someone put it. This led to inevitable frustration: 'Ye could live on it if ye did nothin' else but if ye have nae social life it does your brain in. Usually Ah've got tae rely on folk takin' me oot an' sometimes Ah go "Fuck it!" and go oot an' get pissed 'cos Ah'm that pissed off.' For most, 'If I go out to the pub I don't drink, just sit there', although 'In a Giro week you can do a lot more things'. For most on benefit, 'I go out to the pub once a month, if I'm lucky, and sometimes it's not even that, just Christmas and birthdays.' Similarly with the stereotypically feminine activity of window-shopping (though several girls said they could not stand it), 'I can't afford to look so I don't bother.' 'It's not worth looking if you can't buy.' 'It right depresses me. I sit down and cry if I see things I want and I can't get.' Instead, 'I dream. I get my catalogues out and think when I've got money I'll get that and that.' All those who had rented on Income Support mentioned difficulties in first, getting a landlord to take them, especially finding the necessary deposit, and then, if they were accepted, getting Social Security to pay the rent on time or at all. Income Support, paid two weeks in arrears, unlike Supplementary Benefit, makes it extremely hard to obtain a tenancy. Although legally you can take on a tenancy at 16, many landlords refuse to let to young people. Landlords are also notoriously reluctant to take couples with young children or pregnant women and this also was reflected in interviews where 'hassles with landlords' were mentioned as one of the main difficulties connected with moving. Frequent moving from place to place also led to problems, not only with landlords: 'If ye've moved aboot a lot they'll no' give ye the hire o' a video or onythin'. The same if ye've no had a steady job.' For help and advice most said they would ask their parents or the CAB, while a few had learnt about specialist agencies, like Liverpool's Basement.

While there were no owner-occupiers on Income Support, there were some living in almost as reduced circumstances as their contemporaries on state benefits, and similar to young couples dependent upon a single low wage to bring up children, whether in council or private rented accommodation. Few wage earners could easily afford owner occupation and maintain a lifestyle similar to those other earners of their age who had returned to their parents. Even in Swindon, where average wages were highest (Graph 7), those couples on lower wages were barely keeping up with inflated mortgage payments and some of them must surely have joined those who had already lost their homes there. It was obviously easy to get into debt in these circumstances and debts incurred through incidental expenses, like solicitor's fees and furnishings, were a reason given by those who had lost their homes, while others rescheduled their mortgages in an attempt to hang on. The pressure to buy quickly to gain a toehold on the housing ladder before prices rose beyond them had put a number of interviewees in this situation. The young man in Swindon who had bought on his own and the one in Kirkcaldy whose fiancée quit the flat they bought together were both struggling. In Liverpool only 'the yuppie' (p. 65) was earning sufficient to afford to buy alone easily, although Nick (p. 68) reckoned that he and his girlfriend would manage just as well on his wages in their new house, sacrificing only a holiday to buy. Home owners were not the only people in debt however; indeed the person with the highest debts, of over £700 from a handful of hire-purchase cards, lived with her grandmother.

In sum, while there were a variety of individual experiences in the period of their life course covering the often prolonged transition to independent living, these can be generalized according to the lifestyles of individuals by sex, by whether they had children, were on Income Support, between those living independently and those earners who had returned to their parents. These divisions were related but not coincident with housing tenure. Someone in their own home on low or one wage with children could be living at this stage in their life course in circumstances as reduced as their contemporaries in council or privately rented accommodation. However, single mothers and anyone dependent upon state benefits clearly formed a particularly deprived group, whether they were council, private or housing association tenants or if they had returned to parents unable to support them financially. The proportions of the different groups varied by area. As Daksha's businessman father said to her, 'You're living in your own world here' (on a private estate of three- and four-bedroomed houses in Swindon). 'People in the Parks [Swindon's largest council estate] live the same as people in Liverpool and there are people in Liverpool living like us, only there are less of them.'

THE AREA EFFECT

Young people who leave school at the earliest age, as many interviewees had, are closely tied to their local labour market. With few exceptions, like some apprenticeships (e.g. footballing), induction into the armed forces, live-in hotel work and nannying (these last two requiring usually one additional year in FE at least), they do not have access to the national labour market for which students have often had to live away from their families to obtain the necessary higher-education qualifications. In the locality it is difficult to move primarily because initial wages are usually insufficient to enable independent living. 'In addition,' as has been seen, 'their family and peer group ties are strong' and, as Ashton, Maguire and Spilsbury go on to point out (1990, pp. 178–9), local labour markets are characterized by the relative size of the various segments comprising them and the discrepancy between 'the ensuing demand for labour at the local level and its supply'. This contrast was marked between Swindon and the other study areas, particularly Liverpool. The average earnings gradient for those who were employed in the four localities shows the economic contrast clearly (Graph 7). Ashton *et al.* suggest that such economic factors generate 'distinctive cultures within the local communities which create significant differences in attitude between populations of the respective local labour markets' (ibid.). One effect of this local culture has already been seen in the difference in self-ascribed class by area. Another was the attitudes to the locality shared by young people brought up there, including whether emigration was accepted as a norm. These influenced their willingness to leave or to stay.

Young Liverpudlians characteristically had most to say for and against their city with its falling and ageing population. Many shared the feeling, 'There's nothing for me here.' 'You've got to get out if you want to get anywhere.' 'It's just diabolical.' 'Bloody horrible, like New York.' 'You're just not safe; that's the worst thing . . . gay-bashing and coloured-bashing and accent-bashing – just if you come from a different place and you've got a different accent, 'cos they've got nothing else to do, no jobs, no clubs, nothing.' However, even this view of the place was tempered: 'I don't want to leave my family. The only thing that keeps me here is my family. I think every Scouse person is the same – they wouldn't stay but for their family.' Attitudes were thus ambivalent: 'I love the place but I'd never live here again. I only come back to visit. You see, when you leave the friends that you had they don't treat you the way they did before. Liverpudlians are very friendly people but they don't like deserters.' Then there was the South, which was not all attractive, if attractive at all: 'All my mates went to London but I couldn't go. It's just too big, too many people. They said there was loads of work there but they couldn't stay 'cos they couldn't get digs.' 'There's no jobs for anyone round here but I wouldn't think of moving down South. I've been offered jobs down there on building sites and that but I don't fancy it. I'd rather stay with my mum.' Others changed their attitude while they were away: 'I wasn't a great lover of Liverpool; I thought it was a city on its way out but when I was down there people came up to me saying how horrible it was and so I became defensive. I think it's not such a bad place now.' The South was not what it was cracked up to be: 'You miss your friends. You feel a bit strange. You wonder what it's all about. It's not much really. You find it's nothing really.' 'It's probably just as cold here but it seemed colder there. Plus I missed my parents and being at home. I mean, all my friends are here. There you'd go out to a club and not know anybody.' Others would not consider moving – except for a change, to travel and see the world but then come back. 'I think it's your attitude. If you keep your head straight in Liverpool you're all right.' 'I don't see why I should go away. It's where I live. It's not fair on me.'

In Swindon there was not the same necessity to move to find work, except for the higher sectors of the national labour market mentioned above. Daksha, one of the two Swindon students, realized: 'You've got to move if you want to study and get a career.' But most interviewees would not move for work unless they had to. It was housing rather than work which made young Swindonians think they might have to move out of the area. There was, as well, the attraction of the place in which you have been brought up: 'Once you know a place like I know this place you want to stay there.' This was added to by the combination of town and country, especially in the satellite towns and villages where 'you get the best of both worlds'. There was also a general feeling that things were getting better in Swindon, not only economically but in the number and variety of new facilities that were available. However, there could be too much development: 'They're building too many houses. One day we'll wake up and there'll be houses covering the fields and everywhere. There'll be houses in the park soon.' Socially 'there's more affluence but as a caring society we're going downhill' and George went on to compare the insidious effects with London where he was a student, so that 'Even down here people nowadays are not so willing to give you a helping hand. They're just concerned for themselves.' Perceptively he added,

> 'I think we're going towards a more market-orientated sort of thing, where owning your own house and two cars is the normal thing, but I can see environmental issues becoming more important and these two things are contradictory, though I think we're going to be led to believe they're not.'

Some young people in Swindon felt that the place was rather dull in terms of a social life, and one in four respondents to *The Swindon Under 25 Survey* said that 'Thamesdown is a boring place to live in' (Curphey and Grant, 1985, p. 25). This feeling was more marked in Kirkcaldy, which could be compared with nearby Edinburgh. 'There's only two discos in Kirkcaldy. One's really terrible an' the other's really terrible. There's a few pubs as well: one where aw the idiots go tae get drunk an' one full o' auld men wi' their dugs an' walkin' sticks under the tables.' So a number of interviewees were determined 'there's no way Ah'm stayin' the rest o' ma life up here'. 'It's OK for a wee quiet holiday but no tae live.' Others, in both Swindon and Kirkcaldy, seemed unconscious of this. Their idea of a club was the local social club and among their leisure activities they listed gardening and board games. Theirs was a country style of life centred around meeting family and friends in the local pub at weekends. And there was a reluctance to move to 'the big places, like Edinburgh an' Glasgow, or England'. They also realized it would be hard to find housing there, as Claire had discovered in Livingstone: 'If ye dinnae work there or come frae there ye're really strugglin'. I thought it wid be easy wi' ma auntie an' that there but I didnae really know the way it worked.' In addition there was an intense parochialism so that in Livingstone (only 30 miles away) 'Folk knew we werenae frae there so they were a wee bit stand-offish. They werenae too sure whether tae talk tae us. Tae them Fifers are teuchters [Highlanders].'

It was Sheffield where young people earning a fair wage had the best night life at their disposal. This was in contrast to Liverpool where, although there are more than a hundred night clubs (see Wood, 1990), many of them have lowered their prices so far as to be mainly patronized by school-age youngsters and so are no longer attractive to older people. In fact in terms of night life one young Liverpudlian reckoned the only good thing about Liverpool was that it was near Manchester! More interviewees were unambiguously positive about Sheffield than in any other area. Even if they wanted to move out of the particular part of Sheffield they were in, for instance to move from the Manor because they felt employers discriminated against job applicants from there, no one wanted to leave the city altogether, except to travel and return. (Even Ken, who aspired to move into the London music scene, planned to keep a base in Yorkshire.) They also shared apprehensions about the South: 'It's false.' 'Everyone's trying to impress each other.' 'Northerners are much more friendly.' 'Everyone's considered a lot more equal.' They also appreciated the South's housing problem, even though house prices were rising out of their range in Sheffield as well, with the result that 'It's very hard for young people here. Wages have stayed the same but houses prices haven't because of the Student Games.' The Games and 'all the building going on' had revived the economy however and, as in Swindon, made people more generally optimistic so that, even for those who were unemployed, 'It would take a lot to move me from round here 'cos I know a lot about Sheffield, where to go and that – all the short cuts.'

TYPES OF YOUNG HOME-LEAVER

'You always look at your mum's and dad's house as your home, as your real home.' Leaving it put virtually all young movers at an immediate material disadvantage. Even if they moved to seek employment, for a job or for higher wages, their living conditions and lifestyle invariably compared unfavourably with those at their parental home. It was only a very few who had nothing further to gain materially from living there and they had been more or less forcibly expelled (p. 94). The advantages of leaving home were not material but consisted in the almost unanimous agreement upon 'independence' and 'freedom' to 'be yourself'. 'You can go where you want when you want.' 'Eat what you want when you want.' 'Drink what you want and play loud music early in the morning.' 'Decorate how you like.' 'Leave your room in a mess if you want to.' 'There's nae naggin'.' Plus, 'Ye cannae take women back tae your mum an dad's hoose.'

Nearly all the young movers welcomed this new responsibility for 'something to call my own'. 'We just wanted our own place.' 'Responsibility is what changes you.' 'Having to grow up – I mean, having a baby and a house to look after.' 'Taking my own decisions' 'without consulting my parents' had given them experience they regarded as valuable, especially dealing with bills and budgeting. 'It made me realize I relied on my mum too much.' 'It made me grow up a lot.' 'It made me a lot more wise to a lot of things.' 'It gives you confidence. You realize what you're capable of.' 'You realize what a lot of crap people talk about going out into the big world and all that. You just take it in your stride.' Compared with others their own age, 'They wouldn't know what hit them.' 'They don't know how to stand on their own two feet.' 'The people I was at school with are still like big children, mollycoddled by their parents.' Especially those who had gone to higher education: 'Those students, they're not living in the real world.' In addition, some who had bought regarded their home as an investment which would repay their present privations. There were also physical advantages of moving from what were sometimes overcrowded conditions: 'Peace.' 'Privacy.' 'Not a load of kids running about all over the place.' 'Not listening to about three different types of music coming from three different directions.' So that, 'You don't have to queue for the bathroom in the morning' and 'Ye can watch what ye want on telly.'

All this was compensation for the disadvantages of moving which were 'in a word, money – the lack of it'. 'You have to spend on everything from food to toilet cleaner.' If lack of money was the major inhibitor upon moving, not only financial support was lost but other previously unappreciated services: 'There's naebody runnin' aroond behind ye'; 'Nobody to clean up after you.' Males particularly missed 'Things you took for granted you have to do yourself, like pick up a hoover.' Many therefore still brought their washing home – 'It's expected though; everybody does that.' Nor was it unusual to retain keys to the parental home. Meals, especially Sunday lunch, with their parents were also common and, although most said they did not mind doing their own cooking and cleaning, many missed 'home cooking'. Eight, who had moved out of the area, admitted to being homesick whilst away. They were nostalgic for the place they had come from as much as anything: 'Homesick for Liverpool', 'Where you knew everybody', so that 'Having a game of football with my mates, that's what I really missed.' Whereas, 'Moving away you had to start afresh and make new friends.' If there was too much pressure and sudden responsibility, 'Sometimes I just want to go off and forget everything and do my own thing, like when I was at home in my own room'. Then it was a case of 'sticking it out' or returning. (Compare Fisher's 1988 study of students, nearly a third of whom reported experiencing homesickness. She suggests elsewhere that 'homesickness affects 60 per cent of the population who leave home'.) For those who lived locally with parents coming round regularly, 'It's hardly like living away', especially if, as was often the case, they had not moved far. Even though 'Sharing with strangers is not all that nice at times', 'being on your own' was commonly the worst experience of moving: 'I miss company more than anything', 'just having someone to sit with'. Especially the young mums who were 'on [their] own with two kids all day'. For those living alone it was also harder to economize because 'Shopping for one is more expensive'.

Most felt moving from their parents permanently or temporarily was an important step to have taken – 'a big thing in my life definitely', though some took it as a matter of course: 'It didn't seem important at the time, just something we had to do.' Or, 'It wasn't exactly a big step 'cos it was just down the road.' For those who moved to work it could be 'important to start my career'. For those who moved to marry or cohabit, 'Getting our own house was the most important thing after the baby.'

Half the young movers considered their move had been successful in their own terms; even if they had subsequently moved back, they had no regrets for their actions and would not have done anything differently. Obviously many had mixed feelings, including those who realized they could not have done differently in the circumstances. ('I would have preferred a normal upbringing with my own mother and father' but, as someone else said, 'My mum would have to be a different person for things to have been different.') However, half of them would have done at least something differently if they had the chance again. Given the ethnographic approach to recording the life courses of the cases interviewed from the wider sample, this self-estimation provided the criterion for assessing the common patterns of different types of young home leaver which emerged from the interview cases.

Moving to marry or cohabit

As stated, the main reason for moving was to marry or cohabit. More often than not this was the young person's first serious relationship and, apart from a few who were school sweethearts, most met their partners soon after leaving school, 'going steady' for a year or more on average before the more or less formal commitment of engagement (see p. 93). Moving was facilitated if one partner was older (as was the case for most girls and some boys) and had savings or, better still, their own accommodation. Moving gradually into their partner's accommodation, staying at first odd nights and then for longer, afforded the most painless parting but the process could be speeded up by pregnancy (e.g. p. 40). The pressure to buy quickly also led to rushing into things, not saving sufficiently and preparing adequately so that debts were incurred and the home lost. For others, 'I just wish it had been a few years later so we could've saved to buy a house' (council tenant). Family factors in the lives of the older generation have also been seen to put pressure on children to leave: an impending divorce, remarriage, the arrival of new children or a grandparent coming to live in the family home, for instance. However these were not the primary reasons for leaving for those who moved to marry or cohabit, even if they accelerated their departure. Apart from those whose partnerships had dissolved and who had returned, about half of all movers for marriage/cohabitation expressed regrets about moving sooner than normal: 'I suppose I went ahead a bit early'; 'it happened a bit quicker than anticipated'; 'I would quite happily have stayed at home for a while longer'; '. . . for a wee bit longer.' Others 'would have done things differently – not walked out'; 'not gone so abruptly'; 'I would've planned and will next time'. To the extent that 'I would've changed quite a lot of things. Maybe not got married at all.' 'I wouldn't've gone.' Or, 'Ah wid have preferred tae get my ain place than move in wi' somebody else.' The rest were satisfied with their move, felt 'ready' for it and that they had not 'missed' anything by it: 'We found that we matured quicker than most people our age' (see p. 43). One 'would like to have bought earlier but couldn't afford it'.

Wallace (1987, p. 165) argued that the assumption of domestic responsibilities acts as a spur to the employment commitment of young men but depresses that of young women. In the '16–19' survey as a whole, as elsewhere, the preferred age for marriage was lower for females than males but for women the higher their educational performance the higher their preferred age of marriage. This relation did not hold for men, whose career plans were unaffected by marital considerations (Martens). In various ways, therefore, as Marsden *et al.* recorded for YTS trainees, 'unemployed' (and they could have added semi- and underemployed) girls 'retreat into the domestic role' (1990, p. 123). Certainly among all those interviewed who had moved to marry/cohabit, educational qualifications were lower than average and this had the usual relation to parental occupation and housing tenure, etc. Many had left school early or at the earliest legal age (Easter leavers in some cases). In so far as school leaving still marks the end of childhood (p. 6), these youngsters therefore assumed an 'adult' status sooner than others. Nobody who had left to marry/cohabit had passed A-level for instance, though there was one girl who had failed her A-levels (see also p. 54) and two with Scottish highers, as well as young men with higher technical qualifications. Half the women interviewed had moved to marry/cohabit while unemployed, employed part-time or had held a succession of semiskilled, low-paid jobs. This included all of those women with children. By contrast, all but one of the young married/cohabiting men were working at jobs that afforded wages on or above the average for their locality. In the exceptional unemployed case, his marriage had broken down, though he attributed loss of his job to marital difficulties rather than the reverse. For the others (equally divided between men and women) who had returned to their parental home after moving to marry or cohabit, the dissolution of their relationships had caused their move back, though in one case inability to find accommodation with her partner, or subsequently for herself and her child, had caused her to return and, as seen, the loss of the homes they had bought led to temporary separations from their partners in two Swindon cases (pp. 27–9). Compared to others their age, those who had moved to marry or cohabit did not see themselves as unusual or 'only a little bit earlier than most, I suppose'. Rather than peers, they often compared themselves with others in their family, particularly siblings, thus contributing to 'family traditions' (pp. 22 and 31). Marriers/cohabitees tended to be more home-centred (often of necessity) in their leisure activities and not to regret foreshortening their earlier independent social life (as above). Although most had moved to marry or cohabit with the support, if reserved at first, of their parent(s), where poor relations with parent(s) or step-parent had added to pressure to move, interviewees were more likely to express some regret at the earliness of their move but, as in other cases, their new living arrangements had often brought about an improvement in their relations with their parent(s), particularly with the birth of grandchildren.

Refugees

'Refugees' were movers whose primary reason for leaving their first home was parental pressure in whatever form. They include the two interviewees who had been in care, the two who were homeless and the one who had been fostered. With the exception of one who had fallen on her feet, refugees not surprisingly expressed regret for what had happened and wished they could have done differently, even if they realized this had been impossibly beyond their control. 'It would have been nice not to have people wanting me to move.' 'I would have preferred to have lived my young life more happily.' 'If I'd had my own way I wouldn't've left until I got married.' 'I would've preferred to have stayed until I was ready.' The two who had returned after being kicked out had nowhere else to go and were either planning to move again or were under evident parental pressure to do so. Refugees' family backgrounds were unhappy (divorce, alcoholism, mental illness and suicide were all mentioned) with consequences for their own education and employment prospects (e.g. pp. 53–4 and 71), though in one case (p. 89) her reaction had been to interest herself more in her chosen subject for higher study and the one fostered case was also a higher-education student. Lack of parental support made refugees the most vulnerable group of young home leavers. The resilience of these refugees from their own families, facing such experiences, was striking but then, as Dickens wrote in *Nicholas Nickleby*, 'elasticity of spirit is happily the lot of young persons, or the world would never be stocked with old ones'.

Pilgrims

The word 'pilgrims' is used here in its American or secular sense, though the echo of a quest – a rite of passage like the Aboriginal 'walkabout' – captures something of the shared experience of those who left voluntarily 'to see something of the world' or 'to do something with my life', if only 'to have something to look back on' 'when I settle down'. This could of course also apply to those who left for other reasons, particularly to work (see p. 112) but in addition to leaving of their own volition, which was their essential characteristic, pilgrims left for the sake of leaving. 'Independence', 'freedom' and 'experience' were the purpose of their move and not incidental advantages arising from it as they were for most others. They were also the most likely to return but, if they came back, they were often reluctant returners; 'If I'd found a nice place I would've stayed and not come back.' Such reluctant returners hoped to move again 'as soon as a place becomes vacant'.

Their relations with their parents had not always been happy, at least from their own point of view – they felt 'smothered': 'They still treat me like a little kid', or 'They've got such high standards that's why I don't like living with them', 'She's a heavy-duty Catholic'. But in every case their parents were glad to have them back and 'They said I was stupid to leave' or 'They begged me not to go'. As noted, in some cases where changes in parents' relationships, not only with each other but in/out of employment and with other members of their families, affected their children, it seemed that leaving had extricated children from a situation which 'I couldn't handle any more'. They had returned when things had sorted themselves out (e.g. pp. 65–6). However, in most cases pilgrims left for positive rather than negative reasons, if only 'for a change'. 'I needed a break.' 'I didn't want to go straight to college.' 'I needed time.' 'Maybe I should've gone to college straight away like most of my friends did but, having said that, I don't think you know what you want to do with your life at 18.' 'It did me a lot of good personally. It's all back to realizing what you're capable of and how you can manage on your own on the other side of the world.'

The educational qualifications of pilgrims were higher than for the other groups (with corresponding parental occupations and housing tenure). Three had obtained A-levels before leaving and others had begun if not completed sixth form or FE. Pilgrims had often changed the direction of their lives or at least their course of study, as in the case of Ken and Angus, who had left what were clearly inappropriate further-education courses. For others, their time away was part of their 'young years' that were 'over an' done wi'' so that 'Ah'll no move again until later when Ah get married'. Others again had moved too soon: 'I thought I was more grown up than I was.' They had learnt from their experience and would move again when they felt they were ready. 'I learnt a lot.' 'I'll do it differently next time.'

Migrants

If unemployment speeds leaving to work, especially for young men, it slows moving to marry or cohabit for males (as shown by the employment of nearly all those moving for that reason above) but speeds moving to marry or cohabit for females (also as above). These effects are sometimes mixed, as when an initial move to work led to a subsequent move to marry or cohabit, e.g. p. 62. (In this case also the girl's parents were divided over wanting their daughter to go: 'My mum said, "Get out while you've got the chance of a job to go to", but my dad wasn't very pleased'.) The plainest economic migration was, as with students moving from their locality to gain qualifications for access to national labour markets, 'to start my career' and in this case 'a job in a five-star hotel is the best start you could get'. Moving to a footballing apprenticeship or induction into the armed services, even though these turned out to be false starts, were clear cases of migration for particular employment not available locally. This was also the case with nannying, though this was part of the general lack of employment locally that drove people from the North to work in the South, including those with good educational qualifications who had secured well-paid office work in London. Migration for work, while it may be accepted as a reason for leaving home, is not therefore the unconstrained free choice to leave undertaken by pilgrims, but nor are migrants compelled to leave like refugees. 'There's no work here so you have to go away. It's quite normal.' The effect of economic compulsion as against free choice to move can be seen in the even division among migrants between those who regarded their move as a successful one and those who would rather have done differently.

The numbers in and proportions of those in these different groups, as well as the varying balance of men to women, alters at different ages, places and times (depending upon the local economy, state of the trade cycle, etc.). The majority moving to marry or cohabit, for instance, rises to a peak and then falls with age, and within that group the proportion of women to men peaks and falls with age earlier, more women moving sooner to marry or cohabit and more men moving later on average. Their division into marriers/cohabitees, pilgrims, refugees and migrants is no more than an aid to conceptualization of why social actors do what they do. As far as these are valid generalizations, the proportions between the majority of those moving to marry or cohabit and the roughly equal numbers of pilgrims, refugees and migrants were 3:1:1:1. However, these proportions only hold for young people of the ages and at the time of this study in the places it was undertaken. With the proviso also that the number of migrants is underestimated (since only those who returned from work away were interviewed), overall approximately half of the interviewees moved to marry/cohabit and the remainder divided nearly equally between those moving for the three other main reasons. In Swindon the then buoyant local economy enabled more marriers/cohabitees to move, although hampered by the high prices of the preferred private housing market and cost of borrowing for it. In contrast to the other areas, only one person had moved out of Swindon for work. Similarly, there was only one refugee in Swindon.

Single mothers, students, trainees and others

In addition to the four main types of young mover above there was a small group of single mothers, all of whom regretted their situation: 'I wanted to move then but I want to move back now.' 'I wouldn't have done it all.' 'If I had another chance I'd stay at school and get qualifications and get a decent job.' 'I would've preferred to have had a job and saved up before having a baby.' 'I wanted a nice steady job and then the kids to come along but it seems to have happened the other way round.' Three out of five were early school leavers, if not necessarily through their own choice (Halimah). By contrast, all those students and trainees interviewed were positive about their situation whatever its problems. Not only was such an institutional transition from home to independent living and from school to work endorsed by both the wider society and accepted by their family, it also offered, in the words of a student nurse 'the best o' both worlds'. Their experience and those of the pilgrims, who were also least likely to regret their decision to move, can be taken as the basis upon which to envisage a new transition from dependence to independence for young people in the future.

Finally, the construction of types, while it may aid description, of course omits those who cannot be fitted into any of the above. These include the small group whose parents moved, for instance, or those whose parents died and/or those who moved within their family. Lastly, Mike in Swindon was unique among such a young sample in buying his house on his own as 'a good stepping-stone for my future', although Steve ('the yuppie'), who left Liverpool initially as a pilgrim for a holiday job in London but then decided to stay as a migrant, later returned to his parents but was about to buy on his own when interviewed. He also illustrates the way one type may merge into another.

TOWARDS A NEW TRANSITION

Bound though it is by sclerotic class division, Britain is not immune from the accelerating changes affecting other countries of the developed world. These stem from the way new technology is being applied in a changing world-wide division of labour. Some of the implications of this unprecedentedly rapid and accelerating social change for young people and their families were outlined in Chapter 1. Although this study has shown the continuing importance of their family, including 'extended kin relationships', for young people starting out in life for whom the attractions of neighbourhood also remain strong, traditional communities have been eroded to the extent that childhood and youth are no longer integrated into stable local social networks reproducing class and gender divisions down the generations. Instead, youth is being extended by longer schooling and prolonged apprenticeship to flexible employment. The role of the state, and especially the education system, in this process of sustaining traditional divisions and creating new ones has been suggested by Offe (1984 and 1985). It is a process less negotiated by indigenous cultural forms and more regulated by the mass media, which rapidly appropriate such forms and feed them back as marketable styles, a process celebrated with his usual naïve romanticism and more than usual banality by Willis (1990). During this 'extended transition' or 'post-adolescence' young people are increasingly removed from direct control by adults in the family and at work. Hence the repeated populist authoritarian demands for a return to traditional disciplines and the attempt to force the new relationships back into the box of idealized nuclear family life, also for the return to some sort of compulsory 'national service'.

   Patterns of transition for the new generations basically continue to reproduce those of the old and thus remain fundamentally determined by class, gender and race. Leaving education at the legal minimum age, for instance, makes 'school leaver' and 'working class' virtually synonymous. However, one effect of the introduction of GCSE examinations (even though only designed for the top 60 per cent) has been to raise the age of selection from 14 to 16 for continuing education after 16. The distinction is thus blurred between previously separated O-level and CSE streams in state schools that sorted out the majority of 16-year-old school leavers from the academic remainder. It is predictable and, to an extent, already observable that instead of a parting of the ways at 14, with GCSE (and the Standard Assessment Tests, if they are introduced), there is now a two-year cooling out period in which those who cannot keep up with the course work for GCSE, like Glennis on p. 47, truant and leave. Leaving school early without any qualifications virtually confirms membership of the more or less ideologically constructed and socially manipulated 'underclass', unless the young person can find a 'good' job equivalent to skilled employment through word-of-mouth contacts, as Nick did, p. 68. Paradoxically, more early leaving through truancy also enables the pupils who remain in school to attain better examination results and thus to continue in education beyond the legal minimum. This corresponds to the pattern already established in Scotland, where pupils can legally leave earlier but where more also remain in education (see p. 76). Thus the numbers remaining in education after 16 in England and Wales rose beyond half for the first time at the end of the 1980s, despite the survival of the 'apprentice boy' model in Youth Training, which continued to encourage leaving at the earliest possible date to get places on 'good' schemes leading to employment. The result is a later transition for more young people from school to work and, associated with it through the income required, from parental home to independent living. Not that prolonged education and improved qualifications necessarily lead to security of employment. Even for the 'top 20 per cent' for whom higher-education qualifications guarantee access to careers in supervisory/administrative non-manual employment there is heightened insecurity. This is leading to greater dependence upon academic achievement as the means of reproducing superior status with greater resort by middle-class parents to private schooling as well as to the widening differentiation between schools that the Education Reform Act 1988 was designed to encourage. Meanwhile, the attempt to construct a vocationally relevant education for the rest of the school population has been abandoned. Remaining for further and higher education is encouraged by new forms of accreditation and access, although discouraged by the introduction of student loans to pay full course costs.

The normality and desirability of full-time general education for all to 18 and of recurring returns to learning full- and part-time thereafter for as many people as possible should be recognized and used to emphasize the assumption of full citizenship rights from 18, as they are confirmed by, for example, the US school-leaving 'prom'. As the Confederation of British Industry (1989) has already proposed in its *Towards a Skills Revolution*, no one under 18 should be employed without the integration of continuing education and training in their work but the onus should be on employers to pay for this, not on young people to find training or pay for it through vouchers or credits. This should prevent employers, especially the small employers who are the main culprits, from encouraging young people to leave school at the earliest opportunity. Access to training for 'good' jobs 'with prospects' must remain open beyond 16. This is the single most effective way of ensuring more young people remain in full-time education and do not leave in hopes of getting one of the few remaining skilled jobs still available locally. As it is, the rise in staying on is mainly caused by young women taking courses for the further qualifications now necessary for access to many office jobs. More people (adult and young) are also training and retraining full- and part-time, adding to new patterns of intermittent employment for the majority. In addition, the discontinuities of the housing and employment markets, as well as between the depressed regions and the more buoyant areas of the economy, entail more migration by more people for work.

Given the above, and on the basis of the types of young home leaver that have been distinguished, it is easy to predict that the numbers of young people leaving to marry or cohabit will continue to fall while the numbers of migrants will rise. More tendentiously, it can also be claimed that the proportions of pilgrims and refugees will grow. If the former, as in this study, come from the relatively advantaged and more educated youth, the latter will come mainly from families disintegrating under the pressures of poverty and unemployment. While both types of young home-mover, and migrants also, are therefore placed in new situations, provision for them, while recognizing Erikson's conception of youth as a developmental stage of exploration, should avoid, as Jones and Wallace cautioned, extending to working-class youth 'models of transition to adulthood currently prevalent among the middle class. For young people who lack financial resources, this will represent not embourgeoisement, but a hollow sham of middle-class practices' (1990, p. 153). This contributes to the new cultures of inclusion and exclusion which young people are moving towards in the age of the single European market and what ex-Premier Heath called 'the new imperialism' of a single superpower (BBC1, 7.2.1991).

Rather, variety of provision is needed to meet the new variety of experience.

For housing, this requires cheap furnished and unfurnished rented properties provided for young singles and couples as part of a national programme of house building and refurbishment. The example of Denmark, where public housing is still built, could be followed so that all new public building schemes are required to include single-person units, for the old and the young, integrated with other types of housing provision. Self-build and cooperative housing are also to be encouraged and, while they cannot be the solution for everyone, should play a part in the regional regeneration needed for balanced economic development to improve conditions and use the skills of residents in the depressed areas and inner cities. More special hostel accommodation for young people is also required, particularly for migrants and refugees, including supported, semi-supported and shared facilities, and directed access emergency accommodation. For refugees, most large cities now have specialist refuges for young people, like the hostel in Sheffield visited by the councillor from Swindon (p. 19), though typically these are underfunded and overstretched. Some serve special groups, such as Asian girls, or as in the case of east London's long-running Kipper Project for Bangladeshi youth. For migrants, Knowsley Borough Careers Service runs a 'Working away from home' scheme, which, while it does not aim to encourage migration from the area to work in the South, recognizes that in the absence of any regional policy for local economic development this will continue to occur and that, as in this study, many of the young people who move for work will return after unsatisfactory experiences. A careers officer therefore endeavours to provide preparatory guidance and supported visits to young people moving out of the area for employment. The new transition is extending and so the aim should be to support it rather than attempt to curtail or redirect it. If young people return and leave their parental home a number of times over several years, helping them to do so will not only provide for them 'the best of both worlds' but also relieve pressure upon their parents and families. As stated, young people's benefit rights must also be restored to improve their position in the labour as well as the housing market.

In a wider context, rapid historical and even climatic change pose problems for society that can only be solved by calling upon the energy and imagination of youth. It is a commonplace to note the ageing of the developed countries. The world population as a whole is growing younger, however, and the old cannot continue to dominate the young, dictating to them patterns of development that are driving only to destruction. While young people are often avid consumers, they are also idealistic and have their futures to protect. The world is theirs, as well as ours, but in the last analysis, it is theirs. It has been seen how ready ordinary young people are to take on responsibilities (p. 108) but also how modest are the aspirations of most young people (p. 70). If even these limited ambitions are to be fulfilled in the future, profound changes in society and in its relations with the rest of the human and natural world will be necessary. In this context the widening transition for youth might provide the space for responsible social and environmental action by young people, very different from the National Service of the past or the voluntary schemes canvassed at present.

Meanwhile, this was how 86 young people started out in life in Kirkcaldy, Liverpool, Sheffield and Swindon in 1989–90.

A Statistical Afterword

Sheena Ashford

To what extent do the young leavers presented here differ from other young people? Are they unusual not only in their early departure from home but in other respects as well? Or are they typical of the vast majority of young people who will almost invariably have left home by the age of 25?

Using the data provided by all the '16–19' questionnaire returns, young leavers as a group can be contrasted with other young people who have never left home to gain a clearer perspective of the characteristics of youngsters who left home in their teens.

Of the 2493 young people for whom records are available for all three waves of the survey, 663 or 27 per cent lived away from home at some point during the survey period. Just over a third of these (10 per cent) have gone back to live at home by wave three, while the remainder (17 per cent) were still living away. Some of these may have gone home for a period and left again by the time of the third sweep of the survey, so that numbers of returners, who leave home and then go back, are likely to be higher in reality than is suggested by these figures.

Age affects moving, as has been seen. The older cohort in the survey was two years older than the younger cohort. These two years are important ones for young people leaving home, and the figures show that young people who have not moved away are much more likely to be in the younger cohort – twice as likely in fact.

Who, then, are these youngsters who leave home so precipitately? By the time of the third questionnaire when they were aged from 19 to 21, they were as likely to be males as to be females, but more likely to be in a full-time job or on the dole than to be doing anything else, with, of course, the exception of students. Even so, having a job does not by itself lead young people to leave home: far more young people who have a job remain living with their parents than opt to move out.

For some, leaving home is an inevitable part of the relocation involved in beginning a course of higher education. But what of the others? For them, leaving home may reflect a complicated combination of 'pushes' and 'pulls' rather than a single event. Among other factors, becoming economically independent, establishing a stable relationship, domestic disharmony, responding to cultural expectations and the availability of accommodation may all help to 'prime' young people for leaving the parental home. However, the questionnaire returns show that no one of these conditions is strictly necessary for young people's decision to leave. Moreover, any

Table 1   *Current labour market status and patterns of leaving home*

	At parental home, W2&W3 %	Away from home, W2&W3 %	Moved away by W3 %	Moved back by W3 %	Total %	Number
Wave 2 Status						
Unemployed	66	10	8	16	100	171
YTS	82	2	5	12	101	314
At school	85	1	5	8	99	599
6th form coll.	79	3	6	11	99	237
Univy/poly	24	44	27	5	100	175
F-t job	76	5	10	8	99	754
P-t job	58	8	19	15	100	79
Wave 3 Status						
Unemployed	66	10	9	15	100	137
YTS	80	3	6	11	100	229
F-t education	89	1	2	8	100	415
P-t education	84	3	5	8	100	191
Univy/poly	15	40	41	3	99	204
F-t job	78	3	7	11	99	1043
P-t job	69	11	8	12	100	75
At home	39	35	15	11	100	26
Wave 2 Income, £ per week						
0–17	83	2	5	9	99	591
18–26	77	2	10	11	100	319
27–40	76	5	8	11	100	515
41–60	58	16	13	12	99	372
61+	70	9	12	9	100	699
Wave 3 Income, £ per week						
0–17	83	3	7	8	101	396
18–26	82	2	5	11	100	203
27–40	73	7	8	12	100	401
41–60	59	15	16	11	101	358
61+	73	7	10	10	100	1135
Wave 2 Family circumstances						
Single	75	6	9	10	100	2259
Engaged	58	13	22	7	100	145
Married/cohab.	44	31	12	13	100	52
No children	74	6	10	10	100	2396
Expect a baby	38	8	31	23	100	13
Have children	36	41	18	5	100	44
Wave 3 Family circumstances						
Single	75	6	9	10	100	2103
Engaged	65	9	13	13	100	278
Married/cohab.	53	18	14	14	99	92
No children	74	6	10	10	100	2413
Expect a baby	59	19	9	13	100	32
Have children	48	31	15	6	100	71
Sex						
Males	73	8	10	10	101	1386
Females	74	6	9	10	99	1107

Table 1 *(Cont.)*

	At parental home, W2&W3 %	Away from home, W2&W3 %	Moved away by W3 %	Moved back by W3 %	Total %	Number
Age						
Cohort I	61	14	16	9	100	1044
Cohort II	82	2	5	11	100	1449
Region						
Swindon	71	7	12	10	100	444
Sheffield	75	7	9	10	101	552
Liverpool	77	7	7	9	100	432
Kirkcaldy	71	8	11	11	101	548

one of them may prove to be the deciding factor that finally tips the balance in favour of leaving among young people already 'prepared' to leave.

Table 1 shows that, students apart, leaving home was most likely among the unemployed and those who had a job. Leaving was least likely among young people who had yet to complete their education or training, i.e. those on YTS, or who were still at school, in further education or at sixth-form college. Income plays its part also, with young people in the higher income brackets more likely to have left home than those with the lowest incomes.

Young people who were in stable relationships, i.e. those who were engaged or married, were more likely to be living away from home than were young people who described themselves as single. Especially likely to live away from parents were young people who were married, but even so around half of those who described themselves as married still lived with their parents and around 14 per cent of married respondents had returned to live with parents by the time of the final survey after a period living away. Those who described themselves as engaged were more likely to live away from home than people who described themselves as single, but were less likely to live away from home than individuals who described themselves as married or cohabiting. So being in a stable relationship predisposed respondents to leave the parental home, but was not a critical/decisive factor in the home-leaving process for a substantial proportion of young people.

Like marriage/cohabitation, parenthood is not a particularly decisive event in the development of young people's housing careers. Three-quarters of respondents who had no children lived at home with parents, while nearly two-thirds (64 per cent) of young people with children had moved away. The fact that a similar number of young parents-to-be also lived away from their parental home suggests that the decision to live away was taken either before or during pregnancy rather than after the baby's arrival. The proportions of young parents who were living with their own parents was, if anything, slightly higher among wave three respondents (but note that different questions were asked, which mean that the figures are not directly comparable).

By the time of the wave three returns, girls were no more likely to leave home than were boys, nor were they any more likely to return home after leaving. Age, on the other hand, made an important difference to the numbers in the sample who no longer lived with their parents. Over eight out of ten (82 per cent) of the younger cohort had never lived away, compared to only six out of ten (61 per cent) of the older cohort. Furthermore, moving away among the younger cohort was proportionately much more likely to lead to moving back home, at least temporarily, at a later date: of the 18 per cent who had left home, over half had returned to their parents by the third wave of the survey, compared to less than a quarter of the movers in the older cohort. Patterns varied by area: Swindon and Kirkcaldy had the highest proportion of young people leaving home overall in the age range 16–21. But the young movers in these two regions were more likely than movers in Sheffield and Liverpool to have remained with their parents until wave three and left after they were 19–21.

Where do young people go when they leave the parental home? The shortage of suitable accommodation has been extensively reported and is underlined by many of the interview accounts. The biggest single group – a third (32 per cent) of all young people living away from their parents at wave three – did not have a home of their own in the form of a rented or 'bought' flat or house but instead were living with relatives. The 'hidden homeless' are hidden not only by parents whom they wish to leave but by relatives as well. This corroborates the large part played by relatives in the housing arrangements of many of the interviewees. Only four out of ten (40 per cent) questionnaire respondents who reported living away from parents had managed to rent or buy a house or flat, with a further 8 per cent living in digs. Of the remainder, 9 per cent were renting with friends, 8 per cent were in 'student' accommodation (although students were specifically excluded from this breakdown), and a final 2 per cent were living with friends.

Who lives where? Do girls who leave home end up in the same sort of accommodation as boys? Do married leavers and those with children have the same accommodation as the single who live away? Are the better-off leavers more likely to be found in a house or flat of their own than the poorer leavers?

Girls who had left home by wave three were most commonly found to be living independently (45 per cent), i.e. to have a house or flat which they personally owned or rented. A little over a quarter (28 per cent) were living with relatives, and the rest were living variously with friends, in lodgings, or in student accommodation. Boys, on the other hand, were primarily living with relatives (41 per cent), with just over a quarter (29 per cent) renting or buying a house or flat.

Girls were more likely to be engaged or married by this point, and this goes some way to explaining why girls rather than boys were more likely to have independent accommodation and were less dependent on relatives. The figures show clearly that young single leavers were much more likely to have moved in with relatives than to be in any other living arrangement. On the other hand, for the majority of young people, being engaged or, especially, married or cohabiting meant having a place of their own, either rented or bought.

Young people who had already had a baby were, like the married and the 'nearly married', very likely (87 per cent) to be living independently, away from relatives and friends. Very few young people in the sample were expecting a baby at the time of the survey, but the high proportion (75 per cent) of this group who lived in a house or flat they owned or rented suggests that the move to independent accommodation probably took place before the baby's arrival rather than afterwards.

The next set of figures, in Table 2, shows where young leavers from the four different regions were living at the time of the third sweep of the survey. The variations in the proportions of young leavers who had moved in with relatives is particularly striking: only 17 per cent of young people in Swindon who had left home

Table 2 *Where young people were living at wave three of the survey by gender, by marital status, by parental status*

	Relatives %	Rent with/ home of friends %	Student accomm. %	Rented house %	Digs %	Bought house %	Total %	Number
Girls	28	11	8	27	7	18	99	153
Boys	41	13	8	23	9	6	100	78
Single	45	13	10	15	11	7	101	148
Engaged	12	14	6	36	4	29	101	52
Married	7	0	4	64	0	25	100	28
No children	37	13	9	18	8	15	100	200
Expect a baby	12	0	0	75	12	0	99	8
Have a baby	6	0	3	77	3	10	99	31
Swindon	17	8	11	21	9	34	100	53
Sheffield	32	16	7	25	7	13	100	60
Liverpool	43	10	0	31	8	8	100	49
Kirkcaldy	38	12	13	27	7	3	100	69
Income, £ per week								
0–17	53	6	3	20	13	3	98	30
18–26	44	22	0	22	11	0	99	9
27–40	39	14	0	31	8	8	100	36
41–60	23	12	15	41	6	3	100	34
61+	27	12	11	22	7	22	101	122

were living with relatives by sweep three, but over twice as many leavers in Sheffield (32 per cent), in Kirkcaldy (38 per cent) and above all in Liverpool (43 per cent) were to be found in the homes of relatives. These variations cannot easily be accounted for in terms of regional differences in marital and parental status, and the question remains as to why young people in Liverpool were so much more likely to leave their parents' home to live with a relative. Part of the answer is likely to be money, or rather the lack of it. The bottom section of Table 2 shows that as income increased, the proportion of young people living with relatives dropped so that while over half (53 per cent) of all those with very small incomes (less than £17 per week) who had left the parental home had moved in with relatives, only a quarter (27 per cent) of those in the highest income bracket (over £61 per week) had done so. Similarly, compared to leavers with the poorest incomes, over twice as many young people in the highest income band were living independently in a rented or bought house or flat. This tendency was especially marked in Swindon.

What, in the end, prompts young people to leave home, and prompts some young people to leave home earlier than others? Although young people were more likely to live away if they had jobs or were unemployed, if they were married or living as married, if they had children, and if they had more rather than less money, these transitions – to wage earner, to partner, to parent – were not invariably accompanied by a move away from the parental home and the beginning of independent living. A large proportion of young people married, with children, or earning a wage were still at home with their parents by wave three of the survey. Given the lack of and cost of accommodation locally this is unlikely to have been from choice. Indeed, the large number of young people who moved in with relatives gives support to this supposition. Nevertheless, judging by the substantial proportion of leavers who were not

Table 3   *Young people's attitudes to leaving home*

	Agree %	Uncertain %	Disagree %
Better to have your own place if you've got the money			
Live with parents	88	90	93
Live away	12	10	7
Total	100	100	100
Number	(1334)	(485)	(396)
People are better off living with their parents			
Live with parents	91	89	87
Live away	9	11	13
Total	100	100	100
Number	(911)	(732)	(571)
Feel my parents treat me like a child when I'm at home			
Live with parents	92	85	90
Live away	8	15	10
Total	100	100	100
Number	(575)	(627)	(1016)

living independently, having a place of one's own was clearly not the reason why many young people had left home. Are there, then, along with the desire and means for an independent living which 'pull' young people out of the parental home, other factors which 'push' them to leave? Personal relationships seem an obvious candidate – other things being equal, young people would appear more likely to want to leave home if their relations with their parents were poor than if household members got on well. The significance of personal relationships in young people's decisions to leave home cannot easily be represented accurately by questionnaire items and any attempt to probe this domain by means of a questionnaire should be treated with caution. However, weak though questionnaire items may be, they do at least provide a crude indication of possible sources of family dissent and a valuable background against which to set data from in-depth interviews.

Table 3 shows the proportion of young people who agreed or disagreed with four statements expressing feelings about living with parents or away from home. Young people who were living away from home at wave three of the survey by and large tended to express more positive views about living away from their parents than young people who were still living in the parental home. Because of the static nature of the data, it is not possible to say whether attitudes fuelled the choice to leave or stay or whether the leaving experience brought about a change of attitude. However, it is clear that in all four areas, feelings about the relationship with parents showed only a small difference between young people who were living away from home and young people who were not.

The survey did not provide information about young people's family background and so it was not possible to separate young people with parents living together from those whose parents were separated. Information was obtained about step-parents, but using step-parents as an indicator of family instability necessarily underestimates the percentage of the sample who came from broken homes, since not all those who separate remarry. Furthermore, the children of such families usually remain with their mothers, who are in turn less likely than fathers to remarry. Figures on the

Table 4   *Proportions of young people who did or did not have a step-parent and who had left home*

	Have a step-parent %	Do not have a step-parent %
Live with parents	87	90
Live away	13	10
Total	100	100
Number	(203)	(2000)

proportion of young people who did or did not have a step-parent and were living away from the parental home are given in Table 4. Young people who had a step-parent were some 30 per cent more likely than those who did not have a step-parent to be found living away from the parental home by wave three of the survey. This suggests that family troubles may well have played some part in encouraging young people to find a place of their own to live. The role played by family troubles is more amply conveyed in the interviews.

This book has presented two pictures of young people in the 16–21 age group who have left home on a permanent or semi-permanent basis. Each has its own focus, and each portrays the early home leavers slightly differently. Which portrait best reflects the characteristics of the 'typical' young leaver? The answer is both and neither. Any attempt to produce a statistical portrait of young people who have left home in their teen years must encounter nearly as many difficulties in making the picture represent-ative as finding a set of cases to interview. Changes of address are inevitably more common, and this, combined with changes in civil status, can make the tracking down process lengthy and the contact rate in the second and third years relatively low. Further complications arise when attempts are made to identify young people who have left their parents' home and to compare them with those who have remained with their parents. The home-leaving process is not an abrupt one; many young people leave home only to return for varying periods soon afterwards, before making their final departure. The gradual nature of the leaving experience is an important feature of young people's move towards independence and is one that could easily be lost to any attempt to look at the transition to residential independence by means of a one-stop survey. At any one time, young people may variously be living with parents but have already spent some time away, living away for a short spell before returning home, or living entirely independently of parents. In many ways, of course, and in many cases young people never come to live a life that is fully independent, and parents continue to be a source of financial and emotional support long after young people have established residence elsewhere. What begins initially as an act becomes a process, and only an in-depth approach can furnish the detailed histories without which young people leaving home can become so easily lost from sight.

Appendix 1

Letter Sent to All Respondents

date

Full Name,
Address.

Dear First Name,

Last year you helped us with an important national survey by filling in a questionnaire for the '16–19 Initiative'.

I am especially interested in people in the survey who are (or were) not living with their parents. According to our records you are (or were) in this situation. I will check this with you if I may and if it is the case I would very much like to come and see you to talk about your situation.

I will be in Kirkcaldy/Liverpool/Sheffield/Swindon during April/ from January 22nd until Easter/ from October 2nd until Christmas/ from July 9th to the 21st and I would like to phone or contact you during that time to arrange an interview at your convenience. It will not take more than an hour of your time and can be anywhere that suits you.

I should emphasize that the interview will be strictly confidential and that I have no connection with the housing authorities, social security or any other local or national government department. I hope that it will help to make known the needs of people like yourself in your area.

I look forward to meeting you.

Yours faithfully,

(Pat Ainley)

Questionnaire

Name   Age

Education (date of starting and leaving all courses at school, sixth form, FE, HE, adult education, YTS if not employer-based; qualifications obtained; reasons for leaving):

_____

_____

_____

_____

_____

_____

Employment (dates of and reasons for leaving all employment full- or part-time with pay, including any periods of unemployment, whether claiming benefit or not, and employer-based YTS or apprenticeship, together with CP/ET or other government schemes):

_____

_____

_____

_____

_____

_____

Was there a trades union in any employment? Which one? Were you a member? Reason for choosing/not choosing that union:

_____

_____

_____

Housing (dates of leaving and returning to first and subsequent homes):

_____

_____

_____

Relationships (dates when starting regular dating, courtship, engagement, marriage/cohabitation, divorce/separation, children born):

_____

_____

_____

Other important events that have happened to you or your family:

_____

_____

_____

Any illness causing over two weeks off work or study:

_____

_____

Holidays since 1985: where to? how long? who with?

_____

_____

_____

_____

_____

_____

Type of tenure in present accommodation:

_____

Number of rooms and facilities

_____

Number of people sharing

_____

Their ages, occupations and relations to interviewee

_____

_____

_____

Previous residence(s)

_____
_____
_____
_____
_____
_____

Place of birth (how long lived in locality if not born there)

_____

Housing benefit or other help with housing costs from any source

_____
_____

Dates of and reasons for leaving each accommodation

_____
_____
_____
_____
_____
_____

Distance moved

_____

Help with moving

_____

Problems encountered

_____
_____

Availability of housing

_____

Any advice with housing (Who could you go to for such advice?)

_____

_____

Whose idea was it to move?

_____

Parents' attitude

_____

Advantages of moving

_____

_____

Disadvantages of moving

_____

_____

Where is your home now?/ Have you left home or are you just living away?/ Have you settled down (in your own home)?

_____

_____

_____

_____

How important was it to you to move?

_____

_____

Return to parents or other relatives – from reside occasionally to often (with dates) – but see below amount of time spent with family

_____

_____

_____

_____

Contact with parents/relatives (by visit/phone/letter per week/month/year/ at weddings and funerals/ Christmas/ never)

_____

_____

_____

How do you think your experience of moving compares with other people your age, those you know and those you don't (including siblings and other relatives)? do you think it is 'normal' or 'different'? would you have preferred to have done things differently?

_____

_____

_____

_____

_____

_____

_____

Means and costs of transport: _____

Amount of time spent on: housework/ cooking _____

DIY	_____	with friends	_____
gardening	_____	with boy/girlfriend	_____
shopping	_____	with family (including in-laws/boy/girl-
clubs/pubs	_____	friend's family)	_____
restaurants/cafes	_____	watching television	_____
cinema	_____	watching video	_____
theatre	_____	computer	_____
sports	_____	telephone	_____
board games/cards	_____	playing/listening to music	_____
betting shop/arcade	_____	reading	_____
bingo	_____	hobbies	_____
parties	_____	pets	_____

Smoker/non-smoker

_____

Estimate total amount spent on leisure activities (including smoking) in one week:

_____

Savings?

_____

Debts?

_____

Do you prefer to be called a teenager/youth/young person/young adult/adult?

_____

Occupation: do you think of yourself as a carpenter, student, housewife, etc. since this is your main occupation or what you are training for/working towards?

_____

Do you belong to any [subcultural] group, as e.g. casual/ordinary, soulboy/girl, skin, punk, metal, mod, acid, romantic, etc.?

_____

Would you call yourself middle class, working class or any other class, or do you not think of yourself like that?

_____

Do you identify with or support any political party, organized pressure group or campaign, belong to a church, ethnic or faith community?

_____

Have you voted in any election local or national? If so what did you vote? Will you do so again?

_____

What newspaper do you read, regularly or irregularly?

_____

What are your plans as regards education/training, work, housing and a family?

_____

_____

_____

Do these entail moving out of the area, including for emigration or travel?

_____

Are you confident you will be able to achieve these personal goals?

_____

Do you think things in general are getting better or worse? how do you see yourself in five, ten, fifteen . . . years time?

_____

_____

_____

Miscellaneous:

_____

_____

_____

Appendix 3

Occupations and Educational Qualifications of Interviewees and Occupations of their Parents/ Guardians

(Owner-occupiers starred*)

Father, mother	Self	Ed. Quals
Kirkcaldy, Females		
Process worker, care asst	U/e	—
*Rigger, telephonist	Secretary	6 Ord.
U/e, housewife	School student	5H, 8 Ord.
*Blacksmith, p-t cleaner	Student nurse	4H, 8 Ord.
*Labourer, secretary	Lab. asst	3H, 8 Ord.
*Turner, assembler	Assembler	4 Ord.
U/e, housewife	Housewife	7 Ord.
Foreman, 'lollipop lady'	*Wages clerk	2 Ord.
*Plumber, housewife	P-t shop asst	1 Ord.
Retired postman, retired nurse	Sick	1 Ord.
Retired roofer, retired	P-t market stall	1 Ord.
U/e, u/e	Housewife	—
Kirkcaldy, Males		
Glass enamel sprayer, cleaner	Labourer	7 Ord.
—, barmaid	Bar	C&G
*TV engineer, domestic help	Sick	5 Ord., ONC, HNC
Bricklayer, bar manager	ET	3H, 8 Ord., HND
*Plumber, p-t cleaner/hairdresser	HNC trainee	3H, 8 Ord.
Unemployed, —	U/e	8 Ord., 3 O-levels
Stocktaker, p-t shop asst	Appt paper factory	3H, 8 Ord.
*Asst director KDC, businesswoman	*Clerical officer	4 Ord., HNC
*Roads dept KDC, housewife	*Machine operator	3 Ord.
Fishmonger, social worker	*Clerical asst	7 Ord.
Labourer, housewife	ET	—
Liverpool, Females		
*—, teacher	Nanny	2A, 1 O-level, 2CSE
Chip shop proprietors	U/e	5CSE
*Police insp, driving instructor	Temp. sec.	2 O-levels, 5CSE

Father, mother	Self	Ed. Quals
Kirkcaldy, Females		
*Retired caretaker, cleaner	Housewife	—
*Docker, assembler	Cashier	5 O-levels
*—, p-t barmaid	Student	3A, 8 O-levels, 3CSE
Driver, bar steward	(*)Student nurse	10 O-levels, RSA
*U/e, nurse	U/e	3 O-levels, 4CSE
Gardener, care asst	U/e	5CSE
—, —	Student	3 O-levels
*Ed.Welfare Off., teacher	Hotel recept	Dip. + RSA
U/e, u/e	Care asst	—
U/e, u/e	Sec./recept	7CSE + RSA
*Redundant docker, p-t cleaner	P-t residential social worker	8CSE
—, p-t cleaner	P-t bar	2CSE
Engineer, housewife	P-t army cadet instructor	—
Liverpool, Males		
*Brewery insp, cashier	*Financial consultant	5 O-levels
Publicans	U/e	7CSE
*Butcher, clerical	U/e	2A, 2 O-levels
Lorry driver, cleaner	Trainee engineer	C&G
BT engineer, housewife	Temp packer	—
—, u/e	U/e	—
Fitter/welder, p-t kitchen asst	*Trainee fitter/welder	—
Sheffield, Females		
Steel fabricator, p-t home help	Housewife	—
*Steel worker, shop asst	Hotel recep.	7CSE
*Landlord, housewife	Telesales	2A, 9 O-levels
*Teacher, housewife	*Housewife	3 O-levels, 4CSE
*—, nurse	Admin. officer	6 O-levels
Redundant steelworker, disabled	Student	2A, 8 O-levels
*BR engineer, recep.	Temp. sec.	2A, 8 O-levels
Builder, housewife	Housewife	—
*Retired steelworker, cleaner	(*)Sewing machinist	—
—, press operator	P-t cleaner	—
U/e, housewife	Housewife	—
—, housewife	Housewife	—
Sheffield, Males		
Garage, p-t cleaner	U/e	—
Toolmaker, secretary	U/e	—
*—, teacher	Student	1A, 4 O-levels
Asst cook, machine operator	U/e	—
*Electrician, school dinner lady	Autoelectrician	6CSE
*Carpenter, accountant	*Carpenter	2 O-levels, 5CSE
—, housewife	U/e	—
*Civil servant, social worker	U/e musician	4 O-levels
Swindon, Females		
Retired railway worker, oap	Temp sec.	1 O-level, 8CSE
Curator, housewife	Trainee manager	4 O-levels
*Fitter, housewife	Clerical asst	2GCSE
*Foundry serviceman, p-t cleaner	*Electronics factory	5CSE
*Salesman, office	(*)Key to disc operator	2CSE

Father, mother	Self	Ed. Quals
Van driver, p-t cleaner	(*)Warehouse	7CSE
*Businessman, businesswoman	Student	3A, 8 O-levels
*Lorry driver, housewife	*Housewife	5CSE
*Telephone engineer, secretary	*Telephonist	3 O-levels, 6CSE
*Retired railway worker, oap	Packer	5CSE
*Garage, office	Housewife	4CSE
Disabled, factory	Sick	8CSE

Swindon, Males

*Bricklayer, shop asst	Builder's merchant asst.	6CSE
*Lorry driver, lab. tech.	Building labourer	8CSE
*Fitter, spooler	*Glass operative	1 O-level, 8CSE
*Retired clerk, —	Trainee manager	1 O-level, 5CSE
*Fork-lift driver, office	*Produce foreman	1 O-level, 6CSE
*Taxi driver, office	Computer operator	2A, 5 O-levels
Retired builder, nurse	Roofer	—
*Site supervisor, p-t office	Student	2A, 4 O-levels

(*) = bought and lost home

Appendix 4

Sports and Recreations Undertaken by Interviewees

	Females	**Males**
Keep fit	3	10
Football – Play	1	15
Watch	3	5
Swimming	12	8
Snooker/pool	2	3
Darts	3	2
Aerobics	3	
Badminton	6	
Tennis	1	2
Squash	1	4
Weight training	1	6
Ice-skating	3	
Greyhounds	1	
Running/jogging	1	3
Hillwalking		2
Golf		5
Fishing		3

Plus jig saw puzzles, baby-sitting, word searches ('for hours'), voluntary work walking dogs, crosswords, indoor plants, knitting/sewing/tapestry, 'drinking at home', 'wig making – you could call it a hobby, it's so boring', toy and clothes making, amateur dramatics, Bible study + Scouts and Guides, 'I dream'.

Plus one each: climbing, watching boxing, microlight flying, cricket, watching water-polo, hockey, radio-controlled cars, 'collecting weird things from junk shops', collecting miniature cars, write poems and songs, 'supermarket trolley-racing'.

Pets: dog 12, cat 5, budgie 4, goldfish, snake.

Appendix 5

Young People Moving Out of the Survey Areas

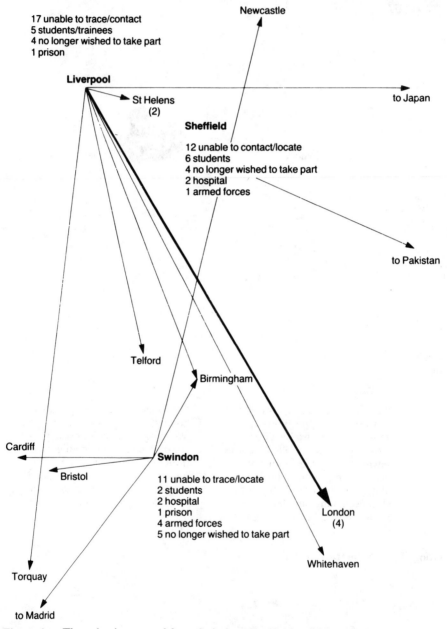

17 unable to trace/contact
5 students/trainees
4 no longer wished to take part
1 prison

Newcastle

Liverpool

St Helens
(2)

to Japan

Sheffield

12 unable to contact/locate
6 students
4 no longer wished to take part
2 hospital
1 armed forces

to Pakistan

Telford

Birmingham

Cardiff

Swindon

Bristol

11 unable to trace/locate
2 students
2 hospital
1 prison
4 armed forces
5 no longer wished to take part

London
(4)

Whitehaven

Torquay

to Madrid

Figure 1   Those having moved from Swindon, Sheffield and Liverpool.

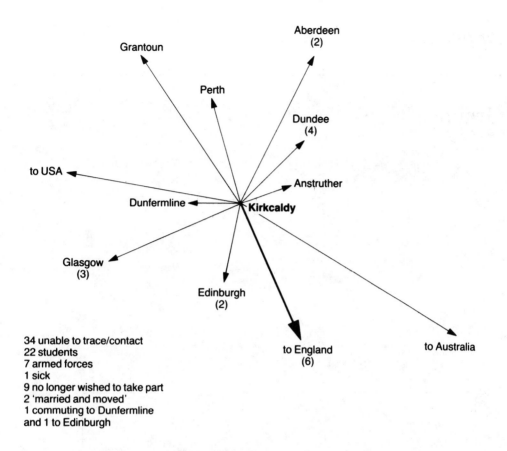

34 unable to trace/contact
22 students
7 armed forces
1 sick
9 no longer wished to take part
2 'married and moved'
1 commuting to Dunfermline
and 1 to Edinburgh

Figure 2   Those having moved from Kirkcaldy.

Appendix 6

Graphs

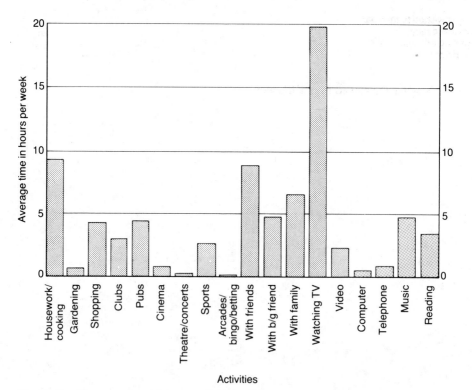

Graph 1   Young movers' leisure activities, all cases.

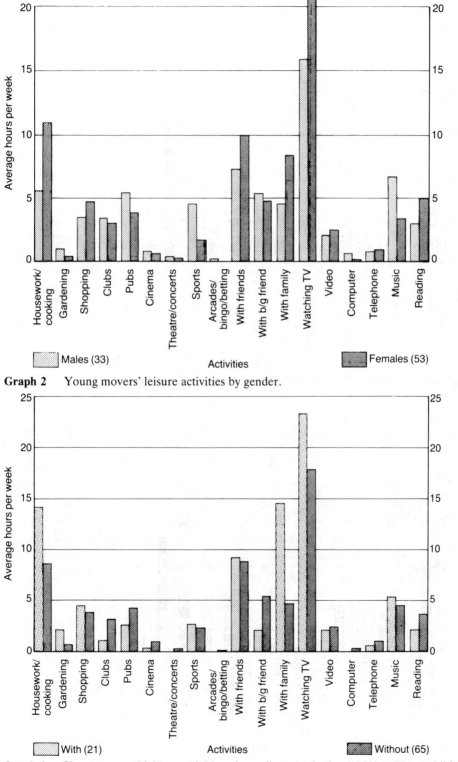

Graph 2   Young movers' leisure activities by gender.

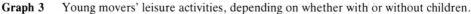

Graph 3   Young movers' leisure activities, depending on whether with or without children.

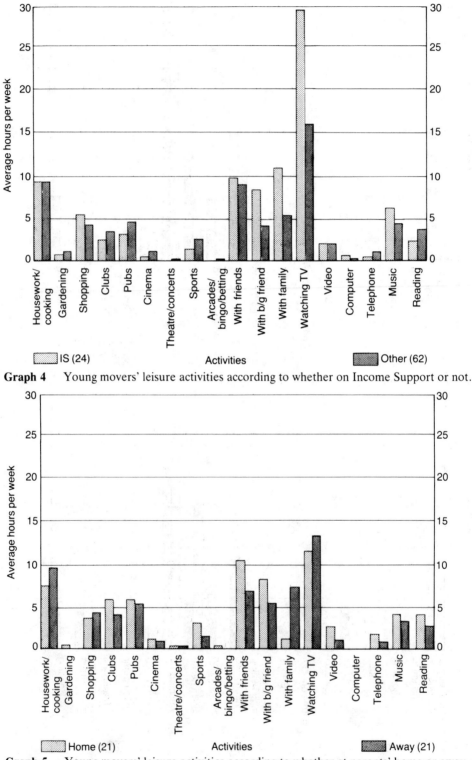

Graph 4   Young movers' leisure activities according to whether on Income Support or not.

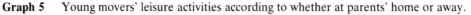

Graph 5   Young movers' leisure activities according to whether at parents' home or away.

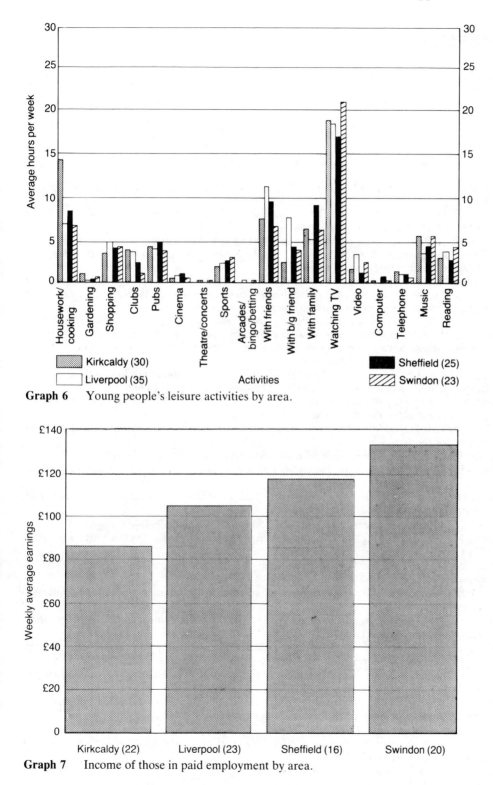

Graph 6   Young people's leisure activities by area.

Graph 7   Income of those in paid employment by area.

References

Adamski, V. and Grootings, P. (eds) (1989) *Youth, Education and Work in Europe*. London: Routledge.

Ainley, P. (1988) *From School to YTS: Education and Training in England and Wales 1944–87*. Milton Keynes: Open University Press.

Ainley, P. (1990) *Vocational Education and Training*. London: Cassell.

Ainley P. and Corney, M. (1990) *Training for the Future: The Rise and Fall of the Manpower Services Commission*. London: Cassell.

Aldrich, H., Cater, J., Jones, T. and McEvoy, D. (1981) 'Business development and self-segregation: Asian enterprises in three British cities'. In Peach, C., Robinson, V. and Smith, S. (eds.) *Ethnic Segregation in Cities*. London: Croom Helm.

Amin, S. (1990) *Delinking: Towards a Polycentric World*, trans. Wolfers, M. London: Zed Press.

Anderson, M. (1983) 'What is new about the modern family: an historical perspective'. In *The Family*, British Society for Population Studies Occasional Paper 31. London: Office of Population Censuses and Statistics.

Ashton, D. and Maguire, M. (1986) 'Young adults in the labour market'. Department of Employment Research Paper 55. London: Department of Employment.

Ashton, D., Maguire, M. and Spilsbury, M. (1990) *Restructuring the Youth Labour Market: The Implications for Youth*. London: Macmillan.

Ball, C. (1990) *More Means Different: Widening Access to Higher Education*. London: Royal Society for the Arts.

Banks, M. *et al.* (1991) *Careers and Identities*. Milton Keynes: Open University Press.

Bates, I. *et al.* (1991) *Ethnographic and Qualitative Studies from the 16–19 Initiative*. Milton Keynes: Open University Press.

Bazalgette, J. (1978) *School Life and Work Life: A Study of Transition in the Inner City*. London: Hutchinson.

Berger, B. (1963) 'Adolescence and Beyond'. *Social Problems* **10**, 294–408.

Bolton, J. (1989) 'Housing aid and homelessness services, note for Shelter visit'. Liverpool: City Council Housing Services and Homelessness Office.

Boyd, M. and Pryor, E. 'The cluttered nest: the living arrangements of young Canadian adults'. Montreal: *Canadian Journal of Sociology* **14** (4), 461–77.

Breakwell, G. (1987) 'ESRC young people in society: 16–19 Initiative'. Guildford: University of Surrey mimeo.

Brown, P. (1987) *Schooling Ordinary Kids: Inequality, Unemployment and the New Vocationalism*. London: Tavistock.

Bussue, L. and Drew, D. (1985) 'Sheffield's Black Population: Key Facts'. Sheffield: Sheffield City Polytechnic, Department of Applied Statistics and Operational Research Report.

Bynner, J. (1987) 'Transition to what? ESRC'S new 16–19 Initiative'. *ESRC Newsletter*, Swindon, November.

Bynner, J. (1989) 'The rise of open learning: a UK approach to work-related education and training'. London: City University Social Statistics Research Unit occasional paper.

Bynner, J. *et al.* (1990) *Youth and Work: Transition to Employment in Two European Countries; A Report for the Anglo-German Foundation for the Study of Industrial Society*. London: Anglo-German Foundation.

Carter, M. (1962) *Home, School and Work*. Oxford: Pergamon.

Caudill, M. and Weinstein, H. (1972) 'Maternal care and infant behaviour in Japan and America'. In Lavateli, C. and Stendler, F. (eds) *Readings in Child Behaviour and Development*. New York: Harcourt Brace.

Clough, E., Gray, J., Jones, B. and Pattie, C. (1989) *Youth Cohort Studies*. Sheffield: Manpower Services Commission/Training Commission/Training Agency/Department of Employment Research and Development publications.

Cobbett, W. (1966) *Rural Rides*. London: Everyman. (Originally published 1830.)

Coffield, F. *et al*. (1986) *Growing Up at the Margins: Young Adults in the North East*. Milton Keynes: Open University Press.

Cohen, P. (1986) *Rethinking the Youth Question*. London: Institute of Education Post-16 Centre.

Community Planning Committee, Thamesdown Borough Council (1984) *Young People in Thamesdown*. Swindon: Thamesdown Borough Council.

Confederation of British Industry (1989) *Towards a Skills Revolution*. London: CBI.

Connolly, M. and Torkington, N. (1990) 'Black youth and politics in Liverpool'. London: ESRC 16–19 Initiative Occasional Paper.

Corr, H., Jamieson, L. and Tomes, N. (1990) 'Parents and Talking Politics'. Edinburgh: University of Edinburgh Sociology Department unpublished paper.

Crow, G. and Allan, G. (1990) 'Emergence of the Modern British Home'. In Corr, H. and Jamieson, L. (eds) *The Politics of Everyday Life: Continuity and Change in Work and the Family*. London: Macmillan.

Cunningham-Burley, S. (1985) 'Constructing grandparenthood: anticipating appropriate action'. *Sociology* **19** (3), 421–36.

Cunningham-Burley, S. (1986) 'Becoming a grandparent'. *Aging and Society* **6**, 453–70.

Curphey, P. and Grant, R. (1985) *Having a Say . . . The Swindon Under-25 Survey*. Swindon: Thamesdown Borough Council.

Cusack, S. and Roll, J. (1985) *Families Rent Apart*. London: Child Poverty Action Group.

Davies, B. (1986) *Threatening Youth: Towards a National Youth Policy*. Milton Keynes: Open University Press.

Dickens, P., Duncan, S., Goodwin, M. and Gray, F. (1985) *Housing States and Localities*. London: Methuen.

Donzelot, J. (1980) *The Policing of Families*. London: Hutchinson.

Economic and Social Science Research Council (no date) *Economic Restructuring and Political Change: Towards a Case Study of Swindon*. Swindon: ESRC.

Elder, G. (1978) 'Family history and the life course'. In Haraven, T. (ed.) *Transitions: The Family and the Life Course in Historical Perspective*. New York: Wiley.

Engels, F. (1969) *The Condition of the Working Class in England*. Moscow: Progress Publishers. (Originally published 1844.)

Erikson, E. (1950) *Childhood and Society*. New York: Norton.

Eversley, D. (1983) 'The family and housing policy: the interaction of the family, the household and the housing market'. In British Society for Population Studies Conference Papers *The Family*. London: Office of Population Censuses and Surveys.

Finch, J. (1989) *Family Obligations and Social Change*. Cambridge: Cambridge University Press.

Fisher, S. (1988) 'Leaving home: homesickness and the psychological effects of change and transition'. In Fisher, S. and Reason, J. (eds) *Handbook of Life Stress, Cognition and Health*. London: Wiley.

Fisher, S. (1988) 'Vulnerability factors in the transition to university: self-reported mobility history and sex differences as factors in psychological disturbance'. *British Journal of Psychology* **79**, 309–20.

Gilliver, D. (1989) 'To the Manor born'. *Manor Matters*, No. **1**. Sheffield: Manor Training and Resource Centre.

Goldscheider, F. and Waite, L. (1987) 'Nest-leaving patterns and the transition to marriage for young men and women'. *Journal of Marriage and the Family* **49** (3), 507–16.

Greater London Council (1985) *The London Industrial Strategy*. London: GLC.

Griffin, C. (1985) *Typical Girls*. London: Routledge.

Hall, P., Breheny, M., McQuaid, R. and Hart, D. (1987) *Western Sunrise: The Genesis and Growth of Britain's Major High Tech corridor*. London: Allen & Unwin.

Hall, S. (1904) *Adolescence*. New York: Appleton.
Haraven, T. (1982) *Family Time and Industrial Time*. Cambridge: Cambridge University Press.
Harris, C. (1983) *The Family and Industrial Society*. London: Allen & Unwin.
Harris, N. (1990) *Social Security for Young People*. Witton Bassett: Avebury.
Haskey, J. (1983) 'Social class patterns of marriage'. *Population Trends* **36**, 12–19. London: HMSO.
Haskey, J. (1990) 'The children of families broken by divorce'. *Population Trends* **61**, 39–42.
Hohn, C. and Mackensen, R. (1989) Introduction to *Later Phases of the Family Life Cycle, Demographic Aspects* (ed.) Grebenick, E., Hohn, C. and Mackensen, R. Oxford: Clarendon.
Hutson, S. and Liddiard, M. (1990) 'Youth homelessness in Wales'. In Cross, M. and Wallace, C. *Youth in Transition: The Sociology of Youth and Youth Policy*. Brighton: Falmer Press.
Hutson, S. and Jenkins, R. (1989) *Taking the Strain: Families, Unemployment and the 'Transition' to Adulthood*. Milton Keynes: Open University Press.
Ineichen, B. (1981) 'The housing decisions of young people'. *British Journal of Sociology*, **32** (2), 252–8.
Jamieson, L. and Corr, H. (no date) 'Earning your keep: self reliance and family obligation'. Edinburgh: Edinburgh Sociology Department mimeo.
Jones, G. (1986) 'Leaving the parental home, an analysis of early housing careers'. London: National Child Development Study User Support Group working paper 10.
Jones, G. (1988) 'Integrating process and structure in the concept of youth: a case for secondary analysis'. *Sociological Review* **36** (4), 342–55.
Jones, G. (1990) 'Household Formation among Young Adults in Scotland'. Edinburgh: Scottish Homes discussion paper 2.
Jones, G. and Wallace, C. (1990) 'Beyond individualisation: what sort of social change?' In Brown, P., Buchner, P., Chisholm, L. and Kruger, H. (eds) *Childhood, Youth and Social Change: A Comparative Perspective*. Brighton: Falmer Press.
Kelman, J. (1989) *A Disaffection*. London: Secker & Warburg.
Kiernan, K. (1983) 'The structure of families today: continuity or change?' London: Office of Population Censuses and Surveys Occasional Paper 31.
Kiernan, K. (1986) 'Transitions to Young Adulthood'. London: National Child Development Study User Support Group working paper 16.
Kiernan, K. and Eldridge, S. (1987) 'Age at marriage: inter and intra cohort variation'. *British Journal of Sociology* **38** (1), 44–65.
Kitchen, P. (1944) *From Learning to Earning*. London: Faber & Faber.
Kobrin, F. and Waite, L. (1984) 'Effects of family stability on the transition to marriage'. *Journal of Marriage and the Family* **46**, 807–16.
Leonard, D. (1980) *Sex and Generation: A Study of Courtship and Weddings*. London: Tavistock.
Levine, D. (1985) 'Industrialization and the proletarian family in England'. *Past and Present* **107**, 178.
Liverpool City Council (1987) *Past Trends and Future Prospects: Urban Change in Liverpool 1961–2001*. Liverpool: Liverpool City Council.
Mac an Ghaill, M. (1990) 'Beyond the 1944–88 educational interregnum: the case of Sands Community College'. In Gleeson, D. S. (ed.) *Training and Its Alternatives*. Milton Keynes: Open University Press.
Macfarlane, A. (1970) *The Family Life of Ralph Josselin*. Cambridge: Cambridge University Press.
Mahler, F. (1989) 'Transition and socialisation': in Adamsky, V. and Grootings, P. (eds) *Youth, Education and Work in Europe*. London: Routledge.
Mansfield, P. and Collard, J. (1988) *The Beginning of the Rest of Your Life? A Portrait of Newly-wed Marriage*. London: Macmillan.
Marsden, D., Lee, D., Rickman, P. and Duncombe, J. (1990) *Scheming for Youth: A Study of YTS in the Enterprise Culture*. Milton Keynes: Open University Press.
Martens, J. (no date) 'Marriage as a factor in career choice: gender differences in Kirkcaldy'. Dundee: Dundee University mimeo.

Massey, D. (1984) *Spatial Divisions of Labour: Social Structures and the Geography of Production*. London: Macmillan.

Mead, M. (1935) *Sex and Temperament in Three Primitive Societies*. London: Routledge.

Mendick, H. (1976) 'The proto-industrial family economy: the structures of the household and family during the transition to industrial capitalism'. *Social History* **3**, 243–76.

Morgan, K. and Sayer, A. (1988) *Microcircuits of Capital, 'Sunrise' Industry and Uneven Development*. London: Polity.

Murphy, M. (1990) 'Unemployment among young people: social and psychological causes and consequences'. *Youth and Policy* **29**, 52–63.

Murphy, M. and Sullivan, O. (1983) *Housing Tenure and Fertility in Post-War Britain*. London: Centre for Population Studies Research Paper 83–2.

Murphy, M. and Sullivan, O. (1986) 'Employment, housing and housing structure among young adults'. *Journal of Social Policy* **15** (2) 205–22.

Musgrove, F. (1969) 'The problems of youth and the social structure'. *Youth and Society* **2**, 38–58.

Newby, H. (1989) 'Changing Tracks: Change and Decade'. Broadcast by the BBC 22.12.89.

Nicholson, L. and Wasoff, F. (1989) *Students' Experience of Private Rented Housing in Edinburgh*. Edinburgh University Student Accommodation Service.

Nissen, M. (1987) 'Social change and the life cycle'. In Cohen, G. (ed.) *Social Change and the Life Cycle*. London: Tavistock.

Offe, C. (1984) *Contradictions of the Welfare State*, edited by Keane, J. London: Hutchinson.

Offe, C. (1985) *Disorganized Capitalism: Contemporary Transformations of Work and Politics*, edited by Keane, J. Cambridge: Polity.

PA Cambridge Economic Consultants (1989) *Sheffield Employment Study: Economic Forecasts for the Sheffield City Area: A Report for the Department of Employment and Economic Development*. Sheffield: City of Sheffield City Council.

Pahl, R. (1984) *Divisions of Labour*. Oxford: Blackwell.

Parkinson, M. (1985) *Liverpool on the Brink: One City's Struggle against Government Cuts*. Hermitage, Berkshire: Policy Journals.

Payne, J. and Payne, G. (1977) 'Housing pathways and stratification: a study of life chances in the housing market'. *Journal of Social Policy* **6** (2), 129–56.

Penhale, B. (1989) *Associations between unemployment and fertility among young women in the early 1980s*. London: City University Social Statistics Research Unit working paper 60.

Pickvance, C. and Pickvance, K. (1990) 'Young people's housing strategies: family assistance, institutional shielding and social inequality'. Guildford: University of Surrey ESRC Housing Studies Group Paper.

PIEDA (Planning Economic and Development Consultants) (1990) *Glenrothes Office Development. Assessment of Recruitment Potential*. Edinburgh: PIEDA.

Pittard, A. (1991) *Young People Leaving Care*. Sheffield: Sheffield City Council Housing Department.

Ragin, C. (1990) 'Issues and alternatives in comparative social research'. *International Journal of Comparative Sociology*. Evanston: Northwestern University offprint.

Riseborough, G. (1988) '"We're tha YTS Boys": an ethnographic exploration of classroom politics'. Sheffield University: paper presented to the ESRC 16–19 Initiative First Findings Workshop.

Robbins Report (1963) *Higher Education*, Appendix 1. London: HMSO.

Roberts, K. (1971) *From School to Work: A Study of the Youth Employment Service*. Newton Abbott: David & Charles.

Roberts, K. (1990) Draft of an unpublished paper for the Department of Employment.

Roberts, K. and Parsell, G. (1988a) *The Political Orientations, Interests and Activities of Britain's 16 to 18 Year Olds in the Late 1980s*. Liverpool: Liverpool University.

Roberts, K. and Parsell, G. (1988b) 'Opportunity Structures and Career Trajectories from Age 16–19'. London: City University, 16–19 Initiative occasional paper 1.

Roll, J. (1990) *Young People: Growing Up in the Welfare State*. London: Family Policy Study Group.

Sanderson, M. (1972) 'Literacy and social mobility in the Industrial Revolution in England'. *Past and Present* **56**, 662–78.

Schnaiberg, A. and Goldenberg, S. (1989) 'From empty nest to crowded nest: the dynamics of incompletely-launched young adults'. *Social Problems* **36** (3), 251–69.

Sheffield City Council (1987) *The Uncertain Future of Special Steels: Trends in the Sheffield, UK and European Special Steels Industries*. Sheffield: Sheffield City Council Department of Employment and Economic Development.

Sheffield City Council (1988) *Black Sheffielders: An Information Pack*. Sheffield: Sheffield City Council Department of Land and Planning Race Equality Unit.

Sheffield City Council (1989) *Annual Statistical Report 1988/9*. Sheffield: Sheffield City Council Housing Department, Housing Research Section.

Sheffield City Council (1989) *Housing Outlook Report 1990–1993*. Sheffield: Sheffield City Council Housing Department, Housing Research Section.

Shelter (1990) 'Rent to mortgage, who buys it?'. *Roof* **9–10**, 1990.

Sivanandan, N. (1989) 'New circuits of imperialism'. *Race and Class* **30** (4), 263–79.

Study Commission on the Family (1982) *Values and the Changing Family*. London: Study Commission on the Family.

Sullivan, O. and Falkingham, J. (1986) 'Unemployment: family circumstances and childhood correlates among young people in Britain'. London: paper presented at the British Society for Population Studies conference September 1989.

Tasker, F. (1990) 'Adolescent attitudes to marriage and relationships following parental divorce'. Ph.D. thesis, University of Cambridge unpublished.

Thamesdown Borough Council (1987) 'Into the 1990s: an economic development strategy for Thamesdown'. Swindon: Thamesdown Borough Council consultative document.

Thornton, R. (1990) *The New Homeless*. London: Shelter.

Townsend, P. *et al.* (1987) *Poverty and Labour in London*. London: Low Pay Unit.

Van Vliet, W. (1988) 'The housing and living arrangements of young people in the United States'. In Huttman, E. and Van Vliet, W. (eds) *Handbook of Housing and the Built Environment in the United States*. New York: Greenwood.

Wall, R. (1978) 'The age at leaving home'. *Journal of Family History* **3** (2), 181–202.

Wall, R. and Penhale, B. (1989) 'Relationships within households'. *Population Trends* **55**. London: Office of Population Censuses and Statistics.

Wallace, C. (1987) *For Richer, for Poorer: Growing Up in and out of Work*. London: Tavistock.

Wallace, C. (forthcoming) 'Sociology of rural youth'. *Youth and Policy*.

Wellington, J. and Hockey, J. (1990) *Sheffield's Information Revolution? IT in Sheffield and Its Implications for Employment, Education and Training*. Sheffield: Joint Initiative for Social and Economic Research.

Wells, B. (1989) 'The labour market for young and older workers'. *Employment Gazette*, June, 319–31.

Willis, P. (1977) *Learning to Labour: How Working-Class Kids Get Working-Class Jobs*. Farnborough: Saxon House.

Willis, P. (1984) 'Youth Unemployment A New Social State'. In *New Society* **67**, 475–7.

Willis, P. (1990) *Common Culture*. Milton Keynes: Open University.

Willis, P. *et al.* (1987) *The Social Condition of Young People in Wolverhampton*. Wolverhampton: Wolverhampton Borough Council.

Wood, A. (1989) *40 Years New, Glenrothes 1948–88*. Glenrothes: Glenrothes Cheshire Homes.

Wood, T. (1990) *Looking for Love*. Manchester: Cornerhouse Publications.

Wright, E. (1978) *Class, Crisis and the State*. London: Verso.

Wright, E. (1984) 'A general framework for the analysis of class structure'. Reprinted in Wright, E. (ed.) *The Debate on Classes*. London: Verso.

Young, C. (1987) *Leaving Home in Australia: The Trend towards Independence*. Canberra: Australian Family Formation Monograph 9, Department of Demography, Australian National University.

Young Person's Advisory Service (1990) *Statistics for the Period January to December 1989*. Liverpool: The Basement, 34a Stanley St.

Index